PAUL OF YUGOSLAVIA

Britain's Maligned Friend

by

NEIL BALFOUR and SALLY MACKAY

HAMISH HAMILTON

LONDON · 1980

First published in Great Britain 1980
by Hamish Hamilton Ltd
Garden House 57–59 Long Acre
London WC2E 9JZ

British Library Cataloguing in Publication Data

Balfour, Neil
   Paul of Yugoslavia.
   1. Paul, *Prince*
   2. Yugoslavia—Kings and rulers—Biography
   I. Mackay, Sally
   949.7′02′0924   DR359.P3
   ISBN 0–241–10392–4

Printed in Great Britain
by Ebenezer Baylis and Son Ltd
The Trinity Press, Worcester, and London

FOR NICHOLAS

Contents

List of Illustrations

Nos. 1, 2, 3, 4, 6, 8, 12, 17, 19 by kind permission of H.R.H. Princess Olga; No. 5 the late Lady Doris Vyner; Nos. 7, 9, 10, 12 Radio Times Hulton Picture Library; No. 11 Mrs Roger Wethered; No. 13 Mr Peter Coats; No. 14 Central Press Photos; No. 15 Interpress, Paris; No. 16 Fox Photos; No. 18 Mrs Cvetković; No. 20 Keystone Press Agency Ltd.

YUGOSLAVIA 1918-1941

Acknowledgements

This book would never have been written by us had not:

—Serena shown inexhaustible reserves of understanding, self-lessness and encouragement during her first two and a half years of marriage to a much distracted and absent husband;

—Richard acted as a glittering example of self-discipline and had been an invaluable support to someone who happily shared two years of exile with him;

—Princess Olga refrained from entrusting the work to someone better qualified to undertake it, and tried in every conceivable way to help us in our task, by giving us unrestricted access to her own private diaries and papers and to those of Prince Paul;

—Sir John Balfour made available to us his family's archives, his own prodigious memory, unflagging enthusiasm and merciless textual criticism;

—Professor Phyllis Auty befriended us and given us the invaluable benefit of her professional advice (for this book would have been better written by her);

—Professor Elizabeth Valkanier and the staff at the Bakhmeteff Archives, Rare Books and Manuscript Library, Columbia University, provided us over many weeks with every facility for the study and selective reproduction of the Prince Paul Papers;

Our task would have been considerably more difficult had not:

—Prince Alexander and Princess Elizabeth helped us piece together certain facts and enabled us better to understand certain relationships;

—Dr Nikitović and Mrs Hoptner shown such singular kindness in terms of translation work and personal reminiscence, to an over-worked young researcher in New York City;

—H.M. The Queen Mother, the late Lady Doris Vyner, Mr Harold Macmillan and Mme Mara Cvetković helped us better to understand complicated facets of Prince Paul's personality;

—Elizabeth's nurse, Miss Ede, been able to recollect certain events with such perfect clarity;

—Professor Elizabeth Barker and Alastair Forbes made important suggestions to the text;

—the following helped us identify and obtain original and other source material: Kosta St Pavlović of the Department of Slavonic studies at Cambridge, Peter Coats, Margaret Davis and Dr J. F. A. Mason, the Librarian at Christ Church, Oxford;

—the following given us permission to quote from letters and other documents: H.R.H. The Duke of Kent, The Librarian at Windsor Castle, Lord Clark, and Paul Channon, M.P.;

—the following helped decipher and type an extremely messy script, not once, but again and again: Valerie Brett, Judy Jenkins, Annabel White, Jane Bateson and Roslyn Kloegman;

To all of these we are profoundly grateful.

NEIL BALFOUR
Palais de l'Europe
6700 Strasbourg

SALLY MACKAY
Mercers Creek Plantation
Antigua
West Indies

Foreword

As the last survivor of a family whose members were among the earliest British friends of the late Prince Paul of Yugoslavia, I am honoured at having been asked to write a foreword to his biography by his former son-in-law Neil Balfour—himself a good friend but no relation of mine—and by Sally Mackay.

Based on painstaking and scrupulous research, this book not only makes a valuable addition to the process of dispelling the unreasoning odium to which the Prince was exposed in Britain at the time of the Belgrade coup d'état of March 1941, but also places the achievements of his seven years of Regency of Yugoslavia in their true perspective. The story speaks for itself of how, as a loyal Yugoslav, he sought with courage and devotion to acquit himself of the hideous burden of responsibility which fate had thrust upon him.

As one, however, who was a fellow undergraduate of Prince Paul in pre-1914 Oxford, and whose subsequent diplomatic career included service at our Belgrade legation during the first two years of his Regency, I should like to pay my personal tribute to a friend whose affection for Britain never faltered in seasons of joy or adversity. To his surviving friends in this country as elsewhere this gifted and sensitive lover of the arts will always be remembered as a highly civilized person of exceptional kindness, courtesy, gentleness, and human understanding. Among many blessings of a long life I am happy to count the memory of Prince Paul which evokes these lines of the poet Yeats:

> Think where man's glory most begins and ends,
> and say my glory was I had such friends.

SIR JOHN BALFOUR, G.C.M.G., G.B.E.

Pronunciation of Serbo-Croat

z   Like s in measure
c   like ts in cuts
č   like ch in chew
ć   like tch in ditch
j   like y in yet
ai   like i in fight
š   like sh in shame

Pronunciation of some of the names is as follows:

Maček	Machek
Stojadinović	Stoyadinovitch
Ustaše	Ustasha (as in Worcestershire)
Šubašić	Shubashitch
Živković	Zivkovitch

PART I

the author's father-in-law

CHAPTER I

1893–1912

Background and Youth

Paul Karageorgević was born on 15th April 1893 in St Petersburg, the only child of Prince Arsène Karageorgević of Serbia and Aurore Demidoff, Princess of San Donato. Why Arsène and Aurore ever married remains a mystery. His temperament and background made him a wholly unsuitable husband, while Aurore was clearly unequal to her responsibilities as mother. They were a profoundly unhappy couple and they did not remain together for long.

Arsène, who had attended the Lycée Louis le Grand in Paris as a boy and later trained as an officer at the Collège de Saint-Cyr, had from an early age developed a way with women and a longing for war. He was a gambler by nature and was to thirst throughout his life for danger and adventure. By the time he was twenty-eight his military citations and personal accounts show him to have been involved as a French cavalry officer on campaigns in places as far apart as North Africa and China, and during the course of his long and unsettled career he was to serve as an officer not only in French but also in Imperial Russian and Royal Serbian cavalry regiments.

Arsène's restless character owed much to his Karageorgević background. He was the grandson of the legendary Kara Djorje ('Black George'), a dark-faced swine herdsman who, in 1804, had risen up against the hated Turks and become 'Gospodar', or undisputed ruler, of Serbia. Kara Djorje's reign had lasted until 1813 when he, in turn, had been thrown out by the Turks and later murdered at the instigation of his rival, Miloš Obrenović. For the best part of the nineteenth century the Karageorgević and Obrenović families had vied for the crown of Serbia and at the time of Arsène's birth, in 1859, his father King Alexander I was forced into exile and made to abdicate in favour of the ageing Miloš. Alexander had settled with his family at Temesvar, a town near the Serbian border, well placed for the dynastic ambitions of the Karageorgević family but unsuitable for the education of children. Arsène and his two older brothers had accordingly been sent to school in France.

Aurore Demidoff, in contrast, came from an older family whose rise to fame and fortune, however, owed less to noble acts of heroism than to their perfect business sense. The story goes that one day in 1694 Nikita Demiditch, a poor blacksmith at Tula, was peacefully hammering on his anvil when a carriage emblazoned with the imperial arms suddenly pulled up outside. A steward ran up to Nikita and asked him to repair a pistol which had jammed on the journey. As he was going about his work Nikita heard a voice inside the carriage curse the fact that it was necessary to send abroad for beautiful and efficient fire-arms. At once Nikita answered back that such weapons were quite easy to make. The man who stepped out and slapped him across the face for his boastful insolence was no less than the Tsar, Peter the Great, himself. Nikita, reeling from the blow, staggered inside his workshop and produced a pair of pistols identical to the one he had been handed for repair. Peter the Great was flabbergasted and immediately invited Nikita to lunch. When the blacksmith left the palace he had been given his freedom and certain lands in the Urals. He turned this extraordinary stroke of luck to good effect for, discovering that his lands were rich in iron ore, he swiftly established a munitions factory. During the war with Sweden the factory in Tula worked round the clock, maintained a crucial level of production and earned for its proprietor the title of Count.

By the time the title was made hereditary in 1780 the Demidoffs were mining silver, platinum and gold but though their wealth was prodigious their position in society remained insecure. Thus it was that Nicholas Demidoff, Aurore's grandfather, was considered to have done well for himself, having married Elisabeth Alexandrovna Stroganoff.

To avoid the social uncertainty of St Petersburg, Nicholas and his bride moved to France. In Napoleonic Paris they flourished. With unfathomable wealth, a Russian title and a thirst for international society they set the stage for the later achievements of their eldest son, Anatole. For it was Anatole Demidoff, uncle of Aurore, who was to carry his father's and mother's social, literary and artistic ambitions to fulfilment.

Anatole was brought up in the magnificent villa of San Donato which his father had built above Florence. He was cultured, charming and handsome and before long made a spectacular marriage to Napoleon's formidable niece, Mathilde.* On account of his wife's exalted name and imperial Russian connections Anatole was awarded the title of Prince of San Donato. But the marriage did not last. Mathilde returned to Paris and Anatole lived on alone at San Donato writing a series of travel books, which were to become famous, and collecting paintings and furniture with which to enhance the beauty of his home.

From Anatole, who had no heirs, the princely title passed down to Paul, his younger brother and father of Aurore. Aurore's mother, Princess Helen Troubetskoy, was Paul Demidoff's second wife. Unlike the much travelled Anatole, Paul and Helen lived in Russia and it was in St Petersburg that Paul's son Elim (by a previous marriage) and Paul and Helen's daughters Aurore and Moïna Demidoff were born. Whilst Elim became a Russian diplomat and eventually settled in Greece, Moïna married another famous and cultured Russian traveller, Prince Simeon Abamalek Lazareff, with whom she lived in a palatial villa in Rome.

It was to the inspiration of Anatole Demidoff's achievements at San Donato, and to the example and encouragement of his uncles Abamalek Lazareff in Rome and Elim Demidoff in Greece, that the young Prince Paul of Serbia was to owe much of his early interest in classical art; and it was to the Demidoff fortunes in Italy that the later Prince Paul of Yugoslavia was to owe his financial independence and thus the means whereby to indulge his lifelong passion for art.

Paul left Russia with his mother and a Russian nurse at the age of one. Aurore appears from the beginning to have harboured no illusions about her own or Arsène's ability to bring up their little boy. First she begged her half-brother Elim to adopt him, but Elim was in a difficult position as a

* Mathilde was also a cousin of the Romanovs and a great granddaughter of George III of England.

career diplomat and he had to refuse. Young, bewildered and deserted, the gentle Aurore continued to seek for a home for her son. At last, in 1896, when Paul was just three, the opportunity presented itself.

Arsène's eldest brother Peter, the head of the exiled Karageorgević dynasty, was then living in Geneva. Since his wife had died, he had determined to send his three children, George, Helen and Alexander—the last and youngest of whom was eight years old—to school in St Petersburg. The boys were to attend the Ecole des Pages; the girl the Smolny Institute. He consequently agreed to take in his nephew and nurse to live with him in his house by the side of Lake Geneva. From the day that Paul left Nice with his nurse and his few belongings, he was to see his mother again only twice. As an old man he would tell how he could remember his mother from only two brief but emotionally powerful encounters. Once, aged about six, he was taken out to a large cruise ship on Lake Geneva where a lady clasped him to her bosom for what seemed an eternity, and in his tiny heart an eternity of bliss, and then introduced him to her friends as her son. Then again, aged perhaps eight, he was taken late one evening in the middle of winter to a station where he was told to wait. Presently a train pulled up and the same lady stepped off, hugged her son tightly for some minutes, then climbed, tears streaming down her cheeks, on to the train again and sped away. Aurore remarried not long after sending Paul to Geneva, to a certain Nicholas Count Noguera from Turin. She died in 1904 leaving twin sons, neither of whom ever knew their half-brother Paul.

Arsène for his part never remarried. He continued his peripatetic life alone and, by the time the Karageorgević dynasty was back on the throne in Serbia in 1903 he had run through a succession of mistresses and most of his inheritance. During the Balkan Wars of 1907 and 1912, he distinguished himself as a cavalry officer and captured the town of Veles. Later, when the Great War began, he was passed over. Furious, he returned to Russia where he was given the rank of General and fought with the Horse Guards until the Revolution obliged him to return to Paris.

Arsène never acknowledged his responsibilities towards his son and Paul grew up as a complete stranger to his father. By nature the two were quite different. Paul was highly sensitive, thoughtful and withdrawn. His father was brash, unthinking and extrovert. They were always to maintain a cordial, almost formal relationship, but in early life Paul scarcely came across his father, whom he saw at infrequent and irregular intervals.

Paul's first two years with his uncle in Geneva went passably well. He became devoted to his Russian nurse who had by then taken over the role both of father and mother. His strict and taciturn uncle was not much in evidence and with his cousins away in Russia and the run of the house to himself, Paul was not unhappy.

Then it was that the little boy's life took a dramatic turn for the worse. At the age of seven he was packed off as a boarder to a school in Lausanne and his nurse was dismissed. The school was cold, bleak and infested with rats. For the rest of his life, the thought of a rat filled Paul with horror. Lonely, miserable and confused, Paul prayed for his nurse. Her love and tenderness was the only real affection he had known and he never forgot her. The sense of rejection was complete. For the next four years he moved between Geneva and Lausanne, between a household composed only of men and a school which he hated and feared. By nature both affectionate and timid, his loneliness and longing for female protection during these years were absolute.

Then, in June 1903, news arrived from Serbia that King Alexander Obrenović and his wife had been murdered and that Paul's uncle Peter had been named to succeed him as King. Paul was removed from school and arrangements were made for him to follow his uncle to Belgrade.

At the time Paul was hardly aware of the feud that had existed between the two families, and he was profoundly shocked by the gruesome murders. Alexander Obrenović and his wife had been hacked to pieces in a closet while attempting to hide from their assassins, and their mutilated bodies had been hurled into the palace courtyard below. Paul was present when the messenger came in to announce the murders and the memory was to haunt him for the rest of his life.

Besides this bloodthirsty story Paul knew little about his native land. On the rare occasions when his uncle had chosen to speak to him it had been to correct his bearing and manner or to discuss schooling and other arrangements. His first tongue had been Russian and at school he had spoken and worked in French. When, therefore, at the age of ten Paul arrived in Belgrade and was shown to his small room at the top of the north-east wing of the royal palace he felt, and could not help but be made to feel, a total stranger. Court life was male, and discipline and protocol severe. It was therefore from foreign visitors, ambassadors and other diplomatic staff that this acutely intelligent, painfully shy and inquisitive little boy began to draw his intellectual inspiration. His knowledge of Serbian and other Balkan history he picked up partly at school and partly at meal-times at the palace when, in full military gear, the all-male court paraded at table with the sombre, meticulous and untalkative King Peter. Apart from his efforts to listen, Paul's main concern at meal-times was to get something to eat. The King had a habit of marching in, sitting down, being served first and finishing his meal before anyone else had been properly served. As soon as he had finished he would stand up, declare the meal at an end, and leave.

Between 1903 and 1912, Paul attended school in Belgrade. Of his cousins the eldest, Helen (Jelena), was nine years older and primarily based in Russia. On 3rd September 1911, she married Prince John (Ioann) Constantinovitch of Russia, son of Grand Duke Constantin and grandson of Tsar Nicholas I. The elder of King Peter's two sons, Crown Prince George, was mentally unbalanced and a sadist. At one point in Belgrade he managed to kill his own bodyguard and manservant; at another, he was caught spreading broken glass over a school playground (where the children were accustomed to run about barefoot) in order to watch the fun. Paul, who already in Geneva had nearly been drowned by his older cousin, and in Belgrade had had live bullets fired at his feet to make him jump, was not surprisingly terrified of George and dreaded—even in middle age—being left alone with him.

Alexander, or 'Sandro' as he was referred to by the family, was different. He was quick-witted, distinguished looking and a determined and dedicated soldier. He was popular with both his seniors and his contemporaries, and although he was five years older than Paul and had nothing in common with the boy, he was always friendly and approachable.

Paul found life in Belgrade relatively easy, though in the completely male-dominated, military atmosphere of the royal household he found little inspiration and neither tenderness nor love. He was from the age of ten to eighteen, through necessity rather than by choice, a solitary child. He was good at his work and scored high marks in all his lessons. He kept as much as possible out of the way and out of trouble. He was not tall for his age but fascinatingly good looking. His dark, sad eyes and pale complexion gave him the unmistakable Demidoff look. His mind, too, having been left unusually unregimented and unindoctrinated, found a natural affinity with beautiful objects rather than with horses, uniforms or firearms. His first and most deeply cherished possession was a small blue Sèvres cup and saucer. He had admired its beauty many times in the house of a foreign diplomat, and when the latter was finally recalled Paul went round to purchase the cup and saucer. In Lausanne he had whiled away his lonely and idle hours learning, reciting and, in child-like fashion, writing poetry. In Belgrade he filled in his days in the royal palace admiring and inquiring about pictures, bits of furniture, sculpture, jewellery, staircases, cornices, china and anything else that took his fancy. Eventually, he found that he was able to pilfer lamps, saucers, small pictures, cups and other objets d'art and assemble them in his room for public display. He would then, after having done some basic homework on his precious borrowed possessions, make a show of inviting palace guests to visit his tiny gallery. He was eventually caught and punished. Palace administration concluded that the young prince was at best some kind of eccentric and at worst, an uncontrollable kleptomaniac. Yet he had found, in his deep and almost sensual love of art, a substitute for parental love and affection.

As Paul grew older he began to arrange small plays and poetry readings in the houses of acquaintances and, very occasionally, in his uncle's palace. He began to be invited out too, invariably by foreigners, and away from his immediate family he found he could enjoy the company of others. Amongst the Serbs whom he knew, there seemed to be a total absence of social life outside the court circle and Paul felt himself increasingly standing apart from his fellow countrymen.

Each summer, for health reasons and in the company of his

tutor or a doctor, Paul was sent to one of the spas of Europe. More often than not, these journeys took him through Florence where he visited his aunt, Moïna, at her villa called Pratolino. Moïna had taken some interest in Paul, particularly since her sister's death, and Paul's short visits were always pleasant. Pratolino was a magic place for a child. It was light, airy and delicate, unlike the palace in Belgrade, and at the end of the garden there was a monumental statue by Gian Bologna which was a never-ending source of fascination. Representing the River Po, it took the form of a huge bearded man crouching over a small lake. Its size was such that a grown man could stand on its toe, or walk upright through the passage between its underarm and stooping torso.

As the years passed by, little changed in Paul's life. His father was bivouacked abroad, his mother was dead and his uncle immersed in diplomatic affairs. No one particularly cared to face the question of what should be done with him. Whereas Arsène had been considered unreliable he had, at least, been officer material. Paul was altogether something different. He was weak rather than strong, feeble rather than tough and had a horror of physical disability and violence which was to remain with him all his life. His robust cousins considered him over-sensitive while his tutors continually praised his excellence and his diligence. By 1911 Paul spoke Russian, French, Serbian, a little German and a remarkable amount of English. His interests were definitely artistic, and his bent intellectual. To the surprise and relief of all who had a responsibility for his further education and development, Paul announced in the summer of 1911 that he wanted to study abroad and preferably at Oxford. Nobody could quite work out why or how the boy had developed this fixation. It was almost certainly the doing of one or other of his diplomatic acquaintances and the result of a recently developed interest in English literature and history.

The Karageorgevićs had been educated, by tradition, proximity and convenience in Russia, Switzerland or France. Oxford was a new departure. However, Paul was not in immediate line of succession. He was to all intents and purposes an orphan and in no way suited to the military career which he would otherwise have been expected to pursue.

Immediately the foreign ministry set to work. Through the

Serbian legation in London, a place was found for Paul at Christ Church and all the details fixed for his admission in April 1913.

His father was notified and it was suggested that Paul's expenses should be shared between Arsène and the State. Paul's allowance was enough to entitle him to a flat in London and digs at Oxford. It was assumed that, in addition to his 'college battels' and other fees, he would need sufficient funds to keep and house a manservant, to acquire and to maintain a suitable wardrobe, to travel and to entertain. In all these things Paul was to depend initially at least on the advice of his uncle's Minister in London, Mr Gruić, and his charming and eccentric American wife, Mabel.

At Moïna's request, Paul passed through Rome in the early summer of 1912, en route to England. Prince Simeon Abamalek Lazareff, whose palace in Rome was almost as richly decorated and adorned as the Demidoff villa at San Donato, was delighted when his young and impressionable Serbian nephew arrived. Immediately, it was plain to both that each had found in the other a kindred spirit. For Simeon it was a real joy to find in Paul an attentive, intelligent and, more surprisingly, a relatively well-informed audience. For Paul, his stay in Rome was a sheer delight. At long last he began to see how his thirst for knowledge and his artistic passions might be satisfied. His stay, however, was all too short for soon he was on a train to Florence and thence, via Paris, to London.

Paul had purchased or borrowed several books for his trip to London. De Tocqueville, Gibbon, Flaubert, Rilke and Macaulay were among them. So too were books on the great houses and galleries of England. His excitement at the prospect of all the treasures that awaited him was overpowering. For him, his trip to England marked the end of an orphan-like dependency. He had chosen a path for himself and the nearer he drew to Dover the more convinced he became of the wisdom of his choice.

In Florence he had become intoxicated with the beauty of San Donato. In Paris he was to lie awake all night unable to sleep at the thought of his impending visit to the Louvre. In spite of all that he had read and heard about these museums and priceless works of art, in spite of his anticipation, the reality of his experience when he actually saw them was a complete

delight. He felt an immediate physical relationship with everything he saw.

When at length, aged nineteen, Paul alighted at Victoria Station with four leather suitcases and two wooden and brass trunks, unusually and inappropriately attired on a stiflingly hot summer's day, his excitement was intense. He engaged the services of an ancient looking porter and barrow and joined the queue for hansom cabs.

It was his first experience of the British art of peaceful queueing—indeed, it was his first experience of British life—and he was greatly impressed. When at length his turn came he climbed into the cab and instructed his driver to take him to the Ritz.

Paul had come armed with letters of introduction from Belgrade and they were for the most part addressed to members of the older generation. He spent some months, before going up to Oxford, getting together an appropriate wardrobe in London and making new contacts. Sensitive, emotional and, to the English taste, a little highly-strung, he was immediately taken up by those whom he met. He was exactly the kind of young man whom the more enterprising hostesses of the day were glad to have to dinner. By the time Paul went up to Oxford he had met a small and interesting cross-section of the English ruling class, and was beginning to feel comfortable in their midst.

He was beginning to understand their ways and some of their inter-relationships. Coming from a country where there was virtually no aristocracy and certainly no ruling class outside the cavalry officers' mess, the position, wealth and power of the British nobility filled Paul with sheer astonishment. The treasures in their houses, their estates, their varied interests, and above all their unshakable self-confidence was a complete wonder to him. He was fascinated by their eccentricities and immediately drawn to what he would describe with admiration, throughout the rest of his life, as their essentially 'civilized' way of life. Not surprisingly, within a short period of time he had begun to fashion himself on their style.

CHAPTER II

1913–1922

Oxford, London and the First World War

In 1913 Eugen Millington Drake, who was one of the most dashing Oxford figures of his day, chose to return to Oxford for the start of his final Trinity term a few days early. He boarded the train at Paddington and sat down opposite what he correctly interpreted to be a Freshman, impeccably dressed and sitting bolt upright reading. The young man had a foreign air about him. His clothes, though well chosen, seemed too new; his manner, though composed, showed that he was nervous and shy. Eugen asked the young man whether he was going up to Oxford and on discovering that he was, proceeded to engage him in lengthy conversation. Eugen found that his companion was going up to read Classics, that he had a place at 'the House' (Christ Church) and that he had decided to go up early in order to get to know the place a little ahead of time. Besides, he rather wanted to visit the Ashmolean before the crowds began to pour in. Paul had a lunch meeting planned with his tutor for the following morning and Eugen suggested that he lunch with him the day after at Vincent's Club, which was opening a day or so ahead of term.

From the windows of his rooms at the far end of Peckwater Quadrangle Paul could look out on his fellow undergraduates. For Paul in particular arrival at Oxford was like a dawn—an awakening which was to shape his mind, his character and attitudes for life. For the first time he found himself free from constraint and among contemporaries who shared his tastes, who gave him the affection of which he had been deprived and who introduced him to a world full of confidence and youthful enthusiasm.

In his first year at Oxford, Paul made close and lasting friends: Walter Dalkeith, Bobbety Cranborne, Serge Obolensky and George Gage from his own college, Christ Church; Luly Palmer from University College; Jean de Ribes from Queen's and, from New College, Jock Balfour, with whose younger brother, Archie, Paul was later to form a particularly firm friendship. Of these, some of the most intimate were members of what was then becoming known as the 'Cranborne Set'. The Prince of Wales was also a friend of Paul's, but he was reserved and shy and unable to enter into undergraduate life, or indeed make real friendships, to quite the same extent as Paul.

Paul's academic pursuits were not limited to his Classics syllabus and he made friends, too, with some of the dons. John Murray of Christ Church, in particular, exercised a considerable influence. He was a discerning collector of lithographs and encouraged Paul's interest in art.

As Paul's circle of friends widened his confidence grew. He had a piano installed in his rooms and soon became a member of the most exclusive and popular clubs, including the Bullingdon. Nor did he shrink from the rituals which all this involved. He surprised his contemporaries when, at a Loder's dinner, he was able to drink without pausing for breath the dreaded 'White Lady'* and the remains of a magnum of port.

With a few exceptions European politics were not of particular interest to his friends. The bulk of the 'Cranborne set' led, and taught Paul to lead, a happy, carefree existence. The storm signals of the Anglo-German naval armaments race and the Balkan wars were too remote to be taken seriously by Paul's circle. He himself, however, remained alert to events in Europe, particularly as they affected the Balkans. When the assassination of Archduke Francis Ferdinand at Sarajevo on 28th June 1914 ushered in the cataclysm of the Great War, his misgivings found ample fulfilment.

Paul spent the summer of 1914 in London preparing, with the help of Mr Gruić at the Serbian Legation, for his return to Serbia. As his instructions began to percolate through from Belgrade (where his cousin Alexander, as Crown Prince, was beginning to assume authority in response to King Peter's

* A large silver goblet with swivel bucket beneath, filled to the brim with champagne.

rapidly advancing senility), Paul must have regretted that his pessimism had so quickly been justified by events.

From about the time when Paul's uncle had returned to Serbia as King in 1903, tensions had been rising in Europe. In part this was due to the build up of arms and to Germany's paranoid obsession with her own recognition as a major world power. And in part it was due to the independence movements in Austria–Hungary's South Slav lands. The Balkan Wars of 1907 and 1912, in which the Serbs had finally driven the Turks out of Macedonia, had served to strengthen these nationalist feelings. In Vienna and Budapest the Hapsburg plans had been thwarted; imperial pride had been wounded and the Dual Monarchy, supported by Berlin, was spoiling for a chance to crush the wilful Serbs once and for all.

On 28th June 1914 a pretext was provided. Archduke Francis Ferdinand, heir to the Austrian and Hungarian crowns, was assassinated at Sarajevo. The culprit was a young Bosnian revolutionary, a member of the Serbian secret society, the 'Black Hand'.

Exactly a month later, on 28th July 1914, Austria–Hungary declared war on Serbia. Within a week Germany had joined forces with Austria–Hungary and Russia, France and Britain had come in on the side of Serbia. Only Italy remained neutral, and eventually in 1915 she too came into the war on the Serbian side against a background of handsome rewards.

Paul, who at the start of the crisis had been in London, appears to have stayed there until the autumn. There were problems with passports and there were duties for him to perform. He was hardly a soldier like his father but he knew that an immediate return to Serbia and a soldier's commitment were required of him: he was Serbian and anxious to give of his best. Some time in the early autumn he made his way back to his country. He passed through Florence where he seems, even then, to have established a rapport with the celebrated art historian and scholar Bernard Berenson and his wife, Mary.

Before leaving London Paul had managed to dine with the Asquiths and to use this connection to ask, on behalf of his government, for a message to be delivered by the Prime Minister's wife to Mr David Lloyd George. In November 1914 he received the following letter from Mrs Asquith, written on the 6th:

I got your letter today and was *so* pleased to hear from you. Over here *all* unite in praising gallant Serbia. You have done quite grandly with the Austrians. Over us all there is the terrible cloud of this ghastly useless, senseless war.

So many of the dear young men you knew here are gone. John Manners, George Cecil, Percy Wyndham, Lord Lovat's brother Hugh Fraser, a dear nephew of mine, Capt. Gordon Duff of the Gordon Highlanders, and many many more and now to think of all those brutes of Turks joining the Germans! I pray the Turk will be wiped out *forever*.

My husband is calm and well and working night and day . . . he is certainly the most extraordinary being though I as his wife ought not to say so. It would have been terrible if the other side had been in office, they have no man of Power among them. I am inclined to think the 1st phase of the war is over and the Allies have won. The Germans have lost heavily and have fought well but their code of Truth and Honour is very low and the cruelty of the Prussian Regime must be smashed. I hope we shall see the end of this war in July or August. Our voluntary system of army has been 10,000,000 fold justified. No conscription would have revealed the spirit of our men. We have been far too easy-going at sea and from carelessness and disobedience have made stupid, tho' I am glad to say not fatal, mistakes. The *Goeben* was our worst and that admiral has been finished poor devil! but it was a terrible blunder not sinking the *Goeben* and the *Breslau*. I shall give your message to Mr Lloyd George.[1]

Exactly what kind of military action Paul, a civilian dressed in cavalry uniform, witnessed in Serbia in the autumn and winter of 1914/1915 can only be imagined. The situation he found on arrival was chaotic.

The first Austrian invasion had been launched on 31st July 1914 in spite of its army's numerical inferiority, occasioned by a last minute re-destination of troops to the Eastern front. The Serbian commander, Radomir Putnik, had brought this first offensive to a halt with decisive victories on the Cer Mountain and at Sabac. Putnik's subsequent counter-offensive up the Sava River had had to be abandoned when the Austrians from Bosnia attacked along the Drina to the West. The Austrians' third attack, which had led to the battle of Kolubara, forced the Serbs to evacuate Belgrade on 30th November.

When the royal palace in Belgrade was bombed, Paul lost all his personal possessions and moved, with the rest of the Serbian Government and Court, to Niš. Half of Serbia had been lost to the enemy, the army had fallen back to Kragujevac, typhus raged and morale sank desperately low. The typhus epidemic was so bad that in some towns near to the Serbian headquarters at Kragujevac no volunteers could be found to go in and face the danger of dealing with it. The Serbs themselves could not cope and the hundred or so French doctors in the country were unequal to the task.

At Niš the disease was spreading fast and people collapsed each day in the streets. Most of those who could wore camphor next to their skins and, since the secret of immunity from typhus was known to be cleanliness, people even bathed in water and petrol. The stench was oppressive and for Paul the experience was horrifying.

Then came one of the most remarkable feats of the war, as the following eye-witness account from a young British diplomat bears witness:

King Peter, who had been ill and had handed over the government to Prince Alexander as Regent, came out of his retirement at Banja Luka. Mounted on a white horse, he reviewed his troops and told them that though he would quite understand if any of them desired to go back to their homes, he himself was determined to die rather than to yield. The effect on the Serbian army was immediate and electrifying. On the night of 2nd–3rd December, it began its great counter-offensive. For eleven days it advanced without a halt, driving the Austrians before it. On the 13th it re-entered Belgrade and by that evening there were no Austrians left on Serbian soil, except for over 60,000 prisoners.[2]

The Serbs had shown themselves to be brilliant soldiers.

The winter and spring of 1915 were relatively quiet in the Balkans, with both sides taking stock. Whilst Austria–Hungary and the Central Powers, smarting from their Balkan reversals, laid plans for a summer offensive to strike through to the Straits and re-open railway connections with Turkey, the spirit of nationalism was beginning to take root in the Hapsburgs' Southern Slav lands. It was the same spirit that had moved the Czechs in Austria's Bohemian and Moravian territories, the Slovaks in Hungary's more backward lands, and the Poles. In April 1915, a 'Yugoslav Committee' was formed in London and Paris. The guiding lights of this South Slav, or 'Yugoslav', movement were three influential and articulate Croats: the political leader Anté Trumbić, the journalist Franco Supilo and the sculptor Ivan Mestrović.

In Vienna some thought had already been given to resolving the 'South Slav Question', for maintenance of the Status Quo had become impossible. The spirit of independence and the democratic institutions of Serbia to the south were a constant example to the Croats and Slovenes in the north, who lived under the rule of Budapest and Vienna. All now clamoured for change.

In the event, the solution which was to emerge from the 1914–18 War and from the declarations of the nationalist committees of Yugoslavs abroad was the union of Serbs, Croats and Slovenes within a single Yugoslav state. But in 1915 the world was not ready for this. Great Britain, France and Russia were determined to get Italy into the war on their side and in order to do so they were prepared to sell the Yugoslav movement short. By the Treaty of London, signed on 26th April 1915, the Allies ceded to Italy many of the South Slav cities and territories for which the nascent Yugoslav state was then hankering, including parts of Gorizia, Carniola, Istria and Dalmatia, regions which were occupied by no fewer than 700,000 Croats and Slovenes. The Balkan campaign was a 'side-show' and the territorial integrity of the Yugoslav peoples a disposable asset in the hands of its Great Power allies.

Paul, who had reached Serbia in the autumn of 1914 was, by the end of the following January, in a pathetic physical state. He had been struck down with a particularly virulent form of hepatitis. Unaccustomed to war and to military ways he was, even when fit, of little practical use in an officer's garb. But to

1. Princess Mathilde Bonaparte, wife of Anatole Demidoff, first Prince of San Donato.

2. Anatole Demidoff, by Robert Lefévre.

his government, desperately in need of Allied munitions and troop reinforcements, he became, sick as he was, a useful diplomatic tool. Towards the middle of March he left for Rome where he delivered, in person, certain entreaties and official documents. From there he passed through Florence to England, arriving in May. Exactly what was the nature of his mission to Rome remains obscure. The ultimate purpose, however, seems to have been to get him to England to recover and to serve in London as a mouthpiece, when needed.

By the beginning of May Paul had returned on a visit to Oxford. There for the first time he met Jock Balfour's younger brother, Archie. Whereas Jock's first impressions of Paul had been somewhat reserved (he had regarded him as rather highly-strung and emotional) Archie and Paul struck up an immediate and intimate friendship. Writing to his mother on 12th May, Archie had this to say: 'Paul of Servia [sic] who was up here and was a great friend of Jock's and the Bobbety [Cranborne] crowd is staying here for a week or so before he goes back to Servia again. He has just come from Rome where he has been on a mission about the war.'[3]

Paul seems to have based himself at Oxford throughout May and June, lending his car to Archie and Derek Milner and occasionally travelling down to London to see friends when they came home on leave. Then, at the beginning of July he went north to stay with the Balfours at Newton Don, near Kelso in Scotland. He was, even then, far from well and the purpose of his trip was to convalesce.

By the end of September 1915, Paul was preparing to leave for the Balkans. The month of October was a difficult one for him. He had already begun to say his farewells when his trip was delayed, and, as is evident from a series of letters from Archie to his mother, the date of his departure was postponed not once, but several times.

On 4th October Archie wrote: 'Paul got back from Chatsworth this afternoon and is now probably going off to Holker to see Bobbety Cranborne. He thinks he is going back to Serbia this week' . . . and on 6th: 'Yesterday I went out to luncheon with Paul at Ciro's at 1.30. There he put on the pathetic face with the uplifted hands and begged me to go to a play that evening as he was going to Serbia on Monday or

Tuesday . . .' Together, on Saturday 8th October, Archie and Paul motored to Oxford for Paul to say goodbye to John Murray, the Christ Church don. That Sunday they attended Cathedral service at Oxford and then drove down to Eton to evening chapel and to have dinner with the Dean ('a perfectly filthy dinner').

On 13th October it looked certain that Paul would leave. 'He was most awfully depressed, poor fellow. He is afraid his country is done for and just because we wouldn't listen a month ago and look ahead by sending troops out there in anticipation of this happening. Now of course we have sent troops out there but nothing like a sufficient quantity and rather late in the day.' The date set for Paul's departure was Sunday 17th October 1915, but on that day he was again, with Archie, staying at Eton for a musical evening. In the intervening time the news from Serbia had gone from bad to worse. 'Poor Paul is in an awful state. It really does seem cruel to have behaved as we have behaved towards Serbia. He was going back this morning but he got a telegram from the Crown Prince to say he must wait and see Asquith and there was a long message to tell him what to say. So now he has had to put off going till Tuesday or Wednesday . . .'

In the event, Paul did not leave till 4th November. He had heard that there might be some important cabinet changes in Britain and he had been charged to keep his ear to the ground. Besides, Asquith became ill, so he was obliged to wait. When the day finally came, parting from Archie was particularly hard. The two friends had been together for the best part of six months and each realized that his chance of seeing the other again was remote.

Paul had only got as far as Florence when he fell seriously ill. He remained bed-ridden till Christmas and then suffered a further relapse. Archie, writing to his mother on 5th January 1916, recorded the facts: 'I heard from Paul whose letter was brought over by Irene Lawley who had just come back from Florence. She said he had been very ill and had recovered and then had another heart attack.'

Exactly how much longer Paul remained in Florence is uncertain, but sometime in February or March 1916 he made his way through Rome and Brindisi to Corfu.

In Corfu at the end of March 1916, Paul found the Serbian court, general staff and government. Much had happened since the spring of 1915. Throughout the summer, which had found Paul in Oxford, London and Scotland, the Central Powers had plotted their thrust through the Balkans. Their prestige required it and so too did their strategy of establishing rail communication with their new ally, Turkey.

On 6th September 1915, Bulgaria signed up with the Central Powers, laying claim to parts of Serbian Macedonia. On the same day, an Austro–Hungarian army attacked south from the banks of the Danube and five days later, on 11th, the Bulgars, undeterred by an ultimatum from Moscow, fell upon Eastern Serbia and Serbian Macedonia.

Relying on the strongly pro-Allied Greek Prime Minister, Eleutherios Venizelos, the Allies landed on 5th October 1915 in the Macedonian port of Salonika to the fury of King Constantine of Greece, whose personal preference had been for strict neutrality. On the day of the Allied landings in Salonika, he dismissed Venizelos whom he had sacked once before in March but had been obliged to re-appoint in August on account of the latter's majority in Parliament.

The troops which landed at Salonika under the command of the French General Maurice Sarrail were Gallipoli veterans. At exactly the time when Paul was preparing to leave England for Serbia, in the late autumn of 1915, the troops had been marched north up the Vardar valley into Serbian Macedonia. But the wedge which the Bulgars had driven across the country had prevented the Allies from joining the Serbian army. That winter, accompanied by most of the court and the civil service, the Serbian army made its famous retreat across the snow-covered mountains of Albania to Corfu. Even if he had been fit, it is doubtful whether Paul could have made contact with his cousin's troops or with the court.

The year 1916 was a period of quiet consolidation for the French, British and Russian troops in the Salonika region. A bridgehead was established between Edessa in the west and Kilkis in the east. In May King Constantine of Greece, who was still withholding help from the Serbians, felt obliged to surrender Fort Rupel at Klidhi on the Struma. Unlike Venizelos, who had moved to Crete to establish an alternative government,

King Constantine saw no obligation on Greece to come to the rescue of the Serbs. When in the summer the Bulgars, pouring through the Monastir Gap, overran Greek Macedonia, Venizelos seized his chance. With his majority in Parliament still technically intact, he sailed to Salonika and there, on 27th November 1916 declared a new government in being, at war with Germany and Bulgaria.

Paul, who appears by then to have obtained a job working for the International Red Cross, left Corfu in the winter of 1916 to spend Christmas with Moïna, in Rome and at Pratolino. He remained in Italy at least until the end of January 1917. Having spent almost a year in an officer's mess and in the relative seclusion of Corfu, he had become something of a recluse. He was aware of this and acknowledged his friends' teasing, signing a letter to Mrs Berenson 'Paul l'Hermite'.[4]

Paul returned to Salonika at the end of January 1917, in time for the preparations for the spring offensive. There were by now 500,000 troops cooped up in the Salonika bulkhead and among them were six Serbian divisions. These had regrouped in Corfu after their previous winter's retreat and been shipped to Salonika by British vessels established in Lesbos and Lemnos. But the plans for a northern advance were continually modified and deferred. On 11th June 1917, the Allies managed to get King Constantine deposed whilst Venizelos, having moved back to Athens, declared war on the Central Powers on 27th. Paul saw less action during his few months in Salonika than he had done in Serbia in the autumn and winter of 1914. But his months in Italy and Macedonia had taken their toll and at the start of the summer he had to be sent back to Britain, his digestive system in complete disorder.

On 6th May Charles Barrington Balfour, father of Jock and Archie, wrote to his eldest son:* 'Archie's delighted at the return of Paul who has been on his front. But Archie writes he is a good deal broken in health, so I suppose he has come over here to recuperate. He only arrived the other day and is being taken by Archie to preside at one of the social meetings of the East End Boys Club where he works. The boys will be delighted and I am longing to hear Archie quote their comments.'[5]

* Jock Balfour had been interned as a prisoner of war in Ruhleben camp near Berlin since the early stages of the war.

During August Paul spent some time touring Scotland, staying with friends. Walter Dalkeith was on leave and Paul was invited to his parents' home at Langholm. He went also to Newton Don where C. B. Balfour was shocked by his poor state of health: 'He is certainly much the better for his stay here—where he has had a massage every day and been on a careful diet. He talks of going abroad again, but I can hardly think any doctor would let him. I hope not. I must say that now we have seen so much of him one really gets very fond of him, and I can understand Archie's great friendship for him.'[6]

Towards the end of September, Paul returned to Newton Don and on 7th October, Jock received a letter from his father saying: 'Paul is still here—certainly better than he was, but he can stand very little. We just went out for the morning to get some partridges on Harrietsfield and shot up till luncheon, but he had to give up after a couple of hours.'

On 21st of the month, the house party dispersed, except for Paul who appears to have had nowhere to go. He stayed at Newton Don throughout November and December and in the end spent an especially happy Christmas there, in the company of Archie and Luly Palmer. On 28th December he wrote to Mrs Berenson: 'As you see I am still in Scotland where I expect to remain for another fortnight before going down to my beloved London. I have become a real country squire and spend my days shooting or chopping trees. I also have a lot of time to read, which is a great blessing. I have had a most delightful Christmas, as my two very best friends were also staying here.'[7]

Without any doubt Paul's experiences in Serbia in the winter of 1914/15 had played havoc with his stomach and he was to remain for the rest of his life, if not exactly a sick man, at any rate abnormally plagued by bouts of ill health. He became, for his years, unnaturally concerned with his physical condition, almost to the point of hypochondria. By nature a confirmed pessimist, he was inclined to think that each chronic attack of the liver was the prelude to something worse. He found the very prospect of illness utterly abhorrent. Being particularly fond of good food and wine, about which he was, even then, immensely knowledgeable, it was a source of permanent frustration to him that he was more often than not on a diet.

At the beginning of 1918 Paul's doctor diagnosed chronic colitis, and Paul was required to remain in London.

In Salonika, during the whole of 1917, the situation had been one of stalemate. And for the first half of 1918 there was little action. Then, in September 1918, events took a dramatic turn. General Franchet d'Espérey, who in July had taken over command, put into action a daring plan of attack, devised with the Serbs and designed to cripple the enemy's system of communications in the Balkans and to rout the Bulgarians. On 15th September 1918, the jubilant Serbs thrust north along the Vardar, the French cavalry moving with them, whilst British troops broke through the Bulgarian lines to Strumica. On 29th September, the Bulgarians signed the Armistice of Salonika, unreservedly accepting the Allies' terms.

Militarily, the Serbs had won a remarkable victory. Constitutionally too, the war had brought about a great triumph. With the conquest of Serbia the wider 'Yugoslav' concept had begun to take on an even greater significance. Already on 20th July 1917, Pašić, the Serbian Premier, and Trumbić, President of the Yugoslav Committee in exile, had issued the famous Declaration of Corfu. This had called for the creation of a single nation, comprising Serbs, Croats and Slovenes, to be formed under the Karageorgević dynasty and styled as 'a constitutional, democratic and parliamentary monarchy'. In this new nation there was to be equality for the two alphabets, and for the three religions, flags and national names. It was left to a future Constituent Assembly to put the Declaration into effect.

After the Allied victories in September 1918 the conditions for such constitutional change came into view, as Austria–Hungary began to break up from within. On 29th October, the Croatian Diet issued a declaration that union with Hungary was at an end and that supreme authority lay with the National Council. The National Council then proclaimed the unconditional desire for union with Serbia and Montenegro. The Montenegrins, for their part, promptly deposed their own king and likewise declared for union with Serbia. President Wilson, who believed in the principle of national self determination, gave his approval to the union and at a meeting on 1st December 1918, between the Prince Regent Alexander and the delegation from Zagreb, 'the Kingdom of the Serbs, the Croats and the Slovenes'* was formally established.

By the time Paul returned to Oxford in October 1918 the situation was everywhere hopeful, except of course in Russia, where in July the imperial family had been brutally put to death. In his own country, the Armistice of Salonika had already recognized the Allied victory and elsewhere the end was easily in sight.

Paul was twenty-five years old and anxious to resume his studies. Through his friend John Murray his return to Christ Church had not been difficult to arrange and, with a year of Oxford life already behind him, he looked forward to the start of term. He had a mass of friends, a flat in London and the expectation of a Demidoff inheritance of not inconsiderable dimensions to look forward to. All in all, the post-war years seemed full of promise.

Financially, Paul's position appears to have improved considerably. This was just as well, for apart from his life of sumptuous dinner parties and balls in London, his visits to the opera, the theatre and the ballet, and the large country-house weekends in England, he was a regular visitor to the major cities on the Continent. In addition he began, about then, to develop a taste for the expensive. Apart from re-establishing contact with his old acquaintances and friends, Paul started to form new, and more eccentric attachments. The deepest and most enduring of these was Henry Channon III ('Chips') who went up to Oxford, like Paul, in October 1918. Whereas Paul's English friends were, with the possible exception of some art-dealers in Bond Street, drawn exclusively from the ranks of the aristocracy and the privileged classes, his new, more cosmopolitan, friends were the product of the New World's wealth. For 'the Bobbety crowd', as Archie had described Paul's friends in 1915, inherited wealth brought inescapable responsibilities. Their wealth was mostly based on possessions —their estates and great houses—and as such these imposed a heavy burden and a sense of duty. Whatever their degree of wealth or social position, their style of life, mentality and sense of values invariably conditioned them for a life of public service

* King Alexander changed the name to 'the Kingdom of Yugoslavia' on 6th January 1929.

and early responsibility. Thus Bobbety (not surprisingly for a Cecil) had immediately gone into political life, Jock had gone into the diplomatic service, and George Gage had become a courtier. Walter Dalkeith, who always managed to look more 'down at heel' than any of his hundreds of tenants and employees, had thrown himself wholeheartedly into the business of running his estates. They were all incapable of ostentation and their time for frivolity and leisure became increasingly curtailed.

Chips, and the world which for Paul he came to represent, was something utterly different. Paul admired the values of the Cranborne Set but he learned to have more fun with Chips. Chips had gone to France in October 1917, at the age of twenty-two, with the American Red Cross. He was four years younger than Paul. Yet as an honorary attaché to the American Embassy in Paris he had already met and become intimate with Marcel Proust and Jean Cocteau. Having been indulged and flattered by the 'two wittiest men in Europe',[8] Chips took Oxford and London by storm. He was immensely rich, for his father and grandfather had made a fortune out of shipping in Chicago, and he was not afraid to show it. Like Paul, he considered himself English by adoption and he came up to Oxford consumed with a love for England. Without a doubt, Paul fell greatly under the influence of his friend's contagious enthusiasm. Paul had himself met, and been much impressed by, Sergei Diaghilev and Vaslav Nijinsky at Lady de Grey's before the war and he had at once been fascinated by the internationalism of the artistic world. In Chips Paul found a contemporary who could boast of having talked with the famous Abbé Mugnier,* of having been befriended by the Duchesse de Brissac, of having thoroughly disliked Gide 'a dreadful, unkempt, poet-looking person'[9] and of having adored the romantic novelist Mrs Elinor Glyn. Chips' capacity for self-appreciation was outrageous and it delighted the less uninhibited Paul, for Chips candidly confessed his 'most unattractive traits' to be 'love of display, grandeur, money for its spending sake and social position.'[10] It was through Chips that Paul met and grew to love eccentrics like Lady Cunard.

* Abbé Mugnier (1853–1944), who lived a life of monastic poverty as almoner to the Missionary Sisters of St Joseph of Cluny, was pursued by Parisian high society.

Paul left Oxford at the end of the 1920 Michaelmas term with a 'War Degree', and took a flat in Mount Street. He was amused by Chips' almost reckless brand of gaiety and, judging from his first investment in a picture, he had picked up some of Chips' fearless approach to money. Paul shared his flat initially with Chips and 'Grubby' Gage and, later on, with Serge Obolensky. In it he was able to display, though in cramped and far from ideal conditions, his beautiful new acquisition, *Forest Fire* by Piero di Cosimo.*

At Oxford and in London Paul also expanded his circle of English friends. Through the Cranborne Set in general he met a new and slightly younger generation. The most notable among these were Elizabeth Bowes-Lyon and her friend Doris Gordon-Lennox. Through his friendship with Archie, Paul was often made welcome at Bisham Abbey. The 'Abbey' was an old moated house beside the Thames near Marlow and Archie's father took it every summer till his death in August 1921. Here Paul spent happy summer weekends with his own contemporaries and, since Lady Nina liked to mix up the generations, public figures of the day.

It was during these immediate post Oxford years that most of Paul's friends married. What the Great War had miraculously failed to accomplish, a stream of wedding ceremonies now succeeded in doing: the ranks of his bachelor friends began quickly to diminish. One by one they disappeared down the aisle leaving only Archie and Chips, both of whom seemed set on a bachelor existence. The effects on Paul were powerful. First, he was left increasingly to rely for companionship on the older generation, on establishment figures like Lady Nina and Lord Curzon and on those who, like Sir Joseph Duveen and Lady Cunard, moved in the world of art. Secondly, he started consciously looking around for a possible bride.

He had from the first regarded Elizabeth Bowes-Lyon as probably the prettiest girl in Britain, with her shining, lively eyes and beautiful smile. But almost as he got to know her, she had become engaged to the second in line to the throne. On her marriage to the Duke of York, Paul was to gain a new and loyal friend. But at the time his own prospects seemed to fade. His dreams of marriage drifted sideways, to Doris

* *Forest Fire* now hangs in the Ashmolean, Oxford.

Gordon-Lennox, and, for a time, their friends began to think that an engagement was in the offing. But this was not to be and Paul remained, throughout his post-Oxford years, concerned to find a suitable bride and apprehensive, like all in his place, lest having found her, he might fail to win her heart.

There were a vast number of parties in London in the years 1919–1923 and Paul was invited to most. He was popular with men and women alike and particularly popular with the parents. His visits to Belgrade and Florence were frequent and regular enough to comply with family obligations but they did not interfere with his London life. Whereas Chips' life-style scarcely left time for him to ponder on whether he should marry, Paul, who was older, felt differently. By the time the 1923 London season started Paul was thirty and longed, more than anything, for a wife.

CHAPTER III

1922–1923

Olga

In 1913 King George I of the Hellenes was assassinated and was succeeded by his son Constantine, Duke of Sparta. King Constantine had four brothers and two sisters.

The third brother, Prince Nicholas of Greece, was an artist and writer. In 1902 he had married Helena (or Ellen) Romanov, daughter of the Grand Duke Vladimir of Russia and they had had three daughters: Olga, born on 11th June 1903, Elizabeth, born on 24th May 1904 and Marina, born on 13th December 1906.*

In 1917 the Greek royal family had been forced to abdicate and for four years they had made Switzerland their base. In the autumn of 1921, King Constantine was recalled to Greece by plebiscite and on 30th October Prince Nicholas and family left Switzerland to return to their family home in Athens. Life at the royal palace of Tatoi was the more enjoyable and close-knit that winter for the fact that its inhabitants had recently lived through an extremely difficult four years in exile. Christmas came and went, and virtually every member of the family was present.

In the early spring of 1922 Princess Nicholas was invited by her brother-in-law, Prince Christopher, and his American wife to stay with them in Cannes. She was accompanied on this trip by her two elder daughters Olga and Elizabeth who were then aged, respectively, eighteen and seventeen. Almost at once Olga's beauty and simplicity of manner caught the attentions of Crown Prince Frederick of Denmark. During the years in exile Princess Nicholas had often discussed with her cousin, Queen Alexandrina of Denmark, the possibility of a match between

* According to the Greek Orthodox Calendar their birthdays were celebrated on 29th May, 11th May and 30th November, respectively.

Olga and 'Rico' (as Prince Frederick was called) and she was delighted at the apparent success of their schemes. The relationship flourished and, in the manner of the day, Prince Frederick's attachment to Olga, the most beautiful princess in Greece and, as she was later to be widely acclaimed, the most beautiful in Europe, became gradually known and accepted. The official engagement followed and he was invited to Athens. His visit, when it came, was a great success and he stayed a total of two weeks.

Olga was, not surprisingly, overwhelmed. She was just nineteen and though in behaviour and manner well trained and therefore seemingly grown up and sophisticated, she was at heart a child, romantic and vulnerable. Her diary, which she began about this time, shows her as a pious teenager, conscious of her role as the eldest daughter and longing to think 'the right thoughts' and feel 'the right feelings'. In some passages her jottings sound self-conscious, artificial and contrived—as though she feared that her mother might read them or as though she wanted her to do so and approve—and in others they are deeply personal, humble, articulate and convincing. For the fourteen months, from August 1922 to October 1923, the diary entries themselves are the best introduction to the girl who was so soon to link her life and fortunes with those of Prince Paul of Serbia.[1]

Princess Nicholas had arrived in Paris with Olga, Elizabeth and Marina in the last week of July. Rico was supposed to meet them there in September to explain his oft-declared intentions. Having been willing in Cannes and in Athens to have his name officially linked with that of Olga, his follow-up letters had shown definite signs of a cooling off. Nevertheless, the engagement was still technically 'on' and both had agreed to meet to discuss the future. The pressure was certainly there for the engagement to continue and though Olga had tried to steel herself for the occasion, she was inevitably apprehensive. She had scarcely had time to fall in love with Rico, but she had enjoyed the flattery and attention and had responded in all the established ways. She had subsequently realized that her dreams of a romantic love affair moving across different countries and ending happily ever after in marriage were an illusion. Here she was in Paris to discuss, in full view of a large cross-section of her family, whether or not the strange behaviour of her betrothed spelt the end of the romance or whether it was to be treated merely as an interlude and to be ignored. If Olga's embarrassment could be spared and the wedding plans be confirmed, so much the better.

On August 20th Princess Nicholas had gone to London with Elizabeth ('Woolly') and Marina as Rico was not expected for at least another fortnight. On 1st September, Olga moved from her room in the flat of her friend, Diddie Vlasto ('which really looks quite nice and cosy now that it is arranged with some of my things!'), to the house of her mother's friend Mme de Croisset at 11, Place des Etats-Unis:

Monday, Sept. 5th

We have been writing and discussing what is best to do as Mummy telegraphed to R. to come on Friday. As we want to be quiet to discuss things and see him privately, Marie Thérèse* thought this house would be best and quietest as the Ritz would be impossible. I only hope now Mummy will consent to come here at once and leave the others at the Ritz with Nursie† and stay here with me quietly till it is all over one way or another. . . . In a few days my life will be decided, I do wish it were over . . .

Thursday, Sept. 8th

Mummy and the girls arrive this evening by the 9.40 train. . . . We have been bombarding Mummy with telegrams begging her to come here alone and that I should stay here to see Rico quietly as meeting at the Ritz would be fatal. Happily the Greek family left last night so there is time to prepare the rooms for Woolly and Marina. Mummy telegraphed yesterday saying she would come here! Marie Thérèse telephoned to the Danish Legation to check when R. was arriving and they said *this* evening at 11 and not tomorrow as we thought. . . . If only I knew in what a state of mind he is in! Is he still bitter and resolved to break off the engagement? I only hope he will listen to me and after that if he still remains the same it means he

* Mme de Croisset.
† Their devoted English nurse, Miss Fox.

never really loved me! God will help me to say the right things! . . .

Sunday, Sept. 11th

All is finished now between Rico and me, he came on Friday at 3 and I saw him first. We remained three quarters (of an hour) talking but he had quite made up his mind to give it up. I said I was willing to try again but he said he had no more love for me (it couldn't have been very strong while it was there). I insisted upon seeing him here quietly to avoid the Ritz. Mummy out of delicacy didn't see him first not to let him think she was trying to influence him, while he without the least decency or tact had already been to the Ritz in the morning to see Christo,* and again, just before coming here, to see Woolly alone, to ask her how to speak to me and what to say!! Before leaving I gave him back the ring and he also said he was glad we had parted 'without bad words'.

It had been less difficult than she had imagined to put on a brave face. But soon, a far worse disaster was to strike and on this occasion the sentimental, religious and family-minded girl was less able to cope. Following the crushing defeat of the Greek army at the hands of the Turks in Asia Minor, her uncle, King Constantine of Greece, was obliged on 17th September 1922 to abdicate and flee the country. His son George was handed the crown but the rest of the royal family were required to leave. King Constantine and his family left for Corfu and from there they moved to Palermo. Prince Nicholas left Greece with his brother in the realization that for him and his family the future would involve considerable hardship. For his daughters, whose ages ranged from fifteen to nineteen, the outlook was particularly bleak: 'The whole thing is such a tremendous nightmare. . . . The thought that this time it is all finished, that Uncle Tino will never rule over the country again and perhaps never see it again. . . . Georgie, King!! and for how long? No one knows if it wouldn't enter their heads to kick him out! Then it will mean a republic and we won't ever see . . . the place . . . again . . . ! Home, the house. . . . Oh! no God won't

* Prince Christopher of Greece.

46

let it come to that, however things are so bad one must be ready for everything. Perhaps God wants to punish us for our lack of faith and principles, thinking we can act without Him.'

Exactly one week after they set sail from Greece, Princess Nicholas left Paris and joined her husband in Palermo. Their most pressing worry was to find accommodation for the winter. They were virtually without means of support and their ability to bring their daughters out into society was severely curtailed. On Monday 3rd October Olga, sitting in her bedroom in Paris, pencilled in her diary: 'I am here at the Ritz since over a week. Mummy left for Palermo on Thursday morning and must have got there on Saturday night. No telegram has come yet. We are just living *sur la branche*, and one can hardly realize this is the second exile and we are once more like wandering Jews with no home to go to! Oh! it is too awful and I feel so stunned, I refuse to grasp it all! It seems one million refugees have arrived in Athens and an order has been issued that every house has to take in two of them and that all empty houses have to be occupied at once!'

From Athens and Palermo the news was each day worse. Prince Christopher, finally out of Athens and safely arrived in Palermo, reported by letter that Prince George was virtually in solitary confinement whilst Prince Andrew and family were actually under guard. In Palermo the exiles were beginning to get on each other's nerves and Olga's parents were longing to get away, either to San Remo or to Grasse, to look for somewhere cheap to rent. Since Woolly and Marina, following the advice of their ear specialist, had departed for a holiday in Chamonix, November in Paris was for Olga a misery of loneliness and uncertainty.

On the 22nd Olga left for San Remo. She realized at once that this discreet little town was to be her 'prison'. But she had no idea how long this nightmare was to last. She was at her most insecure. Longing for happiness, the security of a home and a united family, she realized too that her chances of meeting the right man now, when she was at exactly the age and emotionally prepared for it, were non-existent. She was bored, angry and bitter and yet she knew that for the sake of her parents and younger sisters a superhuman effort was called for.

Yet when on Thursday 23rd November Olga arrived with her two sisters and their old nanny Miss Fox at San Remo their spirits sank to their lowest. Their hotel, 'this Godforsaken place', was perched on the top of a hill. Inside, the rooms were 'perfectly foul, plush on all the furniture, heavy wooden beds and few bathrooms'. In fact, Olga concluded, 'one might as well be in Brindisi'. Terrified that their companion, a Mrs Beaumont (who had rearranged the rooms 'à sa guise' and who found them delightful) might persuade her mother to like them too, Olga anxiously awaited the arrival of her parents—in time, she hoped, for Marina's birthday.

In the event, her parents arrived on 1st December, the day after Marina's sixteenth birthday. Prince Nicholas had not seen his daughters for five months and the reunion was ecstatic. He brought masses of letters with him and Olga especially was thrilled to hear at last from her closest friends and cousins, Sitta (who was by then Crown Princess Helen of Rumania) and Tittum (Sitta's younger sister, Irene), both of them daughters of the now deposed King Constantine. She was also able to report with relief that night: 'P. & M. don't seem very enchanted with the hotel, happily'.

But since her parents were virtually without means and since in the end the wretched hotel proprietor appears to have done what he could for his royal guests, the chances of an immediate move either into a larger villa or to another place altogether vanished. The life of long, windswept, seaside and mountain walks, teas at the English tearoom, bridge games with virtual strangers and the ever-anxious look-out for the postman was oppressive. It made even the prospect of a drive in a rickety Fiat and a day's excursion to Cannes seem like the greatest imaginable treat.

Christmas was a miserable business. Their presents to each other were little handkerchiefs and toy table cloths bought in Paris the previous month. Their governess did best of all: she got a pair of 'washing gloves sewn with black'. Their days were all alike apart from the few though infrequent visits from travelling friends and acquaintances. The Vlastos arrived on 19th December for one day, having driven over from Nice for the night. 'They took us to lunch at the Royal where the hotel and food is not to be compared with this. I was so pleased to see

Diddie again.' They gave the three girls beautiful presents and admired Olga's little black Scots terrier, Yankee.

On 30th December, in the evening, a telegram arrived from Sitta saying that Uncle Tino was dead—he had passed away that morning in Palermo from a stroke. The effect on the family was appalling and that same night Prince and Princess Nicholas caught a train for Naples.

Over the next few weeks Olga went into a deep moral depression. She could not bear the thought that her uncle's death, which meant so much to her and her exiled family, could mean so little to the people in Greece. She tried to uplift herself with lofty thoughts but her misery was intense. 'I can't take my mind away from this awful grief which becomes more acute every day, it is no use, I can't realize it . . . I feel so crushed, my thoughts are no more my own; sometimes I feel I am going to burst.'

Then at last it began to look as if they might move to Florence. Olga was delighted. 'There are such a lot of beautiful things to see.' But their imprisonment in San Remo dragged on and on: 'Here it seems to me more dull and depressing each day, nothing to do or see! Every morning I wake up and wonder and am persuaded it will be like yesterday, I want, I need a change. I am getting too self-centred. I give way to a nasty temper, to depression and hate to speak of it.'

At the end of January, Marie-Laure (Mme de Croisset's daughter and Olga's friend) was married in Grasse. Olga's parents, still in mourning, refused to attend the wedding but Olga and Elizabeth both went.

The cream of Paris society was there and Olga and her sister were a glittering success. The Prince and Princesse de Poix, Prince Murat, Prince and Princesse de Lignes together with their daughters, the Duc and Duchesse de Mouchy and the old Comtesse de Chevigné. Marie-Thérèse showed the sisters off and included them in every gathering over the long weekend. 'Not knowing anyone it was of course very confusing at first.' But there were a few Italians who had passed through San Remo and others whom Olga had met the previous year in Cannes and she enjoyed herself immensely.

Upon their return to San Remo Olga learned that Elizabeth and Marina, whose health had been poor, would be leaving soon for Meran in the Tyrol, where the air was pure and prices extremely cheap. They left on 20th February.

March was a sad month. Olga was lonely without her sisters and to make things worse her little Scots terrier had to be put down. Life in San Remo dragged on with little change and no excitement, though twice Olga managed to get away, at least to the company of others, if not to the high society of which she had had so brief a glimpse. The first occasion was the funeral of Queen Milena of Montenegro where she met some of her more exotic Russian and Balkan relations. The second was a trip to Monte Carlo to visit the dentist and lunch with an uncle and aunt. 'Old Uncle Arthur', Duke of Connaught,* was also present and he was immediately struck by the ravishing beauty of the young Greek princess. Olga was not to know it, but it was thanks to the twinkle in his eye that her reputation as a beauty would precede her to London. And it was thanks to 'Aunt Toria',† who had taken a great interest in her ravishing young guest, that the idea of a visit to London was first mooted.

On 16th March Olga arrived with her parents in Florence. They stayed at the Minerva Hotel and in three weeks took in all the sights. Olga was happy at last to get a chance to visit the galleries, museums and palaces, and her artistic and erudite father was an excellent guide. On 4th April they all moved up to Meran where Elizabeth and Marina were staying, but by then the idea implanted in Prince Nicholas' head by Aunt Toria had begun to take root. Financial considerations permitting, they were all off to London as soon as the two youngest had had their adenoids out. Prince Nicholas was trying to negotiate the letting of their house in Athens to enable them, financially, to survive a London season and at last the deal began to look possible.

The 29th May was Olga's twentieth birthday and she was bursting with expectation and excitement. Five days later they left Meran and on Thursday 8th June arrived in London to stay at the Granby Court Hotel, 88 Queens Gate, for the London season. Was it possible that Olga, with all her beauty might

* Third son of Queen Victoria.
† Victoria, Princess of Great Britain and Ireland, second daughter of King Edward VII and Queen Alexandra.

catch the eye of the Prince of Wales? Her parents can be forgiven for secretly praying that she would.

On 27th June Princess Nicholas took her two eldest daughters to lunch with the King and Queen at Buckingham Palace. Olga was surprisingly unimpressed. 'Today, Mummy, Woolly and I lunched with the king and queen at Buckingham Palace. They were alone, he very talkative and rather noisy, she silent and shy! Enfin lunch went off all right and just before leaving they asked if we cared to go to Wimbledon to see the tennis matches, so he sent word to the secretary there who, on our arrival came to meet us most amiably and took us to the Royal box.'

Paul first saw the beautiful eldest daughter of Prince Nicholas of Greece at a ball given by Lady Zia Wernher. Though he stared at her for most of the evening he was never introduced. When he returned to his flat in Mount Street he was unable to sleep. How could he possibly arrange to see her again? And if he did, what on earth would he say to her?

Olga had not enjoyed the ball very much and had remained oblivious of Paul's interest. On the whole, she found outings with old friends and with her family more amusing than grand formal occasions. 'First of all on Friday afternoon we managed to go to the Horse Show which was marvellous but had to come away early to dress for a big ball given at Zia's house. There were over 400 people and being the first one and not knowing a soul made the whole thing an intense bore! David* was also there but didn't approach any of us. On Saturday evening the Vlastos asked us and U. Christo to the theatre to see *Stop Flirting*, a musical comedy—killingly funny. We shrieked with laughter the whole time.'

It was not till Tuesday 10th July that Paul succeeded in effecting an introduction, but, by an unhappy coincidence, the Prince of Wales was present as well. This was, as far as Olga was concerned, a major distraction. Probably Paul was already in love with her. From the very beginning, he had noted her beauty and innocence and had conceived the wild notion that she might make a perfect wife. On Friday 13th July Olga wrote 'On Tuesday night was the big Red Cross Russian ball at the Hyde Park Hotel to which we all went. That same

* The Prince of Wales.

afternoon we lunched at Claridges with the Alis* and a Spanish gentleman M. Villavieja. After that we had arranged to go to Roehampton to see the polo, such a lovely place, so big and well kept. There the Spanish Mme Merry Del Val was presented and sat with us, also Paul of Serbia. David was playing in the Welsh Guards against the Coldstreams and in the end his side won. After that, the Madrid Cup was given to him by the Dsse de Penagrande. As we were standing just behind him (David) Villavieja presented him; the poor thing was dripping with perspiration and very shy.'

On Friday 13th Paul danced with Olga at the ball given by Sir Philip Sassoon, but though he gets merely a passing reference in her diary, it is clear that he, for his part, had already made up his mind. Though nervous almost to the point of incoherence, he had at last found a means of getting to see her by design rather than by mere coincidence. Villavieja, an elderly Spaniard whom he happened to know well, seemed to know Olga and her family passably well, too. (The old gentleman had already done well by presenting Olga to the Prince of Wales at the polo.) Paul could see clearly enough that an invitation to watch the Prince of Wales at polo was probably his best hope. It would be risky in the extreme but Olga would be more likely to accept and besides, there would be entertainment. The diary entry for Saturday 14th July proved him right: 'Last night was quite amusing, especially watching the people. The host met us on top of the stairs with his sister who acted as hostess for him. The hotel is lovely with lovely pictures and furniture in it. David was already there when we arrived and danced exclusively the whole evening with his lady love Mrs Dudley Ward. She has rather a sweet little face, and it seems she is very tactful (so Paul told me) and he likes her very much too. The Duchess of Sutherland was introduced to Mummy and has asked us on Monday to a fancy-dress ball she is giving. It seems that only married ladies will wear masques and the girls something on the head. Today we are supposed to lunch at Claridges with the Villaviejas and Paul and then to go on to Ranelagh for the polo.'

For the Duchess of Sutherland's ball on 17th Paul chose the

* The Infante Alfonso of Spain and his wife Beatrice (Aunt Bee), daughter of the Duke of Edinburgh.

same fancy dress as six others, including his hostess. 'The Duchess, Paul and five others wore Japanese trousers with short jackets and big things on their heads with long masks!' The Prince of Wales, needless to say, looked original and dashing dressed as a highlander. Paul, however, persevered. On the following Wednesday, in the afternoon, 'Villavieja with his sister-in-law, the Duchess of Salamanca, and Paul came to fetch us to go to Hurlingham to see the polo for the third time. We lunched there but Puppy and Mummy had to leave at four to go to Buckingham Palace to tea. Zuzes* came with us for that reason. In the evening we all decided to go to the theatre at the last minute . . . just Puppy, Mummy, Paul and myself. Woolly had a bad cold so went to bed early. We saw *Lilac Time* with Schubert's music which was charming though very sentimental.'

Whether Elizabeth had stayed home on a pretext or whether it was just Paul's good fortune, from that day the scales seem to have been tilted a little more his way. On the 20th Olga wrote 'last night we went to Hurlingham invited by Admiral Kerr; Mummy and I went there for dinner and Puppy and Woolly with the Villaviejas came after. We didn't stay late as it was such a bore and not a single known person. Paul never appeared as he promised he would with the Duchess from another dinner party. We were back around one. Today I must stay in bed to be all right for this evening as we are going to see *Stop Flirting* for Puppy's benefit. Paul is asking us and I am delighted to see it again! After that we go to the Portlands' ball.'

That was on Friday 20th and the evening went well. They dined at Claridges (the Villaviejas were there too) and at the Portlands they saw the Duke and Duchess of York. In Paul, Prince Nicholas had found a truly kindred spirit and the dutiful Olga was not insensitive to her father's immediate and strong liking for her escort. On the Saturday, Paul arrived at 3.15 p.m. to take them to Hurlingham and afterwards to 'Uncle Ali's and Aunt Bee's' house in Esher. Paul enjoyed himself hugely and accompanied Aunt Bee on the piano after dinner. Monday 23rd saw them again at a ball in Hurlingham. Paul was by then deeply in love with Olga and he would have been pleased to note even the somewhat back-handed praise in her diary:

* Mme Tombazi, a lady in waiting.

'[the ball was] a bore as we knew hardly anyone. Poor Mummy had nothing but old men to talk to! As for myself I only danced twice with Paul and sat out the whole of the evening with him and didn't feel a bit bored.' On the Wednesday they again met at a garden party at Buckingham Palace where Olga witnessed Paul's general popularity and especially his friendship with the royal brothers and with Elizabeth, by now Duchess of York. On the Friday he took Olga's family to dine at the Embassy Club and by the Saturday Olga was writing 'Marina is in bed and I am waiting for Paul to ring up as he said he would at 2.30. Now it is 3.20 and he has not done so yet—Perhaps he has completely forgotten!'

When he called, it was to ask Olga out the next day. He took her to the cinema but seemed unusually preoccupied and nervous. Olga, correctly sensing the mood, leant towards him and prompted in a whisper 'Have you found what you want?' Paul, who a few moments earlier had been consumed with apprehension and fear, turned to her and with a look full of gratitude said 'Yes, at last!'

* * *

The engagement became official on the Thursday when King Alexander's formal consent had been received. After an idyllic long weekend at Brownsea Island as guests of the Infante Alfonso and Aunt Bee, Paul left for Belgrade leaving Olga to answer the stream of well-wishing letters. Alexander's wife, Queen Marie, was expecting a baby in September so the wedding was fixed for Monday 22nd October, to coincide with the christening. Paul invited the Duke of York ('Bertie') to be his best man and the invitations went out at once.

Olga's trousseau was prepared in Paris and Paul made all the necessary arrangements in Belgrade. On Saturday 20th October, in the afternoon Olga, accompanied by her family, arrived in Belgrade for the first time. The royal railway carriage had been sent to the frontier to collect them and Paul travelled out to join them at the penultimate station before Belgrade. He explained, in a high state of over excitement, during the rest of the trip, the detailed arrangements both for the christening and for the wedding the next day.

At the station at Belgrade Alexander was waiting together with Arsène and Sitta, Carol,* Palo and Tittum. It was a great joy seeing them all again! There were also the Ministers, their wives and the garde d'honneur which played our hymn as we stepped out of the train. We drove to the new palace in open carriages drawn by white horses and the coachmen in powdered wigs! Alexander drove first with Puppy then Mummy and Hellen (Mignon† being ill) then Paul and I and lastly Arsène with Woolly and Marina. The others came by motor. On the steps Elisabeta‡ was waiting with Ileana; § I was delighted to see the former again. When we had all assembled, we came upstairs to see Mignon who was in bed and looking much thinner in the face. Mana-Bell brought the baby whom I found very sweet and not in the least ugly! We all had tea in the room next door and talked and neither of us knew from where to begin and what to say! In the evening there was a family dinner and just before, Bertie and Elizabeth arrived. After dinner they all went to the station to meet A. Sophie. ‖ After she came we all retired pretty early to bed and poor Paul was simply dead with fatigue and emotion! We were living in the Old Palace in very nice rooms. Next morning at 11 was the christening. The baby was brought in a shut carriage drawn by six white horses in the arms of an old general and an old admiral. During the ceremony, which took place in the chapel of the Old Palace, Bertie and afterwards A. Missy¶ held the baby. The ceremony over, Alexander took [Peter] with him to the window and showed him to the people. At 1.00 there was a tremendous lunch for 400 people to which the whole of Belgrade was invited, together with the foreigners present.

* Crown Prince, later King Carol of Rumania.
† Nickname for Queen Marie of Yugoslavia, born Princess of Rumania.
‡ Elisabeth, Princess of Rumania married to George II, Duke of Sparta and later King of Greece.
§ Ileana, Princess of Rumania married to Archduke Anton of Austria.
‖ Sophie, Princess of Prussia married to Constantine ('Tino'), King of Greece.
¶ Marie, Princess of Edinburgh, married to King Ferdinand of Rumania (mother of Marie, Elisabeth and Ileana, above).

In the evening there was again a family dinner and a gala concert afterwards. That night we none of us slept very much! In the morning Hellen came to tell us a few details about the service. Then Sophica and her mother came in while I was dressing. Mummy came in to help me put on my veil. Just before starting to church she and Puppy blessed me with a holy picture which they gave me! At 12 the minister of the Court came to say it was time to go so I took Puppy's arm and we walked along followed by the others. They were all waiting in the chapel when we came in and Paul was already standing in his place on the right in front of the altar. When the moment of the crowns came they were placed on our heads and left there and happily they didn't fall off! Bertie exchanged the rings. After the ceremony we went and kissed Puppy and Mummy then the rest of the family. There was a big lunch afterwards but less big than that of the christening. Then we sat and talked a little and I went to change for a short drive round the town, to show ourselves!!!! Then we came back and went to see Mignon and Paul took Mummy, A. Sophia, and me to see his rooms in which A. Missy was living those days! At 6 I came home with Puppy and Mummy to change as we were leaving at 9. I drove to the station with Alexander and Paul, the others following; they all came to the station except A. Missy and Elisabeta. After tender goodbyes to the family (I kissed Puppy and Mummy and sisters in the train) we slowly moved off . . . on our own life à deux!—We had the same train as we came in. We got to Venice the next day at 11 at night feeling tired. We spent three days at the Danielli and on Friday morning we went to the station to see Puppy and Mummy who were passing through on their way back to Paris. We left that afternoon at 3 for Florence which we reached late at night. Princess Abamalek had taken rooms for us at the H. de la Ville. The next day Saturday we lunched with her at Pratolino and Paul took me all over the house and grounds which are enormous!

On the following day they continued by train to Rome where for nearly five weeks they stayed in the huge and sumptuously furnished Villa Abamalek. They saw few people though the

King and Queen of Italy were kind to them and Philip of Hesse, whom they both liked enormously, visited when he was in the city. After three weeks Olga was able to write 'our happiness, mine at least, increases daily and time seems to fly'. Rome could scarcely have been a greater contrast to San Remo where exactly a year before she had arrived as a rejected, miserable and lonely exile.

CHAPTER IV

1924–1932

The Family, Bohinj and the Prince Paul Museum

Exactly twelve days after returning to Belgrade on 16th January 1924 from their honeymoon of eleven weeks, Paul read Olga's diary entry for the 27th: 'I don't want to begin complaining', she wrote, 'but life here is a dreadful bore and a monotony and Paul feels it too—such a queer unhomely atmosphere in the house and no nice family life.' Against his name Paul placed an asterisk and at the foot of the page he added the words 'he does!'. Living in rather cramped and dark quarters within the King's palace was neither fun nor easy. Already in their first two weeks at the palace Paul and Olga had been obliged for ten days to take their meals in separate rooms, following a violent row between King Alexander and Queen Marie. The former had insisted on eating with Paul, leaving Olga to eat with his wife. Neither Paul nor Olga particularly cared for Queen Marie. She was indolent and morose, combining little by way of beauty or intelligence, and she contributed next to nothing to court or family life in Belgrade. She was, moreover, intensely jealous of Olga whose strong appeal to men, and to the King in particular, was obvious, and she would hide away in her room and sulk for days at a stretch. Precisely at the moment when Paul and Olga returned from their honeymoon, the relationship was strained between Alexander and Mignon. By the end of February, the Queen had left for Paris and Olga felt profoundly sorry for her. The King was not an easy man. He was extremely unpredictable and, though he was by nature kind, he could be cruel and unthinking. Belgrade, furthermore, was a dull place and the thought of being tied to it by duty was for Olga, no less than for Paul, depressing. On 20th April, as the Queen was about to return from Paris, Olga wrote, 'Poor thing, how sad she must be to come back. Like beginning lessons on Monday morning, only worse!'

For a short while, early in 1924, it looked as though Paul would be sent to live in Zagreb, the capital of Croatia. The possibility of his fulfilling some vice-regal function was certainly discussed and the prospect was keenly anticipated by the young couple. When, on 2nd February, Paul told his wife that they were to go up to Zagreb to open a huge ball given by the directors of the university she pencilled in her diary, 'I am curious to see what the palace is like where we are to live'. Her impressions of the Croatian capital, its inhabitants and indeed of the palace were good ones and on the last day of the visit she wrote with some enthusiasm about the city which she thought was to become her home:

> The palace is situated in what they call the Old Town, on a hill. The rooms were quite nice but very old and mon-strously furnished. All the same there are a lot of possibilities and I believe one could make something very comfortable out of them, but it would take some time! The ball in the evening was successful but a very exhausting business as thousands of people of all kinds were being presented to us and I had to speak to one lady after another and nearly the whole of the time in German, which is the predominant language there! We both praised Zagreb up to the skies saying what a beautiful place it was and how much we hoped to pay them another lengthier visit some other time to which they seemed enchanted. What made a specially good impression is that Paul attempted to kiss the ring on the hand of the cardinal, and as they are all very Catholic, it made an excellent impression! There were some ladies of good families who have got châteaux round the town where there is fine shooting and hunting in spring and autumn. The next day Paul visited the picture gallery and library but I felt too exhausted to go also.[1]

Immediately after their return to Belgrade, Paul arranged for Olga to start taking lessons in Serbo-Croat.

To Paul Croatia symbolized the less militarist, more

civilized element of Yugoslav life. Zagreb was more outward looking and cosmopolitan than Belgrade, and it was intellectually alive. Moreover, it was nearer Europe. Paul, who made no secret of his wish to fulfil some role in government, let it be known that he would view a posting to Zagreb with great pleasure.

Alexander, however, seems to have had second thoughts. Whether or not he was serious in raising the prospect of the Governorship of Croatia in the first place, he certainly found the keenness with which it was viewed by his cousin irksome. It is possible that he had casually thrown out the idea to test his cousin's sense of duty, misjudging the likely response. Certainly, there was little in Paul's life to date that would have led him to believe that an invitation to settle down in Zagreb would be so enthusiastically taken up. It is also possible—and as the years progressed this explanation was to gain ground even outside royal and government circles—that Alexander was nervous of the likely effects, in an intensely nationalistic and separatist Croatia, of a popular and kindred Karageorgević governor. Though he never doubted Paul's personal and dynastic loyalty, Alexander was acutely conscious of the fragile constitutional structure of his country. It was one that needed a strong dose of centralism. It was not difficult to imagine Paul, once established in Zagreb, taking up the interests of Croatia. If the King feared that his cousin, given the governorship, might take up the cudgels against his own, essentially Serbian, system of government in Belgrade, he may have known Paul better than anyone then imagined. Paul's approach to such a constitutional duty might turn out to be naïve; but it would thereby be the more ruthless. His intelligence, his international education and his open-minded, essentially civilian, approach might go down too well; his analysis of the situation might become too intellectual and his defence of the Croatians a little too articulate for comfort. The last thing Alexander needed, at this point, was a popular champion in Croatia; and it would be just like Paul to go and sink his own personal and even family interests for the sake of some high-flown concept of duty. No, Paul would have to remain in Belgrade and be held, for the time being at least, in reserve.

It did not take long for Paul and Olga to start planning their first trip abroad. Walks in the mornings, often in the pouring rain, and reading in the afternoons might have been all right in their own home and undertaken out of choice, but as guests of the King and Queen in Belgrade, the tedium and monotony of it all was unbearable. During March they began to plan a trip to England. Olga was pregnant and expecting her first child in August and Paul was concerned that it should be born in England. Olga, who was still only twenty, would be better taken care of there and she would be surrounded by her own family and friends. Lady Nina found out for Paul that Bisham Grange, a cottage which Paul had often noticed when staying with the Balfours at next-door Bisham Abbey, would be available in the early summer. The price was a bit steep at £30 a week but it was the perfect place, with a river, five cows, a vegetable garden, enough rooms and within easy reach of London.

Paul and Olga left Belgrade on 11th May 1924. Their first stop was the royal palace in Bled, in the northern province of Slovenia, by the side of a large and beautiful lake. They spent the weekend there in the company of Sitta and her sister Irene and then moved on to Paris where they stayed for the best part of a fortnight surrounded by Olga's family, who were also about to move on to London.

On arrival in London Paul and Olga moved straight up to Bisham Grange, near Marlow. The house was tiny but it was, to both of them, utterly enchanting and the next six weeks were to be some of the happiest of their lives. They had two small upstairs guestrooms and these were almost always occupied, either by Olga's family or Paul's friends. Chips, Lady Cunard, Sir Joseph Duveen, Archie and Lady Nina were amongst those who stayed. Serge Obolensky came too, bringing with him his new fiancée, Alice Astor, and invited Paul to be best man at their wedding.

Paul and Olga made several trips to Esher to see the Infante Alfonso of Spain and the Infanta Beatrice and they were warmly received by the Duke and Duchess of York at Chesterfield House which had been lent to them by the Lascelles. Paul took Olga to Ascot and to Oxford, where he showed her his old rooms in Peckwater, and in London they lunched with the King and Queen, the Portlands, and the Serbian Minister. They also visited Augustus John (whom Olga found 'bohemian and dirty') in his Chelsea studio where he was painting the Infanta Beatrice.*

Compared with Olga's family who had taken rooms in the Granby Court Hotel and who, on account of Elizabeth and Marina, were caught up in the social whirl of the London season, Paul and Olga led a relatively lazy existence. On several occasions Paul accompanied his sisters-in-law to their dances as chaperon, and to his own enjoyment, as matchmaker-in-chief. He got them invited to stay with the Curzons at Hackwood, near Ascot and with the Portlands at Welbeck and was pleased when Lord Ivor Churchill, who had developed a strong liking for Elizabeth, invited the family to stay at Blenheim, parents and all.

Olga's baby was due in August and it was an immense relief to Paul when, on the Friday of Ascot, Elizabeth York took him aside in the Royal Box and offered him their Richmond home, White Lodge, for Olga's confinement during August and September. This was, for Paul, the most generous offer imaginable and a singular act of friendship, and he never forgot it. Elizabeth was there herself, on 7th August, to meet them and show them round. On the 13th Olga gave birth to a nine-and-a-half-pound son. They called him Alexander and the christening, according to the Greek Orthodox rite, took place at White Lodge on 6th September. Apart from the Duke of York, the Infanta Beatrice of Spain and King Alexander, the god-parents were all members of the immediate Greek family circle.

Exactly ten days after Alexander's birth a letter arrived from Paul's old acquaintance, Bernard Berenson, almost thirty years his senior and by then a world famous art historian and acknowledged expert on Italian Renaissance painting. Berenson was proposing to research into Serbian ecclesiastical art with special emphasis on early frescoes and had been told that Paul would be able to help. It was naturally flattering for Paul and he answered on the morning of the christening:

Please forgive me for not answering your letter before but my wife has just had a baby and I've had such an awful lot of

* Augustus John was later to paint a portrait of Olga which was presented by Paul to the Museum of Modern Art in Belgrade.

telegrams and letters to answer and as I have no secretary here it makes it a very slow job. I hope you will understand and excuse me! I was perfectly delighted to hear from you and wish you had told me more about yourself. A propos of the question that interests you, these are the books where you can find descriptions of the frescoes. First, there is Kondakoff who described our churches and monasteries but I fear that it is a very difficult book to get now but perhaps in big libraries such as the British Museum etc. you could still find copies of that Russian work. You will find it easier to get Gabriel Millet's *L'Ancien Art Serbe* (*Les Eglises*) which was published in Paris in 1919. I also know of an English publication which I am trying to find and which I'll send you the moment I find it. I fear I can't remember the name of the author but I trust all the same to be able to send you a copy before long. Do write again. In haste, as my son's christening takes place in a few minutes . . .[2]

For the next thirty-four years, right up until Berenson's death, the two were to maintain an unbroken correspondence. For Paul this relationship was to matter probably more than any other. Berenson became for Paul a kind of hero and mentor, on whose values and standards the younger man would seek to model himself. On the day of little Alexander's christening, however, it served merely to distract Paul from the matters in hand.

During his first three months in England Paul had all but forgotten about his aspirations in Belgrade. Now he waited for news from the King. Even though he had had to put the idea of the post in Zagreb to the back of his mind, he was not without hope that a house would be made available for them in or around Belgrade and that the King would at least define a role for him, if not confer an office. But by the end of September they had still not received anything beyond the usual telegram of congratulations and family news. Both were worried about the immediate future 'as nothing seems to be shaping itself' and since on October 10th the Yorks were due to return from Scotland they were in any case bound to vacate White Lodge by then. Archie and Lady Nina offered them accommodation in London and at Newton Don, but what with the new baby and the fact that they needed to plan ahead for the next few months they plumped instead for a small flat in Claridges. They soon settled on the idea of the South of France and within ten days were in Cannes, staying at the Hotel Gray d'Albion, looking for villas—one for themselves and another for Olga's parents. Eventually they found more or less what they wanted in Grasse. Although it was a far cry from Bisham Grange and White Lodge, Paul could at least console himself that he had succeeded not only in arranging a roof over his little family's head for the next few months but that he had also managed to shoulder some of the responsibility which lay so heavily on his father-in-law, Prince Nicholas. The English valet whom he engaged for himself was highly-strung but the cook turned out to be excellent. He was especially pleased that, at least for Olga, Christmas 1924 would be a happy family affair like the previous year in Paris, for he had been nervous of plunging her into the gloomy and unwelcoming atmosphere of the Old Palace in Belgrade. She was, after all, only twenty-one and particularly tied to her family.

For Paul himself this was a period of complete uncertainty. He wanted desperately to be of help to his cousin and he hoped for a job. It was not so much that he was bored, he longed to be trusted. Not for the first time in his life he wanted to be of use in Belgrade, and for the first time he thought he could be. But the King made no move and, inevitably, Paul felt rejected. He was loath to arrive in Belgrade with Olga and little Alexander to await the King's pleasure. He knew that sooner or later he would have to go there and that unless he went there was little chance of his being offered anything but temporary accommodation but, for the time being at least, it seemed best to keep at arm's length.

When at last his in-laws arrived in Grasse, a week before Christmas, they were pleased with their villa, Les Heures Claires. Ivor Churchill had visited Elizabeth in Paris but nothing had come of it. Now there was nothing for it but to wait for the London season next year. Meanwhile, winter in the South of France was a relatively mild affair with tennis and golf, walks along the sea front, luncheon parties, English teas, dinners, charity balls and occasional expeditions to visit friends and relations. Olga was beside herself with joy. She was deeply in love with Paul and proud of his efforts for her

3. Prince Paul of Serbia in traditional photographic attire.

4. Prince Alexander in military uniform, March 1916.

5. Oxford, March 1920. Left to right: Mr Seymour Cochrane-Baillie (later Lord Lamington), Mollie Lascelles (later Duchess of Buccleuch), Katherine Hamilton (later Lady Katherine Seymour), Lady Elizabeth Bowes-Lyon (later H.M. Queen Elizabeth the Queen Mother), the Hon. Edith Smith, Lady Doris Gordon Lennox (later Lady Doris Vyner), Prince Paul.

6. Royal group at Prince and Princess Paul of Serbia's wedding, 1923. Standing, l to r: Princess Marina of Greece, Prince Nicholas of Greece, Princess Irene of Greece, Duke of York, Prince Paul of Greece, Princess Helene of Serbia, Crown Prince Carol of Rumania, King Alexander of Serbia, Princess Demidoff (aunt), King Ferdinand of Rumania, Prince Arsène Karageorgević, Queen Elisabetta of Greece, Crown Princess Helen of Rumania.
Seated, l to r: Princess Nicholas of Greece, Queen Sophie of Greece, Princess Olga, Prince Paul, Queen Marie of Rumania, the Duchess of York.
On floor: Princess Ileana of Rumania, Princess Elizabeth of Greece.

family. She was enchanted with her little boy and thrilled that the entire family was there to admire him.

Philip of Hesse had become engaged to Mafalda, the King of Italy's second daughter,* and a grand wedding was in the offing for the following year. As luck would have it, Olga had received Fr. 5,000 for Christmas, from Paul's Aunt Moïna, and she immediately set this aside for wedding clothes.

Meanwhile there were friends galore and ample time to see them all. Lord Derby was there, the father of Paul's old friend Lady Victoria Bullock, and so was pompous Dom Manuel of Portugal and his wife Mimi. In the middle of January 1925 Paul went for a few days to Paris to see his ailing father and 'to meet up with Sandro and Mignon'.[3] By February, Arsène had arrived in nearby Nice and, in spite of his extremely debilitated condition he began to hit the gambling tables hard, making a point of arriving every Sunday for lunch at Villa Otrada with his son and daughter-in-law. Arthur, the elderly Duke of Connaught, was at Cap Ferrat and so too was Mme Balsan (Ivor Churchill's mother and ex-Duchess of Marlborough). There were a few Italian royalties at the Villa Regina Madre in Bordighera, including Mafalda and Crown Prince Umberto ('Bepo' to the family) as well as Philip of Hesse. The Queen of Italy, an aunt of King Alexander's through the Montenegrin line, was, as always, hospitable and speculation began to grow about Elizabeth's chances with Crown Prince Umberto. In March Parisian society arrived in force with Charles, Duc de Noailles, his wife Marie Louise and her mother, Marie Thérèse; the Duchesse de Vendôme; the Comte de Rougement and the Prince de Polignac. Princess Marie-José of Belgium came too, and from London the Wernhers made a brief appearance.

Just about the time that Olga's parents were arranging to take a house in Portland Place from the 1st June, Moïna offered to rent for Paul a house in Fiesole, not far from Pratolino. Olga, not without provocation, was prompted to complain: 'Why not give us one of the twenty she possesses around Pratolino?'[4]

Paul had already telegraphed his cousins to ask if he could

* Mafalda was to die in Buchenwald concentration camp, a victim of Italy's decision to desert the Axis cause, on 27th August 1944.

bring his family to stay in Bled for the summer, thinking that this would be the easiest way to re-establish contact. The reply on 7th May consisted of six words and was a bitter disappointment: 'We are not going, love Mignon.'[5] Olga, who like Paul was developing something of a complex about their relationship with the King and Queen, burst forth in indignation. 'So that settles it!' she wrote in her diary. 'They don't seem to want us ever to come back, because certainly it's not amusing for Paul to go and live there never having anything to do and if we went to Bled now it was simply to see them!'

On 20th May 1925 they left by car for Paris, where they remained for a fortnight. On 6th June they moved to London. Paul, who had had an expensive time of it in the South of France and Paris and who was obliged for the sake of his tiny son to keep on the house in Grasse, had neither the inclination nor the resources to run two separate establishments. He accordingly stayed at the Bath Club whilst Olga stayed with her parents in Portland Place.

Suddenly, out of the blue and when their spirits needed lifting, came a telegram from Alexander and Mignon (already at Bled) saying that they would be 'welcome any time'[6]. Exactly two weeks later they left for Bled, planning to fetch their son from Grasse at a later date and as soon as the question of their home had been settled. But, when they arrived at Bled, again they were disappointed. Not a word was said either about work or about independent lodgings. By the end of July they were both back in Paris. Arsène was not well and Paul was worried for the old man. Olga remained in Paris with her parents and sisters after Paul returned to Bled, and then moved down to the South of France to be with her son on his first birthday. Their plans were for her to wait for Paul, whose health was again low, to take a cure in Vichy in September and from there to go together to the Palace of Raconiggi outside Turin for the huge Mafalda-Hesse festivities on the 27th. 'How I wish we could have a settled home at last! I wonder if the Zagreb question will crop up now that the Croatians are invited with the others. It would be such a good thing!'[7]

Almost as Olga was writing these lines, Paul was scribbling an ecstatic telegram to her from Bled. The King had offered them a house in Slovenia near to Bled by the side of the lake of

Bohinj, which Paul described as 'a perfect summer residence for the baby'.[8] Here at last was what they had been hoping for. It was not much, of course, but still it meant an important element of independence and, above all else, a home of their own. Olga packed up her things and left the very next day for Milan, Trieste and Ljubljana. There she was met by Paul who took her at once and in a state of great excitement to see their precious new house.

Whilst the car sped along the twenty-five kilometres from Ljubljana to Kranj he described the house, its situation and potential. As he talked, they passed the rich lowland grasslands and woods of the Sava valley decorated with the wooden hay-lofts and cottages of the Slovene farming communities, gathered in clusters around the cupolas of their tiny, well-positioned churches. Twenty kilometres beyond Kranj, at Lesce, their driver at last swung their car to the left on to the short and familiar road up to Bled. The lake, its surrounding Alpine back-cloth, its island church and ancient castle were magnificent, like some gigantic Turner, in the morning haze. Exactly at the point where the road branched left to Bohinj stood the palace of his cousin, but Paul ordered the driver to push on westwards up the valley, unwilling, in his excitement, to let his young wife unload or change her clothes at Bled.

The river valley grew steeper. Along the centre, on either side of a perfectly clear and smooth-running river, ran a narrow belt of grazing land and as they neared the lake at the top, the little hamlets grew smaller and more frequent. Paul pronounced their names one by one: Bohinj Bela, Nomenj, Lepenc, Bohinj Bistrica, Savica, Kamnje and Polje.

The sense of anticipation was infectious and Olga was thrilled. Not only could she see that Paul had at last found what he clearly considered a perfect home but she was herself overcome by the indescribable beauty of what she saw. When at length they reached Bohinj Jezero, where the world, in the form of the towering Julian Alps, seemed to gather round a clear and perfectly still mountain lake, Paul pointed up to the right and there, perched on a rise overlooking the lake and the beautiful mid-eighteenth-century parish church, was their house. They climbed up the bank and went straight in. The walls of three main floors were of slatted wood and the top

67

two floors had overhanging balconies, which looked out across the river valley. Stone steps led up to the front door, while inside, the ceilings were panelled in polished hard wood. Around and above the main hall chimney piece, which was inlaid with shining brass, ran the central staircase. They immediately planned the lay-out. There were to be two nurseries on the top floor with their own bathroom and a room for the nurse to sleep in. Apart from the main bedroom with its dressing room and bathroom there were to be two guest rooms with separate bathrooms and servants' rooms to house at least a cook and butler. The whole thing would be decorated inexpensively, in whitewash and a mass of chintz. All around there were rivers, lakes, forests and glorious views. The garden could accommodate a tennis court. They would be able, as Olga recorded ecstatically in her diary, 'to grow [their] own vegetables and to keep [their] own horses.'[9] Altogether the prospects were utterly overwhelming.

When they arrived in Belgrade on 10th September 1925, they had been away for an unbroken period of eighteen months. They still needed to pay Moïna a visit, to attend Mafalda and Philip's wedding and, most of all, collect their 'beloved tiny' from the South of France; so after spending three days in Belgrade, where they visited the vast new palace complex at Dedinje (which even King Alexander was forced to admit was 'overdoing' it a bit), they left for Turin via Venice and Milan. They were met in Milan by the Duke of Aosta ('Bouby') and his brother Bob. At Turin they were met by Crown Prince Umberto. The whole town seemed to be infected with the festive air and, beneath the gaze of ancient and sometimes stiff relations, they acted out their various parts. There were dinners, quadrilles, jewels, sashes, chiffon, giggles, rows and jealousies, and at the end of it all the wedding ceremony and procession graced by the Italian leader, Benito Mussolini, as well as by members of the Italian, Greek, Austrian, Serbian, Montenegrin, Belgian and Rumanian royal families. It was a splendid show and everyone enjoyed it immensely.

Afterwards, some of them went to inspect the Fiat factory. Olga fell head over heels in love with a 'delicious little two-seater with new square bonnet and a round dickie, dark blue with black mudguards'.[10] She was allowed to test drive it all around the wide factory roof and, as it was going for a knock-down price of £160, Paul bought it on the spot as a Christmas present for her.

In Florence they found Moïna extremely fat but amiable. In Grasse they shopped for chintz and furniture and baths for their new home in Bohinj. From there Paul went on to Paris where he stayed a few days in Lord Derby's flat and thence to London. Olga left for Belgrade taking Alexander with her. The King was at the station to meet her and was completely taken by his little namesake. He clasped the tiny child to his chest and, when their car pulled up outside the palace, ran up the stairs to show him off to his wife saying 'Look what I've found!' and dumped him on her bed. This was probably the most tactless thing he could have done, especially since he never seemed to care about his own son Peter who was a thin and timid little boy, approximately one year older. Yet he meant it well and wanted Olga to feel at home. She was of course flattered and surprised— it was a real welcome and came straight from the heart.

For Paul, however, the road ahead was still unmapped. Though he was in London when Queen Alexandra died, it never crossed Alexander's mind to ask him to represent Yugoslavia at the funeral. The omission was, in Paul's opinion, less a demonstration of his country's lack of diplomatic savoir faire than a sign that he was still superfluous in Alexander's scheme of things.

Paul was back in Belgrade in time for the traditional Te Deum on 1st December to commemorate the Corfu Declaration of 1917 and the creation of 'the Kingdom of Serbs, Croats and Slovenes', as Yugoslavia was then still technically styled.

1925 was their first Christmas together in Belgrade and Olga introduced a genuine element of excitement and of homeliness. Alexander eagerly helped her with the tree and with every other kind of decoration. They ate their meals together, as they were to do in Belgrade for the next eight years, and after lunch and dinner Paul would sit and talk with Alexander. Every con-ceivable topic of conversation was covered from palace gossip to cabinet intrigue and world politics. For Paul, these talks were both instructive and alluring. For Alexander, they came as welcome relief. He learned, through the years, to trust his cousin's judgement and to listen to his views, but all the while he kept Paul out of politics and, surprisingly, even out of public view. Understandably, Paul turned increasingly for inspiration to his many friends and contacts abroad. His consuming passion remained artistic and he never failed to find excuses to visit London, Paris, Munich, Florence, Rome and Vienna—in short, wherever there was an exhibition or a picture to be seen or studied.

The New Year of 1926 was somewhat ruined by the news from Bucharest that Carol of Rumania had deserted his wife Helen and had gone abroad to live with his mistress, Mme Lupescu. Sitta remained a virtual recluse, unable to move about, whilst her little son Michael was acclaimed Crown Prince. On 4th January Queen Margherita of Italy died and after fulfilling their immediate duties in Belgrade, Paul and Olga left for Rome. All of Olga's family were there and Philip and Mafalda were already installed in their new villa a few miles outside the city. Paul and his father-in-law spent many mornings wandering about the ancient monuments, museums, villas on public view and galleries. Though Paul was never particularly close or affectionate with his mother-in-law, he loved and admired Prince Nicholas. Gay, relaxed, artistic and charming, Prince Nicholas was a welcome balance to the somewhat cliquey and pious family in which he moved. Paul himself was God-fearing and outwardly correct in his religious observance, but he was essentially a humanist. Prince Nicholas recognized and understood this secular trait in Paul and together they secretly and irreverently poked fun at some of the odder manifestations of their family's religiosity.

After the old queen's funeral in Rome, they moved north to Florence where they heard from an excited Duke of York that Elizabeth had been delivered of a baby girl on 21st April.* After spending Easter in Rome and a short stay in Paris, where Olga, in response to a generous offer from Arsène, was able to order some new dresses at Patou's, they returned to Belgrade to prepare for their house-warming in Bohinj in June. 'We have a butler called Doušan who has been here for years, a manservant, a Slovene who was four years with Prince Windischgraetz, a chauffeur and open motor (polished up for us here) and a woman help in the kitchen. There will be English,

* The future Queen Elizabeth II.

French, Italian, German and Serbian spoken in the house.'[11] The great day eventually arrived, and on 17th June 1926, Olga's diary entry was ecstatic:

Ermitage

Here we are at last and it's too good to be true to be in our own house surrounded with our things! We arrived on Tuesday morning very comfortably and found that the cook had arrived by the same train as well as both my little motor and the big one; so that Pacey and I drove in the little one and Baby and nurse in the other. We were given a touching reception by the inhabitants of our village who received us with bouquets and speeches and we were conducted to the house by half a dozen farmers dressed up in helmets and swords mounted on fat cart-horses with coloured paper tassels tied to their tails! The first day we ate at the hotel but now have our own food. We are almost installed except that there are some bits of furniture missing still. The air is divine and I hope it may do us all good. I long for the family to come! Mignon and Peterkins arrive in Bled tomorrow.

Their life in Yugoslavia was at last more regular and subsequent trips abroad were undertaken for specific purposes only. In September of that year Olga's grandmother, the exiled Queen Olga of Greece, died in Rome and they attended the funeral service there and the burial in Florence. Occasionally they would slip off to Munich or to Vienna to see the opera or listen to concerts. Paul would from time to time pay his respects to his aunt Moïna in Pratolino and take advantage of such visits to see his mentor, Berenson.

In 1927 they spent part of January and all of February in Cannes with Olga's family. By the end of March, however, they were back in Bohinj and, with nothing in Belgrade to lure them south, began to plan ahead for the season in London. This time they decided to rent Lord Ednam's house in Chelsea, 96 Cheyne Walk, and to take Marina with them. It seemed to pay off; for in the midst of all their parties and family gatherings the Prince of Wales appeared to take an unusual interest in her. It is difficult to make out which of them was the most excited, for his attentions were more than passing and went far beyond

71

the call of duty and politeness. Paul was near certain and Marina completely overwhelmed, whilst Olga and her mother scarcely dared hope. They stayed on an extra three weeks 'just in case' but it was all to no avail. Still, they had had a wonderful time and had managed to see most of their friends and family. To crown it all, Alexander had decided to give Olga a Rolls-Royce and it was made ready for their departure. Paul and Marina drove it, while Olga returned by train and within days of their arrival at Bohinj, Alexander and Paul had driven off in it to Munich 'incognito'.

Queen Marie was expecting her second child in January 1928 and that winter and spring Paul and Olga strayed only as far as Bucharest. Sitta was in a terrible state. Old King Ferdinand of Rumania had died, making his grandson, Michael, king. Her husband posed a constant threat from abroad and Olga, as her dearest and closest friend, was there to comfort her from February to April. Paul went to and fro with Elizabeth. Olga herself was again pregnant and her doctors advised Paul that she should be allowed to have the baby in England. It was expected in June and so Paul made plans accordingly. Again they went to London with Marina, Olga this time praying 'May God grant this year to be more satisfactory for Marina than last.'[12] In the event, it was not, but, as always, the round of parties was exhausting. More often than not, Paul was required to be Marina's escort and although he complained that it made him 'feel like an old dowager chaperoning her grandchildren'[13] he nevertheless enjoyed the opportunity of catching up with a mass of friends.

On 29th June, Olga was delivered of another son. He was christened Nicholas and soon afterwards was taken by Olga to join his elder brother, Alexander, at the Beresford Hotel, Birchington, where the latter had been enjoying a seaside holiday since early June. Paul took this opportunity to go north to Scotland to visit the Dalkeiths, the Balfours and his other friends scattered about the Lowlands.

By the middle of August they were back at Bohinj and Paul could write 'I fish for trout and shoot chamois with not too much disgust but spend most of my time reading.'[14]

Olga's mother, meanwhile, had spent most of her summer with Elizabeth at the Villa D'Este, home of the Italian royal family. Everyone was keen to further a match between Elizabeth and Crown Prince Umberto. Olga, as always concerned for her sisters' future, was hopeful of the result. 'I wonder if he'll look at Woolly. . . . Poor Mummy sacrificing her whole summer . . . God give it will bring some good results!'[15] But God did not, on this occasion, give, and Prince Umberto thought the whole thing obvious. He was not unnaturally put off.*

Even the unambitious and unpushing Prince Nicholas was beginning to wish his younger daughters would marry, though with him it mattered less that they should walk off with an emperor or a king than that they should find men whose values mirrored his own. If his Romanov wife considered Olga's marriage to a Karageorgević a little less than her entitlement, Prince Nicholas could have wished for nothing better. In June 1929 he wrote to his wife: 'How sweet of Paul to have said such nice things about me. I am very touched. He knows, of course, that I am particularly fond of him and never miss the chance to say so right and left. Wherever I am I sing his praises, his intelligence, erudition, artistic sense and knowledge—above all my gratitude that he has given so much happiness to our Olga. I suppose he knows all that. What a blessing it is that Providence sent us a man like that at a time when all young men of the present generation are so lacking in every way the essential qualities that make life bearable. If only we could find two others like *him* for E. and M.'[16] It was to be some years before Prince Nicholas' hopes were to be fulfilled.

Paul and Olga gradually became accustomed to their life, with headquarters at the Old Palace in Belgrade in the winter and Slovenia in the summer. Bohinj, which had a relaxed and cosy atmosphere, became a regular meeting place for all the family and everyone looked forward to it eagerly. Trips to the South of France, to Paris, Florence, Venice, Munich, Vienna and London were undertaken to visit family, shops and doctors and, in the case of Paul, art dealers, galleries and theatres, but these seldom lasted more than a month. Occasionally the spectre of Zagreb would be raised and the prospects of public office would be dangled before Paul's eyes; but these never came to much and gradually Paul learned to live with the fact, difficult though it was to accept, that, though his

* Prince Umberto married Princess Marie-José of Belgium in 1930.

cousin liked and admired him, he had no use for him in government.

The period from 1928 to 1934 was the nearest Paul ever got to fulfilling the role for which, by nature, he was obviously best suited. Even as an undergraduate at Oxford he had confessed to his contemporaries that, in different circumstances, his ultimate ambition would have been to become the Curator of the Ashmolean. When he had said this, probably over a glass of port and only half in earnest, he was inevitably comparing his own potential in the peace and beauty of Oxford with his probable future in the turmoil of post-war Serbia. But as the years wore on and his character developed, his late night quip of 1920 became increasingly appropriate.

His first real experience of the art world as a profession rather than a pastime had come in 1925. In January of that year, when living in Villa Otrada in Grasse, Paul had travelled up to Paris to see the King and Queen. He had on that occasion put forward his suggestion for the creation of a museum of modern art in Belgrade. Alexander, apprehensive about the prospects of his thirty-one-year-old cousin distributing largesse from an extremely hard pressed national purse, as if he were some kind of latter-day Renaissance prince, said that he would have to think the matter over. By the time Paul arrived at Bled in July, Alexander had come to the conclusion that he should let Paul have his head. Paul was told, however, that he should speak to the Minister of Finance.

The King had still not discussed the matter with his government. He was naturally suspicious of the plan and reckoned it would most probably come to naught. When he told Paul that he should discuss it with the Minister of Finance he thought he had effectively put an end to the idea. But Paul was more resourceful. As he explained to Berenson in January of the following year, 'I suggested to the Finance Minister that I was willing to guarantee him the nucleus of a gallery of modern art, cost-less to the State, on condition that he'd give me a nice building. No sooner said than done. I had always had an eye on a delightful XVIII Century Turkish Konak with a nice "hamam"—a round room with a cupola and niches which will do admirably for statues. I immediately started a campaign and wrote to heaps of people.'[17]

Paul wrote first to Archie who suggested he should get in touch with Mr Aitken at the Tate Gallery, whose opinions he reckoned would be invaluable. He then wrote to several possible donors, including Joseph Duveen, Ivor Churchill, Emerald Cunard and his cousin Alexander. The latter was immediately pressurized into donating some contemporary Serbian works and, on the whole, the response from the others was excellent.

Emerald Cunard, in particular, was not only prompt, but generous in the extreme. 'My dear Paul,' she wrote on 1st September 1925, from the Bristol-Britannia hotel where she was staying in Venice. 'I was delighted to get your letter and above all to hear of your intention about founding a Gallery of Modern Art in Serbia. Of course, I shall give you some pictures of the best modern English school. I'll give you a Duncan Grant (as I have bought three of them), also a fine Lavery (as I have bought four) and a lovely drawing by Augustus John of boys' heads and I must give you one flower picture. I bought a very beautiful one by your protégé Hammond and, if you like it, I will love to give it to you. Also from time to time I can give you a new picture. Would you also accept a bronze by Riccardi, the Roman sculptor? He did the busts of Lord Buckmaster and of Delius and also Lord Londonderry. You may remember them in my house . . .'[18]

Paul showed a copy of her letter to King Alexander who at once agreed to send her the Order of St Sava of Serbia. The decoration worked wonders and on 9th September, this time from the Grand Hotel in Venice, she wrote again:

Dear Paul,

I am overcome with delight, for the most beautiful decoration has arrived from the King and it is such a joy and such an honour to possess it. I can't thank you enough, you are an angel and I only feel I have done nothing to deserve this mark of your and the King's distinction. Thank you from my heart, I shall wear it with such pride.

I wired thanking His Majesty yesterday, directly it arrived.

I long to have you choose the pictures you want. I will ask people to give you pictures for your Gallery as well. Sir

Joseph Duveen who is now in Paris, is delighted to give you several modern pictures by eminent painters and Lady Abdy will also give you one or two fine modern pictures. I wish you could give me a list of people living or dead, in France and England, whose works you would like to acquire. As English, I suggest, Augustus John, Lavery, Walter Sickert, Steer, Duncan Grant, of course Sargent, Guesara, Hammond, Tonks, Bages, Gertler, Miss Rolls, Miss Bland, Miss Picquart, Nicholson and many others. There are now beautiful French and English painters. I will do all I can to give and to collect for you . . .[19]

By the time Paul arrived in London after the Mafalda–Hesse wedding, a few of his early appeals had begun to show results. This in itself was encouraging, but what pleased Paul almost as much was the fact that discerning people, like Sir Joseph Duveen, seemed wholeheartedly to approve of his scheme:

. . . I am intensely interested in what you tell me about the museum of modern art in Belgrade. It is a great scheme, and, entre nous, it is perhaps rather a good thing that you will not be over-supplied with funds to buy old masters. You know my ideas on this subject, and that I would much rather possess a really good modern work than an inferior old work of art. I am at present engaged in compiling a long article for the press on this very subject, advising the public along these lines. Personally, I would never buy an old picture unless I could buy a really great masterpiece, but to purchase second or third rate pictures or objects because they happen to be old is to my mind all humbug. I do not agree with the people who decry modern art. There are so many good things being produced today, if only one has discrimination. A copy of my article will be sent to you as soon as it is ready in a few weeks' time, and I have left instructions here to that effect. I would even now send you a rough copy of it, but it will not be finished until I am on board ship.

Reverting to your own plan, I certainly shall be delighted to send you some pictures for your museum, and will continue to do so, if you will write and tell me where I shall send them. . . . You will be interested to know that I have been buying some great pictures of marvellous quality, all of which you shall see, please God . . .[20]

Paul was thrilled and at once decided that he should widen the scope of his appeal. After innumerable crossings out he settled on the following draft letter:

Knowing your interest in modern art, I venture to put before you a scheme in the hope that, if it interests you sufficiently, you will be very kind and assist me.

My country, Serbia, possesses no art gallery of any sort and for many years it has been my wish to open one in Belgrade. My government have recently set aside a building for this purpose on the understanding that I shall secure at the outset sufficient pictures to form the nucleus of a national collection. I propose that the Gallery shall be representative of modern art and exclude therefore any picture earlier than the nineteenth century.

I have already approached a few individuals such as the King of Serbia, Sir J. Duveen, Lady Cunard and Lord Ivor Churchill who have generously presented me with a number of pictures. The artists so far represented include the following . . .

If you could see your way to helping me by any means I should indeed be grateful. I shall be leaving for Serbia at the end of this week and my address will be 'H.R.H.PP of S., G.C.V.O., The Palace, Belgrade. I hope to be returning to London in January.

Yours . . .[21]

Conscious that he would soon be entering the market not merely as a beggar but as an agent of the Serbian Government Paul realized that he would need professional advice. He knew something about modern art but nothing like enough for his purposes. At Archie's suggestion he had already made contact with Charles Aitken at the Tate Gallery and he now sent him a copy of his final draft appeal letter. On 18th November, Aitken replied to Archie with his comments:

The letter, as drafted, seemed to meet the case, if you let

me know, when you send it out, I could write a note personally to one or two of the people to back it up. You cannot, of course, expect to get many pictures of first rate importance given, except where Prince Paul has personal influence, as in the case of the Steer, but I think a few quite good pictures could be got. Later on I think a few of us could give useful advice and information, if Prince Paul cares to consult us—Tonks, Muirhead Bone, Daniel and Witt (N.G. Trustees) and myself. All these are fairly in touch with things and disinterestedly keen on the best art and free from the commonplace of the R.A. and the fashionable crafts of the 'Smart Set' painters . . .

Prince Paul came in yesterday afternoon and I showed him one or two things. I have always had a feeling for Serbia and it is most cheering to meet an 'important' personage who really takes art seriously and has such a keen and personal appreciation of pictures, so that any little help one can give with the scheme of the Serbian National Gallery will be a real pleasure . . .[22]

By the spring of 1927 Paul had been given or promised about fifty pictures,* and his dream of a museum of modern art was about to become a reality. On 22nd April he wrote, from Belgrade, to Mrs Berenson to thank her and her husband for the gift of a Pissarro:

You were both such angels to me in giving me that lovely picture for my museum and I can't find words to express all I feel for your generosity. When I returned I found my museum ready which is more than I could hope for and only the pictures remain to be fixed to the walls. I thought originally of having them [the walls] covered with a sort of sackcloth but yesterday I came to the conclusion that it would spoil the character of the rooms and that pictures don't look too bad on whitewashed walls. The house being an old Turkish building I've left on purpose all the various niches and fountains which are put into the walls and I fear that any

* For a list of the pictures, prepared by Prince Paul about this time, see Appendix II.

form of stuffs might spoil the atmosphere. Since we are here the Congress of Byzantologists took place in Belgrade and I profited of the presence of the director of the Spalato antiquities and museum to ask him the information concerning the Lotts. Yes, it is still where it was in a Franciscan(?) cloister at Spalato . . . After London we expect to be stuck to our little place in Slovenia (near Laibach) till late in the autumn with a possible excursion to Munich end of August. I've been made president of our Jockey Club and in consequence am obliged to go to races which is more than I can bear! Of all the forms of entertainment this is certainly the poorest invented by the human brain. I think I'd prefer football a thousand times![23]

Once the museum was established Paul's interest in art began to take on a more personal note. His aim in the previous couple of years had been to build up a collection of modern pictures and in this he had been influenced by dealers like Vollard and by patrons like Duveen and Emerald Cunard. From 1929 onwards, however, a passion to learn more about and eventually possess old master pictures gradually took possession of him and for guidance he turned to Bernard Berenson.

Paul's wish was clearly to build up a collection of his own but at first this was more or less out of the question. Instead he set to work on some pictures belonging to his uncle, Elim Demidoff, which he had long been convinced were Italian Renaissance and of good quality.

In September Paul wrote to Berenson for his opinion: 'I am sending you three photos of pictures belonging to my Uncle Demidoff and would be so grateful if you could tell me what they are and also whether they are worth anything. I saw them in his house in Athens 17 years ago and thought they might prove to be something good and always tried to induce him to have them photographed which I have at last succeeded. One is supposed to be a Luini and was bought by Ricard (the painter) for my grandfather in Italy in the sixties. The other two were in the Demidoff country place in the Ural mountains since the end of the XVIII Century and were bought by my great great grandfather. They remained in Russia till 1914 when my uncle fortunately brought them over to Greece. This is all the information I can give you.'[24]

Berenson's reply was prompt and Paul was immensely gratified to have his own conclusions, which were based on some original research, confirmed by the great Renaissance expert. 'How kind of you to answer my letter directly. Thanks ever so much. I was exceedingly proud when I read it as I had come to the same conclusions, with my father-in-law, only we thought the Lippi might perhaps be an original. I was quite sure about the Giovanni Utili as I looked, by chance, through a little book on the "Christ Church pictures" by Borenius and there in plates XV and XVI there is a baby Jesus and a madonna so exactly similar to our picture.'[25]

Almost exactly one year later, after an exhilarating 'motor trip round Germany', Paul was writing to Berenson again, principally to thank him for sending a copy of his latest book *Studies of Medieval Painting*. 'The subject of the book thrills me and I'll start reading it immediately. I was much struck by the Christ belonging to Mr Kahn which is very much alike to an old Byzantine icon belonging to my cousin who found it in a church at Ochrida. It is painted on wood and on the back has an unfinished religious subject painted as well. When I am in Belgrade (about the middle of the month) I'll have it photographed for you although I fear we won't get a very good photo. . . . I am sending you the photos of a Poussin I discovered in Munich and which came from the collection of the Schloss at Bückeburg. The subject is *Le Maître des Failisques* and I believe I've got the first version of the Louvre picture which is known to have been painted in 1637 for Passart and which was lost. Tell me if you like it, I've also bought some lovely old Spanish Portugalete carpets. I had never seen any before and fell in love with them.'[26]

Paul's art interests were, and would remain, eclectic. As well as pictures he bought china, glass, tapestries, carpets and books. But pictures were always his great love and over the years he was to amass a collection of beauty and considerable interest. In the early 1930s, however, he had little spare cash to fritter in the salerooms and no home of his own in which to hang even those pictures that he already possessed—Bohinj was only a summer house and, being tiny, was hardly suitable. Although Zagreb had been mentioned again in 1930 nothing had come of it.

CHAPTER V

1933–1934

Elizabeth and Marina

When Paul had returned to Belgrade, in 1924, with his beautiful young bride he had cut more of a cosmopolitan, Renaissance figure than that of a Serbian prince and it was known that he hankered for his weeks in London, Florence, Paris and Munich and for the company of his friends abroad. Although he had seemed willing to become involved in affairs of state it was obvious that he mistrusted politicians and their trade and that he had little in common with any of his compatriots. But as the years passed and he and Olga spent more of their time in Yugoslavia, Paul's attitude changed. Living in Belgrade in almost daily contact with the King and his ministers and as a frequent guest at most of the embassies and legations, he had almost no alternative but to take an interest in the domestic affairs of his country. Gradually he began to form his own opinions and even to judge his cousin's performance.

The rôle that King Alexander, then the Prince Regent, had accepted on 1st December 1918 was not an easy one. The Kingdom of Serbs, Croats and Slovenes had been composed from no less than nine separate regions—Slovenia, Croatia, Slavonia, Vojvodina, Dalmatia, Bosnia and Hercegovina from Austria–Hungary and Serbia and Montenegro, two formerly independent kingdoms. Even at its inception the unity of the new kingdom was a shaky one for, underlying it, there was a long-standing and bitter argument about the form of government that should be adopted. The Serbs in Belgrade, led by the reactionary old conservative, Pašić, favoured a centralist government based in Belgrade and Serbian in style. The Croats and Slovenes in Zagreb, along with other less articulate minorities, called for federalism and the right to retain their separate identities. The King's position in all this was supposedly a neutral one, but although Alexander believed in unity he had been brought up amongst Serbs and had served in the Serbian army. It was difficult for him to remain unbiased.

Of all the federalists, the Croats were the most vociferous. Slovenia, after all, was further from Belgrade and the Slovenes believed that distance and a separate language would save them from rigid control by a centralist government. In Croatia, however, feelings ran high. The Croats had enjoyed a fair degree of autonomy under Hungarian rule and they objected to the high-handed way in which their less civilized Serbian neighbours were attempting to take over. The immediate result within Croatia was a split between the extreme separatists and those who wanted to achieve some kind of compromise with the Serbs. Anté Pavelić was amongst the former and he was to become by far the most notorious. At the outset he was a member of the Frankist party, a catholic oriented pro-Hapsburg group, but soon he was to raise a campaign for outright separatism. Pavelić was an ambitious and ruthless man and he saw, in an independent kingdom of Croatia, a position for himself as king.

Of those who favoured compromise, the majority were members of the Croat Peasant Party, led by Stepjan Radić. The Peasant Party had been founded by the Radić brothers at the beginning of the century. From the start, its aim had been as much to organize and educate the peasants as to activate them politically. As a result, it had gone from strength to strength. By the 1920s Stepjan Radić could command almost the entire peasant vote, and in a region where the peasants accounted for between 70 and 80 per cent of the population this was a considerable political force.

When the first Skupština, or parliament, assembled in 1920 the key figures were Pašić, leader of the so called Serbian Radical Party, and Radić of the Croat Peasant Party. The form of government was still to be decided. On 28th June 1921, Pašić presented to Parliament the 'Vidovdan Constitution' (so named because it was St Vitus' day). It was so obviously centralist that the Croats, following Radić, walked out without voting and as a result the constitution was approved. From that moment on Pašić adopted a policy of centralization and the

Croats remained in opposition. There was no agreement between the two sides, there was squabbling amongst the Serbs, Radić was thrown into prison for a time, and to all intents and purposes Parliament was unworkable.

It was King Alexander himself who finally persuaded Radić to take his seat in the Skupština. Pašić had died and for a moment there was hope of a conciliation. But it did not last. The unfairness of the system had engendered too much resentment and unhappiness. On 20th June 1928 in the Skupština, a Radical party representative from Montenegro shot down several representatives, mortally wounding Stepjan Radić and killing his nephew Pavlé outright. Although King Alexander saved the situation by rushing to the old Croat's bedside, he dealt leniently with the assassin (a notoriously reactionary Serb of uncompromisingly centralist convictions).

Stepjan Radić was succeeded as leader of the Peasant Party by Vladko Maček who immediately repudiated the constitution with the phrase 'there is no longer a constitution but only king and people'. The murders brought about a constitutional crisis of far-reaching importance.

King Alexander's first move was an attempt at negotiation. He invited Maček and the leader of the Slovenes to call on him and asked them if he should amputate Croatia and Slovenia. But neither politician favoured a solution which endangered the survival of an independent Croatia–Slovenia, exposed, as these would be, to both Italian and Hungarian pressure. Their federalist solution was immediately and firmly rejected by the Serb leaders. Left with no alternative, and encouraged by the Zagreb Press to take personal command, Alexander dissolved parliament on 6th January 1929 and annulled the 1921 Vidovdan Constitution.

At first, his bold and decisive action met with general approval. The measures to secure his dictatorial power were necessarily strict: every kind of political and other association was made conditional on government consent, local councils were disbanded, press controls were summarily imposed and the Judiciary made subject to the Executive. The Croats, and particularly the artful Dr Maček, assumed that this would at least mean an end to Serbian political domination. But their hopes were dashed by the appointment of the unswervingly

Serbian General Živković* as head of government. Ten months later (on 3rd October 1929), in a massive central and local government reorganization, the name of the country was changed to that of the 'Kingdom of Yugoslavia'.

Alexander tried to impose a sense of national unity by coming down fiercely on separatist institutions and organizations. Even the Serbian army was obliged to exchange its traditional and much loved flags and standards for new, Yugoslavian ones. There was unrest among the Serbs and some Croatian leaders fled the country. Anté Pavelić was one of them. He went via Vienna to Bulgaria where he made contact with the enemies of his country and began to organize the secret and revolutionary Ustaše (insurrectionary) movement, the aim of which was to fight by all means for Croatian independence.

Prompted by the upheaval in Spain and the need to win support abroad, especially from his ally, France, Alexander recalled Parliament in 1931. On 3rd September a new constitution was established by royal decree. But it was a bitter disappointment. Civil liberties were restored only 'within the limits of the law' which forbade political, local and ethical associations, and ministers were to remain exclusively answerable to the Crown.

Unrest was widespread and early in 1933 leading figures in Croatia, Bosnia and the Vojvodina signed a political manifesto calling for the re-establishment of the 1918 Constitution and the recognition of popular sovereignty. Fr Korošeć, leader of the Slovene Populist Party followed this with a request for autonomy for Slovenia, and Mehmed Spaho, head of the Bosnian Moslem Organization, claimed the same for Bosnia. The government over-acted, interning Maček and Korošeć and imprisoning Spaho and others. This was considered so unreasonable that even the Serbian Radical Party joined in a clamour for the restoration of political peace by democratic means.

Paul witnessed only the latter part of this long saga, but what he saw he thoroughly disliked. By instinct and training averse both to autocratic rule and to Serbian militarism, his general outlook was basically sympathetic to a federal solution and to an understanding with the Catholic Croats. He was

* General Živković was an old and close friend of King Alexander's.

nervous of centralism and of Alexander's interpretation of Vladko Maček's declaration at the time of the Skupština murders, and above all he was concerned about the circle of advisers that Alexander had collected round him. They were all men who encouraged and played upon the rigid, authoritarian side of Alexander's personality. On 6th February 1933, Olga recorded that Paul 'was very worried [at] Sandro's inconsistent policy; listens to wrong people; now on advice of Demetrović attacks Catholic Church! So much so that Herriot, a mason, criticises him! [Paul] sees rightly and can do nothing.'[1] On 17th March she noted after Sir Nevile Henderson, the British Minister, had been to lunch (as he usually did at least once a week): '[Paul] discussed political situation here which he sees clearly. Very worried about S. [the king] wavering and choosing wrong people.'

For many years Paul had shown a willingness to involve himself directly in Yugoslav affairs, but Alexander had consistently refused to recognize his abilities. Now, in 1933, Alexander took a step which virtually severed all relations between himself and his cousin and almost drove Paul abroad. The reason remains obscure. It may have been because of Paul's increasingly noticeable political awareness or, more likely, because of an understandable jealousy of the respect which Paul commanded abroad, and of the way in which he was cultivated by the diplomatic corps in Belgrade.

Towards the end of June 1933 Alexander, who had built himself a vast new palace complex at Dedinje, determined on converting the Old Palace in Belgrade into a national art museum. Having made no provision for Paul or his family who had been in residence for the best part of ten years, he allowed the news of his decision to reach Paul indirectly. On 27th June Olga's diary reports: 'Pacey came back at 10.00 was told by Dr [sic] the cheerful news that S. [Sandro] has given this house over to [the] town for a museum, so we must clear out— abroad . . . as no house suitable here.' Paul's letters contain no mention of this episode. His pride was hurt and he could hardly admit even to himself that the King had effectively decided that he and his family were of no further use in Yugoslavia. Yet this was exactly how it seemed to them both. The next day Olga wrote, 'felt knocked on the head all day with the awful thought of the coming changing of our home after 10 years! Where will we go? Such mountains of things to sort and pack up. It's so hard on poor Pacey who is by far the best friend S. will ever have.'

Another reason for the king's high-handed and insensitive treatment had something to do with Olga and Queen Marie. The queen, who was idle, unattractive and given more to the company of women than men,* had had enough of Olga's beauty and obvious 'hold' on Belgrade society and court life, and she was certainly behind some of the stories which at that moment seemed to be poisoning Alexander's mind.

The pretext came one day in June when Olga and her sisters came across a military manoeuvre during their afternoon ride. Unwisely, as it turned out, they engaged the commander in conversation, complimenting him on his men's high standard of dress, especially on such a hot afternoon. The effect on the men was stunning and the manoeuvre was, not surprisingly, a shambles. When the officer in command reported this to Alexander, he became furious and unreasonable: 'Pacey had been to see S. Had v. unpleasant talk with him; he insulted me, said I was 'une intriguante' and 'Gaffeuse' and God knows what. Someone must be telling him lies he believes. Too awful. Poor P. very upset told him a few truths. He is jealous and wants an excuse to get rid of us, so attacks me.'[1]

Olga may have been tactless out riding, but as the grand-daughter of the Grand Duke Vladimir of Russia and of King George of Greece she was not accustomed to such treatment. On 1st July she described her confrontation with the King: 'Ghastly day for me. Went to Dedinje with sisters to see S. Faced him alone to tell him it was all lies that I posed as a martyr and said he was kicking us out. Nothing would persuade him. Said we were ungrateful after all he had done for us, that P. refused to see the plans he had made for that house! P. never even saw them! This too he refused to believe. Said he had nothing to blame himself for and that I was not to mix in his army!'

That night they left for Bohinj. Olga especially was hurt. Sandro had always made a great fuss of her in front of 'la

* Since 1928 Queen Marie had spent almost all her time in the company of a Miss Crowther.

86

grosse', as he referred to his wife, and she had tended to hero-worship him with his beautiful uniforms and military bearing. Pathetically, she recorded on 2 July 'all illusions about him gone. Can never feel the same again.' Inevitably she felt home-sick for Greece, from which her family were still exiled. That same night she noted 'so anxious to know the results of elections in Salonika today. They say if the Government wins, Monarchy is not far off. If only it could be at last! . . .'

After a month in Bohinj, however, and after efforts by a repentant Alexander at a reconciliation, Paul and Olga forgot about the incident and soon relations were back to normal. The King and Paul started shooting together and the King's attentions were once again bestowed on Olga and on the little Alexander ('Quiss' to the family). A new house was to be built, near to Dedinje and Paul was to choose between three alterna-tive plans.

The rest of the summer was spent in idyllic conditions in the company of Olga's parents and sisters at Bohinj. Afternoon tennis, bathing in the river and in the new pool, fishing, riding in the woods, weeding and lunches in the rose garden were combined with strenuous match-making efforts on behalf of Olga's sisters Elizabeth and Marina. Paul as always found time, whatever the motive for the particular trip, to visit the galleries, art dealers and theatres of Paris, Munich, London and Florence—but he was restless and without purpose. His love of his own family and of his two sisters-in-law and father-in-law and his attachment to Bohinj did something to cheer him. But he seemed, at this point in his life, to lack both direction and confidence.

Alexander consulted him on matters of state and welcomed his opinions, but at the same time regarded him, together with his ravishing wife and children, as more of a show-piece than anything else. Whenever visiting royalty or heads of state needed entertaining in Belgrade or at Bled, or whenever Yugoslavia needed to be represented on state occasions abroad, the urbane and cultivated Paul invariably obliged. But the rôle of *legatus a latere* was not always welcome, let alone con-venient. On 25th November 1933 Olga, who was then in Paris with Paul and intending to stay there with her parents, sisters and son Alexander (over from school in England for Christmas), recorded: 'Sandro wrote to Pacey asking us to be there on December 10th to help entertain Boris* and Giovanna and Kiril! Delightful prospect! Que faire?'

Throughout 1932 and 1933 Paul's letters show him as increasingly sensitive to the fact that within Yugoslavia he was under-utilized and as a result suffering from constant bouts of insomnia, lumbago and an appalling digestive system. In a letter to Bernard Berenson in July 1932 and again in one to Berenson's wife a year later, Paul comes over as a nervous and apprehensive parent pessimistic about his health, his prospects, his finances and the condition of Europe in general.

My dear B.B.

If only you knew how often my thoughts fly to I Tatti and how often I consult you mentally; few events happen in my life without my wondering what you would have done in that particular case, yet my letters are scarce and appearances are against me no doubt. I never even thanked you for your last publications received in the Spring, on the eve of my departure to Paris where I was sent—in an awful state of health—to attend the funeral of the president. After that I went to London where I spent 2 months under my Dr. He gave me injections, 2 a day and the result, I am glad to say, is good. I certainly feel better and have a good colour which I never had since childhood. Also, my diet has become more varied but unfortunately I don't seem to put on in weight which is disturbing as I weigh so little. My insomnia has also somewhat abated although it returns periodically. It is the thing I dread most in the world and I dare hardly even mention it so much I am in awe of that terrible complaint. I have also lost most of my money—90% of what I have saved the last 12 years. Unfortunately I put practically everything in Swedish Matches which I sold just before the final crash for a song. I ought not to complain as, thank heaven, I have enough to live on at the moment, although I have hardly any capital left. This is also a great source of worry when one has a family. An allowance is very pleasant, of course, but it is always temporary and gives one a feeling of dependence . . .[2]

* King Boris of Bulgaria.

88

My dear Mrs Berenson,

How kind of you to have sent me your book. I found it on my return from Paris where I spent over a month and started reading it immediately. Strange to say your book doesn't inspire me with the desire to visit the lands which you describe but rather makes me long for I Tatti and your and B.B.'s presence. Fanaticism of all kinds has always been distasteful to me and however beautiful the places haunted by it may be they [repel] me rather than attract me . . . What difficult times these are: one never knows from day to day whether one will wake up a ruined man, and one regrets having children whose future is more than uncertain. My eldest boy was 9 two days ago and I will probably take him to school to England in the autumn. How is one to bring up one's boys nowadays is a problem to which I find no solution . . . My only refuge remains art and it consoles me of many things. I have been studying Greco these last months and wonder if you know a picture known as *The Lady with the Hermine** owned by Stirling Maxwell in Scotland which modern Spanish critics attribute to the Venetian school. Is it possible? I can't imagine that it could possibly be a Tintoretto or any other Venetian, as it strikes me as being a typical earlyish Greco. I just finished the last volume of Genji—so delightful and as good as the early ones. When shall we meet I wonder? One grows old without ever seeing the people one loves and spends one's life seeing people one dislikes. What a fate . . .[3]

Four things changed Paul's gloomy outlook. First, at the beginning of September 1933 he was named head of all the museums in Yugoslavia; secondly, and probably as a result of the excitement and joy with which he threw himself into his new job, his health seems to have considerably improved; thirdly, his financial circumstances took a slight turn for the better; and fourthly, Elizabeth and Marina got married, the youngest, Marina, to a man who was to become one of Paul's most beloved, intimate and loyal friends.

Paul, who to all intents and purposes had been brought up an orphan, derived a particular satisfaction and at least as much

* El Greco's portrait *La Dama del Arminio* is now on view at Pollock House, Glasgow.

pleasure as Olga from the fact that by marrying, Elizabeth and Marina swelled the ranks of the family. But it took months and a considerable amount of effort on everyone's part to bring the matches off. On 5th March 1933, Paul, Olga, Elizabeth and Marina had gone to Munich. The three sisters had been grandly and hectically entertained from dawn to dusk in everything from cinemas to palaces by Albrecht of Bavaria, his father Rupprecht and Toto Toerring.* Ernst ('Erny') of Saxony and his wife Sophie of Luxembourg had also been much in evidence. Throughout their trip the watchful gaze of the elder sister had never lifted. On arrival at the Hotel Continental Olga noted in her diary: 'Toto . . . same as usual. Very shy. What will his attitude be? Woolly doesn't dare hope too much and knows nothing of his real feelings.'[4] A week later she complained 'We try to let Toto walk alone with Woolly and be near her as often as possible—always jokes. Nothing serious—Wish he was less reserved!'[5] But all was not lost. Two days after their return to Belgrade, Elizabeth received a letter from Toto.

On 18th July, ten days after the arrival of Olga's parents in Bohinj, Paul again left for Munich. His visit was partly prompted by his wish to get away from the unpleasant atmosphere created by Alexander at the end of June and partly in order to test the temperature with Toto. Paul saw a lot of Toto but was unable to report any of the signs of a love-sick man, and Olga's comment after Paul's last telephone call from Munich was pessimistic. 'Toto like a shut drawer, though P. gave him plenty of chances to speak.'[6]

It was not until September, when he came to Bohinj with Albrecht (the latter in every sense the chaperon, the former, it was hoped, as suitor) that Toto was sure in himself of what he wanted. Even then, on 11th and on the day before Paul, Olga, Marina, and little Alexander left for London, Olga noted: 'Toto quite amiable, sat beside Woolly in the garden—seems attracted but no further. What can be the cause?'[7] But on 22nd September 1933, when Paul and Olga were in London with Marina, a telegram arrived from Bohinj. They had left Olga's parents in charge of little Nicky and of their final outrageous matchmaking effort. The telegram read quite simply and, since the signatories were staying in the home of the person to whom

* Count Charles Theodor Toerring Jettenbach.

it was addressed, economically: 'So happy. Woolly—Toto.'

The rest of the winter was spent between London, Belgrade, Paris and Munich. For Christmas, 1933, they were in Paris where many of the Greek royal family had also gathered. Quiss joined them there for his holidays from Ludgrove but Nicky stayed in Belgrade. The improvement noted in Quiss was immediate. From having been stubbornly unwilling to concentrate on his lessons and a source of constant worry and irritation to his parents he was now calmer and more attentive. During the course of 1933 it had become clear to both Paul and Olga that the King much preferred his namesake to his own first-born, Peter. Although flattered to see their son so obviously favoured—given huge presents, allowed to accompany the King in his carriage, to go shooting with him and to stand beside him all day—Paul and Olga found it increasingly difficult to discipline the boy at home. Besides, they found the relationship an embarrassment in front of little Peter. Peter was a year older but by contrast seemed rather backward. Already in February Olga had found Peter 'doing prep for ages. Doesn't seem to have a set time like Quiss. So pathetic; heard him read very slowly.' But her conclusion was that his life and lessons were 'not made interesting enough'.[8] The fact that Sandro seemed incapable of hiding his preference did not help Olga's relationship with Mignon; on 2nd August she recorded: 'Boys went to Bled for tea yesterday. S. made a fuss of Quiss; ignored Peter and the others! So embarrassing! Miss Smith [Quiss's governess] said Mignon seemed cross.'[9]

The main reason for the prolonged stay of Olga, Elizabeth and Marina in Paris over the Christmas season was, of course, to get their clothes made ready for the big event. Elizabeth was ecstatically happy and the family overjoyed. Everyone appeared to be indulging in a moment of extravagance, but for Olga's parents the prospect of an expensive wedding was frightening. Even at the best of times, their financial position had been weak. In the past it had scarcely sufficed to give their daughters the start in life to which their rank and name had entitled them. Though Prince Nicholas was an accomplished landscape painter, the excellence of his paintings was at no stage put to commercial advantage. The improved financial atmosphere of the times, moreover, which had helped raise the morale of those with capital, had done little for those who lived off an allowance. In June they had been obliged to let their house in Athens to an Italian for an inadequate rental and in letters from Paul to Olga, written in July 1933, while Paul was undergoing treatment in Paris, the parents-in-laws' finances are a frequent topic.

My own beloved Angel
I feel ashamed not to have written to you yet but you know how hectic Paris life is, especially the first few days before one gets used to it all. My journey went off well but it was icy on the way till my arrival here where it is warm and lovely. In Vienna I spent an hour in the town and ate cakes at Demel! I was met by Achileia* who told me that Puppy [Prince Nicholas] was arriving from Rome practically at the same time. He did let the Italians have his house for 130.000 lire a year which is little but apparently he had to accept everything for fear of remaining without tenants. Their money affairs seem to be in a very precarious state and I'm trying to help . . .[10]

Paul's own financial position had improved considerably. So much so that he was buying a ring at Cartier's for Olga and a picture which he dared hope might, after cleaning, turn out to be a genuine Rembrandt. But his promise to try to do something about Prince Nicholas' difficulties was not an idle one and in October he conceived a way to help which was both dignified and delicate. Olga's dry, matter of fact diary entry on 23rd October did little justice to her sense of gratitude and pride: 'Pacey bought from Mummy for me her lovely diamond crown brooch for our ten years. She is thankful for the money as they are hard up for Fael's† trousseau. I'm so pleased he could do it.'

Their match-making efforts on behalf of Marina, too, had begun in September 1933, in London. She had been introduced to 'Georgie', Duke of Kent, and from the beginning he seemed to respond. Chips, always perceptive, spotted the possibility in May, recording in his diary on the 8th: 'Paul of Serbia and Princess Olga and Princess Marina lunched with us

* Prince Nicholas' valet.
† A nickname Olga used for her sisters, on this occasion Elizabeth.

here. They are surely two of the most beautiful Princesses, if not women, in the world. Princess Marina is very much thinner, and I hope one day she will make a suitable marriage with the House of Windsor. About seven years ago her affair with the Prince of Wales was progressing very well, but Freda Dudley Ward, at the last moment, interfered and stopped it.'[11]

Once again it was at Bohinj that the final decision was taken. After Elizabeth's wedding was over, but before the romantic dust which it threw up had had time to settle, Paul had arranged for the Duke of Kent to come out, via Salzburg and Munich, to spend the best part of the summer with them at Bohinj, after Cowes week in August. If Marina learned at Bohinj to love Georgie with an adoration and devotion that was never to diminish, Paul learned to cherish him as a friend. The relationship between the two men from the beginning was strong and mutual. For Paul it meant more than that his youngest sister-in-law had married his own 'best man's' youngest brother. He felt himself not only to have gained a real blood brother but to have gained one whose interests, values and sense of fun mirrored his own. Paul was overjoyed, and so too was Georgie. His ecstatic letter of thanks to Paul, for his summer at Bohinj and for having helped secure his future happiness, was written from York House, St James's Palace, on 26th September 1934:

I am so sorry not to have written you a proper letter but I've now got to the stage when it seems impossible to settle anything—but I'm sure it will all come all right. Anyway, I want to thank you a million times for *all* your kindness and for taking me to Salzburg & Munchen which I loved and for letting me see Marina and so get engaged to her! It's all so lovely and I am so happy that I can hardly believe it. Everyone here is so delighted with her—the crowd especially— 'cos when she arrived at Victoria Station they expected a dowdy princess—such as unfortunately my family are—but when they saw this lovely chic creature—they could hardly believe it and even the men were interested and shouted 'Don't change—don't let them change you!' Of course she won't be changed—not if I have anything to do with it. My parents were charming and so pleased with M. and me! They couldn't have been nicer and Mama was endlessly making

93

lists and producing jewels and making arrangements—she was sweet. In a short time all the main essentials were fixed, which was indeed clever. As to the bridesmaids, as they would have 8 (it's the custom for royalty here!) I thought much better have all family—that's why they are so assorted and Tim* has been asked. It's a good thing really and makes for peace and let bygones be bygones! It's not so much fun here in London as it's always full of crowds and it's impossible to go anywhere together but everyone is so pleased that one really shouldn't complain. I wish you were both here but you will come in October won't you? and I hope to come to Paris on Oct. 19 for a few days. We went to see Aunt Toria—who started again about the matchmaker! She was well squashed and took it back. And then she told M. that she was for David and I was for Tim! But poor old lady she's rather gaga! We saw David last night at midnight— he wouldn't dine—the parents-in-law (mine) he wouldn't see. I mean, he never even mentioned or asked about them. He *did* send a cable to Salzburg but it got lost. He was very nice but nothing if you know what I mean. M. is dining with me and I must dress—we're longing to see you to tell you everything. Again a million thanks . . .[12]

Marina's marriage, which took place on 29th November 1934, at Westminster Abbey, was the happiest conceivable occasion. But by the time Paul arrived in London for it, he was already Prince Regent of Yugoslavia.

* A nickname of Princess Irene of Greece, Princess Olga's first cousin.

PART II

CHAPTER VI

1934

Assassination

Even members of the British diplomatic staff noticed that, in 1934, King Alexander seemed to be pushing his cousin more to the forefront of political affairs. At home, certainly, Alexander was as close to Paul as he had ever been. This may have been a direct result of the rift which had, for a short time, separated them completely in the summer of 1933. Equally it may have been due to an increasing awareness, on Alexander's part, that he was living a life of constant danger.

The dictatorship had driven many of Alexander's enemies abroad but it had not rid him of them. Far from languishing in exile these men had regrouped into efficient bands of terrorists, aided and encouraged by their host countries. At the root of the problem lay the boundaries of Yugoslavia, as drawn up after 1918, which included within the kingdom territory claimed by Albania, Hungary, Bulgaria and Italy. These last three countries, at least, were determined to regain what they considered to be their own, and were prepared to go to almost any lengths to do so.

In the case of Italy, the lands in question were those which she had been promised in the secret Treaty of London, but had not received. Mussolini had coveted the strategically valuable stretch of Dalmatian coastline and he felt slighted and cheated, and at once set about devising a way to undermine the structure of the new country. His obvious tool was Croatian separatism and it was common knowledge that, after 1928, he had received Pavelić and other fleeing Croatian terrorists with open arms.

Alexander was by no means oblivious to Mussolini's intrigues and between 1929 and 1934 he made personal attempts to negotiate with him. But Mussolini refused to co-operate and eventually Alexander gave up, frustrated and angry. No sooner had he done so than he obtained direct proof of the Duce's malicious intentions. From Zagreb, on Boxing Day 1933, he wrote to Paul to explain what had happened:

Dear Cousin,

I want above all to send you and all your little family my best wishes for the new year . . .

We left at midday yesterday for Bled, where we shall stay until 5 Jan. then return here for la grosse's birthday and also for the conference of the Petite Entente. Here they have given us a terrific reception. It is true that the day of our arrival we were in very great danger and it is a real miracle that I am able to write to you today. The people who were waiting for us at Jelatchitcher Try with bombs and revolvers were arrested with all their arms and, what is really important, have confessed all. They had come straight from Trieste where a school for assassins has been founded under the protection of the great fascist! When the fuss has died down I will do what is necessary to open the eyes of the world to what are the fascist methods in foreign policy. I was right not to trust and not to have anything to do with those scoundrels . . .[1]

With Bulgaria the disputed territories were in Macedonia. Bulgaria and Serbia had been quarrelling over the division of this region since the expulsion of the Turks, and it was Macedonia that had been the cause of the second Balkan war in 1913. After the Great War both Serbia and Greece had been awarded large parts of Macedonia and Bulgaria was thoroughly unhappy with the new boundaries. King Boris made no attempt to conceal his dissatisfaction nor did he make any effort to stamp out the Internal Macedonian Revolutionary Organization (I.M.R.O.), a secret terrorist organization whose aim was a united and independent Macedonia.

King Alexander's foreign policy, which he conducted largely himself, had been aimed at securing the frontiers of his country. In 1921, with Rumania and Czechoslovakia, he had signed the Little Entente, to counter Hungarian irredentism and prevent a Hapsburg restoration, and in 1934 he succeeded in bringing together Greece, Rumania and Turkey to form the Balkan

Entente with Yugoslavia. To all intents and purposes this latter treaty was a mutual protection pact against aggression by any Balkan state acting alone, or in league with a non-Balkan power. Alexander had hoped to include Bulgaria in the Balkan Entente and to this end he had visited King Boris in Sofia before the inauguration in February 1934. It was a brave thing to have done for Alexander knew well the kind of risk that he was running. When Paul offered to accompany him he refused on the grounds that Paul should remain in Belgrade in case anything untoward should happen. This was the first time that Alexander hinted to Paul that he relied on him in this way and it increased the bond between them.

As it turned out the visit passed without mishap and although Bulgaria did not become a signatory to the Balkan Entente Alexander exacted a number of promises from King Boris, amongst which was an agreement that he should clamp down on the activities of the I.M.R.O.

In the period between the two pacts King Alexander had concentrated on finding an ally amongst the great powers. At first he had looked to France, for with Germany defeated, Great Britain not interested and Russia communist and therefore no longer acceptable, she was the obvious answer. But just when the internal situation in Yugoslavia was at its worst and the economy most depressed, France cut off her aid. As if this was not enough, in 1934, the French foreign minister, Louis Barthou, embarked on a new scheme for a grand alliance against Hitler. For the alliance to work France needed to get both Italy and Yugoslavia on her side.

Alexander was highly suspicious of the French plan, for he was certain that France would not hesitate to jettison Yugoslavia's interests in order to gain Italy's support against Hitler. However, Barthou was insistent and in June he arrived in Belgrade to discuss the matter further with the Yugoslavs. Alexander, who had already begun to turn to the Germans for support, was non-committal but eventually he reluctantly agreed to travel to France in October to continue the discussions.

Paul and Olga were with Alexander the night before he left for France. He was in a jolly mood and when Olga begged him to take his bullet-proof vest he laughed and said 'For Bulgaria, yes, but surely not for France?'[2] As Queen Marie was suffering from gallstones and was shortly to undergo an operation it had been decided that she should travel by train direct to Paris. It was thus Paul and Olga who accompanied Alexander to Split and saw him off on the destroyer *Dubrovnik*.

On 9th October, Paul was restless all day. In the afternoon he went for a drive by himself, but returned to have tea with Olga and her aunt who was staying in the house. They were sitting in the drawing-room when a servant entered to announce a telephone call from Marseilles. Paul turned pale and hurried out of the room. The telephone call lasted a long time. When Paul came back, he broke the news that there had been an attempt on Sandro's life, and that he was mortally wounded.

The attack had taken place shortly after the *Dubrovnik* landed in Marseilles. Louis Barthou had met King Alexander on the quay and the two of them, together with General Georges, had immediately embarked on a drive through the town. Welcoming crowds lined the streets and in order that they should be able to see the King better the police motor cycle escort had been withdrawn, leaving only scattered troops and a mounted guardsman riding in front of the car. Suddenly a man had emerged from the crowd and leapt onto the wide running board of the car, shouting 'vive le roi!' Such was the lack of security that he had been able to fire at the King, at Barthou and at General Georges before he was pushed aside by the chauffeur and finally cut down by a stroke from a guardsman's sabre. King Alexander died almost instantly and Louis Barthou soon afterwards.

Paul told all he had heard quietly, in a detached tone of voice. He felt sick and horrified at the thought of the scene in Marseilles, and yet he could not give way to his grief for part of his mind was racing over the things that he had been told to do in precisely such an emergency. Alexander had found no rôle for him in his lifetime but Paul knew that, in death, his cousin would have left him to pick up the reins. At least twice before, attempts had been made on Alexander's life and for both of his most recent visits, to Sofia and to Paris, Alexander had specifically asked Paul to remain behind. He had told Paul that if ever anything should happen to him he was to proceed immediately to Dedinje where, inside his desk, he would find two wills, one for the Prime Minister and one for himself.

Still unsure exactly what his murdered cousin had in store for him, Paul drove immediately to the palace. Scared and lonely, he felt a sudden pang of remorse. How often had he questioned Alexander's methods, how many times had he complained with bitterness that he had not been trusted with governmental responsibility! Prompted as much by a desperate need to feel wanted as by a real sense of duty, he had longed for the respect and trust of Alexander as of an elder brother. Now at last, and when he least expected it, it seemed that he would have to bear the brunt alone. As his motor car swept through the gates of Dedinje, the thought that Alexander might have left him in sole charge of his young kingdom began to fill him with a sense of dread.

Upon arrival at the palace Paul summoned the Prime Minister, Mr Užunović, the Commander-in-Chief of the Royal Guard, General Živokvić, and the head of the Belgrade police. Together they opened the wills and read the names of the men whom King Alexander had selected to act as Regents until King Peter should reach his majority in September 1941. Paul was to be first Regent and alongside him were to be two others, Mr Perović and Mr Stanković. Both these choices were unexpected. Perović was a Serb, the governor of Croatia and a good administrator. But he was not a popular man. Stanković was also a Serb, a professor of medicine at Belgrade University, and reputedly a freemason of the Grand Orient Order. He had gained the confidence of King Alexander and had been appointed Minister of Education in 1932. But soon afterwards he had been held responsible for the fall of the cabinet and had been dismissed. Paul had never met Perović and what he knew of Stanković he disliked. Neither was particularly powerful and it must have been clear to Paul, even then, that their rôle would ultimately depend on the extent to which he himself would be prepared to take the lead.

Whether or not Paul had known that he would be named Regent remains an open question. Certainly Alexander had intimated that he expected him to take charge in an emergency and for this Paul seemed prepared. The speed and manner in which he assumed authority was a surprise to many, including the British Minister, Sir Nevile Henderson: 'Immediately after the session I proceeded to the palace, and was received by the Prince Regent of Yugoslavia, as he is henceforth to be known. His Royal Highness described to me the actions which he had taken on first receiving the news by telephone from Marseilles. He appears to have shown remarkable promptitude, and an energy and decision for which I admit that I had not previously given him credit.'[3]

Besides having to organize King Alexander's funeral, Paul had to arrange for the return of Queen Marie, who had been stopped at Lyons and told of her husband's death, and of the young King, who was at preparatory school in England. Above all, he had to maintain order in the country. The Yugoslavs were grief-stricken and angry at the murder of their King and it was likely that there would be reprisals. At first the identity of the murderer was not known and this was fortunate as there was no single direction in which the people could vent their fury. They blamed the French for failing to provide adequate security and they suspected that both Croat terrorists and Italians had been involved. A few windows were broken at the Italian consulate in Sarajevo and minor incidents occurred at the consulates in Zagreb and Ljubljana—but this was nothing, considering what might have happened. Later, when the results of the French enquiry became known, the people began to demand some form of revenge.

Alexander's body was brought back from France by boat and by train. For three days it lay in state in the ballroom of the Old Palace in Belgrade which Olga had prepared with lilac drapes and a silver cross. The funeral took place on 14th October. It was a solemn and grand affair, with most of the family and representatives from all the major countries present. In fact, the only notable absentee was King Boris of Bulgaria. Germany sent Field-Marshal Goering, Italy the Duke of Spoleto, France President Lebrun and Marshal Pétain and England the Duke of Kent. King George had been unwilling to send one of the royal princes as he considered the situation in Yugoslavia too dangerous but pressure from Sir Nevile Henderson via the Foreign Secretary, and the readiness of the Duke of Kent to go, had finally persuaded him to relent. The day was a long one. First the King's body was taken from the Old Palace to the Cathedral in a procession, with the mourners walking behind the coffin and the crowds in the streets wailing and crying as the cortège passed. Then followed the Orthodox Church service and finally the train journey to Topola, north of Belgrade, where King Alexander was buried in the family mausoleum.

It was an exhausting time for Paul who had to receive all the foreign dignitaries and cope with the grief and uncertainty in the family. The question of what should become of the young King Peter and his mother arose almost immediately. Queen Marie, encouraged by her flatterers, took it into her head that she should have been made a member of the Regency. Her mother, Queen Marie of Rumania ('aunt Missy'), who happened to be staying at Dedinje at the time, immediately broached the subject with Paul. But he stood firm and nothing more was heard of the matter. However, Marie remained sensitive about her position and within thirty days of her husband's death she sent a document to Paul entitled 'Queen Marie's Requests'.[4] In this she laid out exactly what she considered to be her rights. In the main, Paul went along with her wishes. Between them they agreed that she and her children should remain at Dedinje and that Paul and Olga should move into the new palace which Alexander had started to build in the grounds and which he had intended for his children. The original plans for this second palace had been for an English style cottage with a gabled roof. As it had hardly been begun when Paul took it over, he was able to change its style. When completed, the palace was a completely white Regency house approached through an avenue of limes and named by Paul 'Beli Dvor'. As for Peter it was decided that he should not return to preparatory school in England but should remain with his mother in the care of his English tutor, Cecil Parrott, and various Yugoslav tutors.

When making these arrangements one of Paul's considerations had to be the state of his cousin's finances. Alexander had been a generous man and extravagant with his own fortune as Paul later explained in a note for the young King:

> . . . I must make one thing clear from the start and that is that Sandro left his affairs in a very confused state and it took years to clear them up and even, at first, to make both ends

meet. He was a very dynamic personality and when he wanted something it had to be done immediately and regardless of cost. He used to start innumerable works and undertakings simultaneously. At the time of his death Beli Dvor was being built. . . . Then he was building an enormous castle at Bled. . . . The monument to the unknown soldier on Avala was paid by him personally and for years it was a heavy drain eating up millions of dinars yearly. He had taken a granite quarry in Dalmatia and a whole company of soldiers were installed on Avala helping with the works. . . . Then we must mention Miločer. . . . These are only a few items which I can remember at the moment but there were many more. Sandro's decoration of Topola church where the mosaics cost a fortune, the purchase of Demir Kapija and the work there (a huge property with farms in Macedonia). The resources were great but not inexhaustible . . .[5]

In the midst of these arrangements Paul was well aware that his own life could be at risk. As always in his moments of despair he turned to his friends for comfort and support. To Archie on 3rd November he wrote:

My life has been hell for the last 3 weeks and it is a miracle that I've been able to stand the whole thing. I can't tell you how much I appreciated your letter and what a comfort it was. You know, I trust, how much I value your friendship which has been one of the joys of my life. There is a lot you can still do for me and I fear I'll occasionally have to bother you on various questions. Should anything happen to me—it would be a wonder if it didn't—I beg of you to look after Olga and the children. I've already told her to consult you on every occasion where she needs sound and reliable advice . . .[6]

Paul had other things beside family matters to occupy him. Over the following weeks information began to filter through from the French enquiry. It turned out that the assassin was a Bulgarian and a member of the bodyguard of Mihajlov, leader of the I.M.R.O. He had been trained in bomb throwing and shooting at Janko Pušta, a farm and school for terrorists in

Hungary. As to the organization of the plot, everything pointed to Anté Pavelić, the leader of the Ustaše movement, who was by then living in Italy, under Mussolini's protection and in great comfort, in a villa near Turin. Pavelić had not been in Marseilles on October 9th but he had been there a few days before. Besides, Italian pistols had been used. The extent to which Mussolini and his government had been involved in the murder of King Alexander was to remain a mystery, but Paul was convinced that they were ultimately responsible. Like Alexander, he had mistrusted Mussolini from the start and his natural suspicions were reinforced by the rumours and reports of secret conversations which reached him from Italy and France. From 'a high standing person in Paris' he heard that Signor Suvich, the Italian Under-Secretary of State for Foreign Affairs, had expressed his views on the assassination as follows:

> For the time being Italy has no intention or desire to enter into any discussion with Yugoslavia with a view to any political rapprochement. The Marseilles assassination is a very important event which has created a new situation in Central Europe. It is a new factor in European politics. Therefore, Italy assumes in this regard a policy of expectation. She awaits all those issues which in the internal life of Yugoslavia should follow the removal of the late King. In any event, Italy possesses no interest in reaching a decision until all the consequences of the death of King Alexander grow clearer.

And when questioned about Italian support of Croatian terrorists, Suvich had answered: 'We do not conceal the fact that we cherish sympathy for Croatian separation and the Croatian separatists who are at present in Italy; we consider them as our allies.'[7]

From another source Paul received confirmation of these views. The Italian Ambassador in Paris had confided 'to a well-known Frenchman', with whom he was on friendly terms, that Italian assistance of terrorists against Belgrade was only a 'modality of the subterranean war which Italy was carrying on against Yugoslavia'.[8]

Paul's diary, over this period, contains numerous references to scraps of conversations about Italy. At one point he noted: 'Mussolini sees film 3 times [film of Marseilles]'[9] at another he recorded the remark made by the Italian Foreign Minister, Count Ciano, 'Nous allons voir si la Yugoslavie tiendra le coup!'[10] In May of the following year when he saw Paul Boncour, the lawyer whom he had hired to represent Queen Marie at the French enquiry, he recorded Boncour's view that 'en lisant les documents on ne peut plus avoir aucun doute sur le rôle et la culpabilité Italo-Hongroise'.[11]

Paul's evidence of Mussolini's involvement was mostly circumstantial but the evidence that both Italy and Hungary were guilty of harbouring the murderers was not. The facts had been stated in the French court and the Yugoslav people were demanding some form of action. The government decided to take its case to the Council of the League of Nations, it stated at the time it believed 'in the efficacy of the League of Nations, the guardian of peace and of the international morality on which peace depends'.

But the case of Yugoslavia was not to be judged on its own merits. At the end of 1934 Britain and France were trying to improve relations with Italy while France was on the point of discussing a common foreign policy with her. The last thing either country wanted was to upset Mussolini. When Paul travelled to England in November for Marina's wedding he saw both Laval, the French Foreign Minister, and Sir John Simon, his British counterpart. He had a long talk with the latter and explained the state of public opinion in Yugoslavia and his own views on Mussolini. He asked Britain to use her influence to stop the organization of terrorist camps. Sir John Simon was sympathetic but made no promises. As he informed the British Ambassador in Belgrade: 'I said that we well understand the feelings of Yugoslavia, and thought that the protest was not only excusable, but natural. Our difficulty was to see what results would be obtained by this means, and how it could best be obtained. Protests in Geneva could not bring back the dead to life, and, terrible as the event was which had thrown Yugoslavia into mourning and roused such widespread indignation, there was still a more terrible thing which we must all work to prevent, and that was war.'[12]

When Paul returned home empty-handed except for this

piece of advice, he found that the Yugoslavs were becoming impatient. Feelings were running high on the borders with Italy and Hungary and a mass expulsion of Hungarians was under way. It seemed as if the majority of the Yugoslav peoples were in no mood to accept a peaceful solution—after all, as they all well remembered, when an Italian general had been killed on Greek soil while delimiting the Graeco-Albanian frontier in 1923, Italy had responded by bombarding and seizing Corfu.

The debate in the Council of the League of Nations began on 7th December, and on the 10th Anthony Eden, then British Minister for League of Nations Affairs, presented a resolution to the Council. This resolution consisted of a verbal rebuke to Hungary for harbouring members of the Ustaše and tolerating the existence of terrorist camps, and made no mention at all of Italy. The resolution was immediately accepted and back in Britain Eden was praised for his diplomacy. In Yugoslavia, however, the resolution was bitterly resented and the sense of isolation ran deep.

Almost immediately after the resolution of the League of Nations had been announced, the Yugoslav government fell. The effect of the dictatorship had been to splinter the Serb parties and simultaneously to strengthen those in other provinces; and the ageing Mr Užunović had soon found that he was unable to maintain authority with the cabinet of old, hard-line Serbs that he had assembled after the assassination. Paul, who throughout his cousin's reign had been denied access to the political scene, was thus suddenly faced with the main responsibility for resolving the crisis.

In principle, Paul believed that the only way to achieve real unity in Yugoslavia was to work towards an agreement between the Serbs and the Croats. To this end, one of his first moves on becoming Prince Regent had been to grant political amnesties to Korošeć, the Slovene, and Maček, the Croat. In the case of the former, this action had come as no great surprise. Father Korošeć was sixty-two years old and he had had a long career in politics both as a member of the government and in opposition to it. Although he had gone too far in 1933 Alexander had respected and trusted him. At the time of the assassination the King had already let it be known that he intended to release Korošeć, and when the ageing prelate asked for permission to pay his last respects to the dead King, Paul at once granted it and removed all restrictions. In the case of Maček, however, the situation was rather more awkward and Paul's action more controversial for, in 1933, Maček had been tried and sentenced to three years' imprisonment as an ordinary criminal rather than as a political prisoner, on the grounds that he had worked for the total separation of Croatia from the Yugoslav state.

With very little help from his fellow regents, Paul set about looking amongst the Serb politicians for a suitable candidate to form a government. It was his first experience of the reality of Serbian politics and the succession of interviews which he recorded in his diary reflects something of the utter bewilderment he felt. There were plenty of people willing to advise him and many different opinions and he was at a loss as to whom to believe. Eventually, however, he was persuaded that a Mr Jevtić would be most suitable. Jevtić had been Foreign Minister under King Alexander and had presented Yugoslavia's case at the League of Nations. He had also, it was rumoured, engineered the fall of the Užunović government. Having made his decision Paul lost no time in summoning Jevtić for an audience, and by the end of December a new government was in being.

CHAPTER VII

1935–1936
Regency I

During the first ten months of 1935 Paul was preoccupied with the internal politics of Yugoslavia. Jevtić seemed unable to achieve a proper balance between the radical and the extreme right wing and Paul became increasingly pessimistic. He was beginning to get an insight into the web of intrigue and double dealing that overlay political life in Serbia and he was utterly disgusted by it. But he still held out some hope for a settlement between the Serbs and the Croats, and he realized that the crucial element in all this would be Vladko Maček.

Already in October 1934, Paul had first had word that Maček, who was then still in prison, was interested in whether or not his views might meet with the approval of the Prince Regent. After Maček's release in January 1935, Paul met a Mr Harrison, correspondent for Reuters, at tea with the British Ambassador. Mr Harrison had seen Maček and, on 15 January, Paul recorded the following in his diary: 'tea with Sir N. Harrison saw Maček who expected to be sent for; round table conference; desires interview with *Daily Mail*; would like to see Jevtić; wishes his friends to be released before coming here; on the whole much more reasonable than ever before.'[1] He seemed quite hopeful, but as it turned out, a meeting was not arranged for months. Elections were due on 5th May and Maček became engrossed with the organization of an opposition party. His Serb-Croat coalition was formed solely for the purpose of the election, with no plans for future political co-operation. In the event, it polled 40 per cent of the votes, but because of the way in which the electoral law favoured the government, Maček's opposition party received only 67 out of the total 273 seats and its members once again boycotted parliament.

Although the Jevtić government had been returned, the political situation was highly unstable. Throughout the country, Croatian terrorism was increasing: bombs were exploding in public places, and there was a general feeling of tension in the air. Paul was tired, worried and discouraged. Just after the elections he had been approached by an intermediary with a message from Maček. The Croatian leader wished the Prince Regent to know that he remained loyal and had every confidence in his leadership, but that the Croats felt they had been cheated. The intermediary had announced that Maček strongly advocated a change in the constitution to give the Croats greater autonomy. But Paul, though sympathetic in principle, was not prepared to take such a step.

On the 22nd May, Paul had a long interview with Father Korošeć. During the course of this he was informed that the Jevtić government was failing and that he should try to get Jevtić to form a union of radicals. On the same day, Paul received a letter from Dr Milan Stojadinović, Minister of Finance under Jevtić: 'Enclosed is the report by Mr Belin, about which I had the honour to speak to you. He is a very serious person, secretary general of the Zagreb Stock Exchange, non-politician, but sympathizes with the Opposition. His information is very significant, and I beg you keep it strictly confidential in order not to compromise the beginning of a work of fateful importance for the future of this country.'[2]

The enclosed report concerned Maček whom Mr Belin had seen the previous day. Maček had claimed that the only hope for a solution to the dangerous political situation was for himself and Prince Paul to meet. This would not be easy to arrange as he refused to take part in Parliament and therefore had no excuse to ask for an audience with the Prince Regent. The simplest way he could suggest to establish contact was for a cabinet crisis to be engineered. In such a situation, Maček, as leader of the Opposition, would have to be invited for consultations. He added that he did not think it would be difficult to bring about a cabinet crisis, even if it were to end with a renewal of the existing one.

There is no record of Paul's reaction to this letter, but not long afterwards the Jevtić government fell. A Croatian colleague of Jevtić accused Maček and the Croat Peasant Party of sympathizing with the murderers of King Alexander. Immediately three Croatian and two Serbian ministers resigned. The Serbs were General Živković and Dr Stojadinović.

On 21st June Paul and Maček finally met in their respective capacities as Prince Regent and leader of the Opposition. The Croat had not moved from his original position of insistence on a radical change in the constitution to give the Croats more autonomy. He wanted Prince Paul to form a bureaucratic interim government, under General Zivković, to administer the country whilst the politicians worked on an agreement. Paul was opposed to a change in the constitution, even though he realized that the existing one was plainly undemocratic. He saw his rôle as Regent quite clearly: he was a caretaker and bound to hand the kingdom over in the same condition in which he had received it. It is possible that other factors influenced him too. The country was in a turbulent state and foreign policy had been neglected. Above all it needed a stable government. A change in the constitution would have been extremely unpopular with the Serbs and would have involved protracted negotiations—'a tedious and slow job'[3] as Paul remarked in his diary.

By the time he saw Maček, Paul had already set in motion an alternative solution. He had asked Stojadinović to look into the possibility of forming a new government. Throughout the course of June, Stojadinović was involved in talks with party leaders and, as a result, was able to propose the formation of a new party, the Yugoslav Radical Union (Jugoslavenska Radikalna Zajednica (J.R.Z.)). The party combined all the pro-government elements and was to be run by an executive committee including the leaders of the Serbian National Radical Party and Radical Party, the Slovene Populist Party, and the Yugoslav Moslem Organization. Paul accepted the concept and on 23rd June the regents officially invited Stojadinović to form a cabinet which would introduce liberal reforms and ease political tensions. The opposition neither opposed, nor agreed to participate in, the new government. Paul was satisfied with the outcome and, writing on 26th June to Bernard Berenson, added as a postscript 'have been awfully busy but am satisfied with the results and look to the future with confidence'.[4]

Milan Stojadinović was a tall, heavily-built and impressive-looking man. He had had a distinguished career. A graduate in law at the University of Belgrade, he had gone on to study economics at French, German and English Universities. During the 1914–18 war he had been employed in the Ministry of Finance and it was allegedly he who, as the enemy were preparing to enter Belgrade, had packed the contents of the Treasury into a small boat and managed to get them to the Yugoslav government in exile in Corfu. During the 1920s Stojadinović had served as a director of a number of Serbian and British companies and had been elected a Vice-President of the Belgrade Stock Exchange. On two separate occasions he had been appointed Minister of Finance by King Alexander. But during the dictatorship he had fallen out of favour with the King and had only regained office in the Jevtić cabinet of 1934.

Paul's decision to back Stojadinović is understandable. He was a dynamic and able man and he seemed to have the authority with which to hold together a wider coalition than had previously seemed possible. He had also appeared both capable and willing to resolve the Serb-Croat problem. The sincerity of his commitment, as expressed in his letter to Paul of 22nd May, may have been genuine enough at the time he made it, but once he was elevated to the Presidency of the Council he made little further effort to come to terms with Maček, and it began to seem increasingly likely that his earlier concern had been no more than a ploy to gain the Prince Regent's confidence.

A factor which exerted considerable influence on Paul was Sir Nevile Henderson's opinion of Stojadinović. Sir Nevile had been British Minister in Belgrade since 1929 and had been on excellent terms with King Alexander. During the first nine months of his regency, Paul had had few people with whom he could discuss affairs objectively, and he had accordingly seen a lot of the Minister. Sir Nevile (who would later claim, with some degree of justification, that Stojadinović owed much of the success of his political career to him)[5] had a strong admiration for the Serb, not least because of his abilities as a sportsman. Whether or not the appointment was in the long run beneficial for Yugoslavia, the immediate effect was good: tempers cooled, Croat terrorism ceased and Paul at last could feel that he had a President of Council who was in control.

In the new cabinet Milan Stojadinović appointed Father Korošeć as Minister of the Interior and took up the post of Foreign Affairs himself. Besides a vague attempt on the part of the Jevtić government to move back to the protection of France, there had been little change in the direction of Yugoslav foreign affairs since the death of the late King. Yugoslavia belonged to the Little Entente with Rumania and Czechoslovakia, and to the Balkan Entente with Greece, Rumania and Turkey. This system of alliances was all very well but it afforded Yugoslavia little real protection against her most aggressive neighbours. Italy had definite ambitions on Yugoslav territory and so too did Bulgaria. The rivalry between Yugoslavia and Bulgaria was deep-rooted and, since the eighth century, the two countries were known to have waged seventeen wars against each other, only one of which had ever been declared. Their quarrel, since the end of the First World War, had been over the question of Macedonia. By the Treaty of Neuilly it had been divided almost entirely between Greece and Yugoslavia, a fact which the Bulgarians bitterly resented. The King of Bulgaria, Boris, was mistrusted by the Serbs. They had more justification for their suspicions than the mere fact that he was the son of King Ferdinand, 'the Fox'. Paul liked Boris personally but regarded him as a rogue and scarcely more reliable than his father. As he warned the British Foreign Secretary, Anthony Eden, when he met him in London: 'He is all things to all men: an Englishman in London, a Coburg in Berlin, a Parma in Italy.'[6]

If Yugoslav foreign policy had remained at a virtual standstill, there had been changes elsewhere. Fascism in Germany and Italy was beginning to threaten the stability of Europe. In March 1935 Hitler had admitted to the existence of a German air force and had announced plans for rearmament and conscription. In May he had used the pretext of the proposed Franco-Soviet treaty to denounce the Locarno Pact. At this stage the French believed Germany to be a greater threat than Italy, but opinions in Britain were divided. In Yugoslavia neither Stojadinović nor Paul was particularly alarmed by the increasing power of Hitler and his National Socialist Germany. Paul regarded the Nazis as an uncouth bunch, but at the same time he admired what they had done for Germany. More important, he approved of Hitler's policy towards Russia. He believed that Hitler's loathing of communism was sincere, and, as his own abhorrence of it amounted almost to a mania, he regarded Germany as a final bulwark in Europe against the further spread of Bolshevism.

Besides, Hitler had made every effort to cultivate good relations with Yugoslavia. Goering had represented Germany at King Alexander's funeral and shortly afterwards Paul had received a letter from his friend, Philip of Hesse, who was later to become Hitler's intermediary in negotiations with Mussolini. After commiserating about the Marseilles tragedy and the new responsibilities that had fallen on Paul's shoulders, Philip went on:

> Goering, in whose house I am staying for a few days, came back greatly impressed from the funeral and his stay in Belgrade. He was full of admiration for you and for all he had seen and spoke in the most enthusiastic way about it to Hitler and to me. You have made a good friend of him which pleases me very much because you can always rely on his loyalty. His greatest wish is that you should come here as soon as you have got a chance so that Hitler and he can show you the new Germany and would be able to prove their friendship . . . [7]

Paul did not visit Goering for some years, but in June of 1935 Philip of Hesse arrived in Belgrade with Goering. It was at the time of the government crisis, and as Goering disregarded Jevtić as an ineffectual francophile, his focus of attention was on Paul. During the course of this visit, he told the Prince Regent that Germany would never support the Hungarian revisionists against Yugoslavia and that he was trying to persuade the Hungarians to give up their claims. He promised that Yugoslavia would have nothing to fear when the Anschluss came, as Hitler would give her a guarantee, written or in any form she wished. He complained about the inconsistency of the Italians and grumbled at the Czechs for becoming a Russian air base. As for Russia he thought that only war could make changes there, and Germany did not want war. He concluded by suggesting that Prince Paul should meet Hitler and by inviting him to come and shoot in Germany.[8] Altogether it was a friendly visit, and it was followed by a further visit from Philip of Hesse bearing presents of toys for the children and two beautiful Augsburg silver *cache-pots* for Paul from Hitler.

From the other fascist nation Yugoslavia had more to fear, in so far as Mussolini had never adopted anything but an aggressive stand towards Yugoslavia. At the beginning of 1935 Mussolini had been preoccupied with his plans for an attack on Abyssinia. This was a cause of much anxiety in Western Europe. The French, at least, did not want to drive Mussolini towards Germany and in January 1935 Laval, the French Foreign Minister, had virtually promised to let him have a free hand in Abyssinia. The British attitude was less clear. Many people realized the importance of keeping Mussolini on the Anglo-French side, but the government was pledged to supporting the League of Nations which promised collective action against any aggressor. For most of the summer, the British and French discussed plans for common action.

By September the issue had reached a climax. The British had asked the League of Nations to impose sanctions on Italy in the event of an attack: France, after much hedging, had declared her support for the League of Nations, and Mussolini had flatly refused to listen to the League.

At first Yugoslavia was not involved. From her point of view there was little to choose between the possible outcomes. On the one hand a campaign in North Africa would divert Mussolini's attention away from the Balkans: on the other, firm treatment by the League of Nations might make him wary of further aggression. Stojadinović, who had just taken up his new post, sent the following memorandum to Prince Paul: 'Concerning our attitude I think we should be—as the Bible says—"wise like a snake and tame like doves". We alone will neither save nor destroy Mussolini and in addition to this, who can tell what the policy of a post-Mussolini Italy will be? After Mussolini, to which side will that rapidly expanding population turn? I would prefer them to go to Abyssinia, rather than to the Balkans. Certainly as long as France has not decided on which side she will come down we have no reason to.'[9]

But Yugoslavia could not remain impartial for long. On 3rd

October 1935 Mussolini invaded Ethiopia. On 7th October the League of Nations declared Italy an aggressor and on 11th the League voted to impose sanctions against Italy. Yugoslavia voted for sanctions along with the others and, in so doing, lost her main trading partner. Up until 1935 Italy had bought about a quarter of all Yugoslav exports and while sanctions were in operation the Yugoslav economy suffered badly. Even after they were lifted trade never resumed its former proportions and the Yugoslav government was forced to seek markets elsewhere. This was to have far-reaching consequences.

So too was the intriguing which went on after the League of Nations' decision. Paul realized that the affair was not over when he passed through Paris in October, on his way to London for a private visit. Whilst in Paris he discussed European affairs with Laval, who since June had been Prime Minister, and noted part of the conversation in his diary: 'Reads me Mussolini's letter, who seems to have taken a fright and considers Laval as his only friend. Italy willing to keep a few provinces leaving the rest to Abyssinia and even offering them an outlet on the sea . . . [Laval] said that if Italy attacked England he would defend the latter and asked me to explain in that country that he was unjustly suspected of not being a friend. When I asked what would Abyssinia answer he jumped and said "vous l'avez decrié, Voilà la question!" Laval wishes to keep Italy's offers secret and hopes to make them still more moderate.'[10]

Laval wanted to work out a series of proposals which could form the basis of peace negotiations between Italy, Abyssinia and the League of Nations. Despite what he said to Paul he was eventually able to get Sir Samuel Hoare to co-operate. Hoare had been a strong supporter of the League of Nations and was well aware that British public opinion was firmly behind the League. At the same time he could see the importance of not alienating Mussolini. Unfortunately for him the Hoare-Laval pact was leaked to the press before it reached the League. The British public accused him of carving up Abyssinia for Mussolini's benefit and of betraying the League, and on 18th December he resigned. The new Foreign Secretary was Anthony Eden, then only thirty-eight years old and at the height of a brilliant career.

Paul and Eden had been at Christ Church together after the Great War. For the latter, Oxford had been a convenient stepping stone; for Paul it had been an end in itself. Eden had arrived at Oxford after four years on the Western Front, certain of his future and confident of his position. Paul had returned to Christ Church after four years' upheaval and chronic illness completely unsure about both his future and his position. Paul had known and liked Anthony's elder brother, Timothy, at Oxford before the war but with Anthony he failed to hit it off. Anthony considered Paul over-emotional, over-sensitive and somewhat foppish, whilst Paul considered Anthony, who was five years his junior, over-ambitious, humourless and arrogant. Anthony had pursued his Persian and Arabic studies with all the seriousness of a scholar in a hurry to move on to other things. Paul had longed for nothing more than to be allowed to drag out his Oxford life for ever. From the start they had regarded each other with a certain mutual contempt and although they were to maintain, throughout their lives, the strictest civility they were to remain basically antipathetic towards each other. This mutual dislike was later to have unfortunate consequences for Yugoslavia.

The visit Paul made to Paris and London at the end of 1935 was the first real break from Yugoslavia that he had had for a year. He had only crossed the border on two other occasions: once for a couple of days' shooting with King Carol of Rumania and once on a secret trip to Munich with the family. The Kents had come to stay and had decided to move on to the Toerrings' in Munich, taking Olga with them. Paul, who had been feeling low at the time, had decided to accompany the party. It had been a short weekend but the drive, early on a Friday morning in the Duke of Kent's motor and unaccompanied by detectives, had been a welcome change.

Paul's life since October 9th of the previous year had changed completely and, as far as he was concerned, it had changed considerably for the worse. He regarded his existence in Yugoslavia and the prospects of his seven-year regency as a sentence: something which he was bound to fulfil and which involved no pleasure and would end with no reward. Where before he had been free to travel about Europe as he pleased and pursue his various interests, he had, overnight, become involved in the day to day running of a country whose army was reluctant to accept him and whose politicians drove him to distraction.

Sitting alone in his study in the middle of a mid-February blizzard in Belgrade, feeling miserable, lonely and seemingly cut off from all his friends, Paul poured out his heart to Mrs Berenson: 'As B.B. must have told you, no doubt, I lead a hard, difficult life with hardly any leisure. I have had to give up all that I cared for and must now lead the existence of a galley slave. The job is honourable certainly, but you know yourself how little we are responsible for the success or the failure of our actions. Without a good dose of what we call luck little can be achieved! . . . Here it is Siberia and we've never seen such snow before—a most depressing sight to my eyes. How often I think of I Tatti and long for your library and specially for you both. Close contact with politicians doesn't improve one's faith in human nature!'[11]

Perhaps what Paul missed most in his first year as Regent was sheer companionship. He had no one with whom he could talk things over and relax. Alexander had been his only real friend in Yugoslavia and he was dead. Visitors to the house, besides the constant and welcome stream of Olga's relatives and some old friends, were mostly either ministers or diplomats. Of the diplomats, Sir Nevile Henderson was probably closest to being a confidant. He had been in Yugoslavia a long time and knew all the politicians. He was, besides, both amiable and kind. But in character he was not a bit like Paul. He was a solid, predictable Englishman whose main passions in life were hunting and fishing. Paul felt isolated. It was not quite so bad for Olga as her family ties were strong and she was constantly in touch—by wire, letter or telephone—with her mother and sisters. For Olga the ups and downs of the family and the births, marriages and movements of her sisters and cousins were of more immediate interest and concern than Yugoslav politics. Besides she was absorbed in the upbringing of her two small sons.

The first six months of 1935 were spent in Belgrade and were fairly gloomy. Though Paul fulfilled his constitutional duties to the letter and though to some extent he began to understand and even to work up an interest in Belgrade politics, his mind was frequently elsewhere. He read continually, craved the company of his erudite friends and the proximity of museums, galleries and dealers. To Berenson he wrote on 17th March: 'I don't suppose that the desire for possessing pictures would be as great if I lived in a big centre with fine museums but in a town like this where the vicissitudes of history have destroyed every vestige of tradition one feels sometimes starved for beauty created by man.'[12]

On most days Paul's routine was much the same. Work began at 10 o'clock when he received various officials such as the Governor of Belgrade, who came each day, and the Inspector of the Army who came every seventh. After them came the Minister of Court, Mr Antić, with his daily report, and then any other ministers or civic leaders who had requested an audience and any foreign diplomats who were visiting Belgrade. At 1 o'clock he stopped for lunch. Sometimes this was just family—perhaps including Queen Marie and Peter—but often there were guests. In the afternoon Olga would take him for a drive, or in summer they might play tennis at the British Legation or golf at Dedinje. After tea Paul would cope with further interviews lasting until dinner. When they were not officially entertaining or being entertained, the evenings were spent quietly as Paul was usually exhausted: Olga would read to him, or he would play Chopin on the piano, or they would go up to Dedinje to watch a film with Queen Marie in the cinema that Alexander had had built beneath the palace.

At the beginning of July 1935, just after the question of the government had been settled and Stojadinović had been appointed Premier, Paul and Olga left Belgrade to spend the rest of the summer in Slovenia. But Bohinj was not as enjoyable as before. On account of the stifling heat in Belgrade, the entire court moved up to Bled for the summer and so work continued for Paul. Olga's parents and the Kents and other friends came to stay but Paul did not have much time to spend with them. He still had to see 'his daily bores' in the morning, and as well as this received frequent visits from Stojadinović and other ministers. The formation of a new political party was a tricky business and, one after another, ruffled politicians came to him for comfort and support for their own views.

In addition to their new and time-consuming political pre-occupations, Olga and Paul were both unwell during the

119

summer of 1935. Olga had just found out that she was expecting her third child and for much of the time she was feeling weak and sick. Paul was suffering from a poisoned arm. By August his left bicep had become hard and swollen and was so painful that he had to retire to bed. The doctors diagnosed the trouble as myositis, a rare disease, and seemed incapable of curing it. Paul became increasingly anxious and depressed. Towards the end of August he agreed to have the swelling cut out. The operation took place in the bathroom at Bohinj and was conducted by the doctors and two nuns who arrived with an operating table and all the necessary equipment. The operation was not entirely successful. On 10th September he wrote to Berenson, complaining: 'Am just back from Belgrade where I had to ride with my arm in a sling suffering all the time. I was so afraid of falling off the horse and making "una brutta figura", but mercifully all went well. My wound won't heal and they had to put a "tampon" inside it. When it's removed the pain will be exquisite!' He tried to concentrate on other things—'if possible I'll try and organize next Spring an exhibition of ecclesiastical art in Belgrade and collect all the treasures of the land, it won't be easy as churches and monasteries are jealous owners'[13]—but it became clear to him that he would sooner or later have to go abroad to have his arm properly treated.

The trip to London in October 1935 was partly for this purpose. They were met at Victoria Station by the Duke of Kent who took them straight to Belgrave Square to admire Marina's new baby. From then on the days were full of engagements: luncheon, tea, theatre and dinner parties, shopping expeditions, and trips to the country to see Alexander at his preparatory school. To a great extent their social life revolved round Belgrave Square* and by extension the other royal households. As Olga recorded on 27th October: 'Very warm. Went to the Greek Church with Mummy. Then to see Attinse [Marina], then went to Buckingham Palace to lunch. Found poor Uncle George very abattu this time and sad. Rested in M's room after as I was exhausted from standing about while Aunt May showed us her latest treasures. Pacey took Georgy to see the Wallace Collection. Went to Hanover

* The Duke and Duchess of Kent were living at No. 3 Belgrave Square.

120

Lodge to tea to see Alice's babies. Pacey, Georgy and I had dinner with David [Prince of Wales] at the Fort. Also "Wallis" Simpson, Lady Colefax, an American couple and Godfrey Thomas. Pacey played the piano and David sang—dressed in kilts v. smart.'[14] About Wallis Simpson, Paul had heard little beyond what Chips had written to him in April of that year. 'She is a jolly, plain, intelligent, quiet, unpretentious and un-prepossessing little woman, but she has the air of a personage who walks into the room as though she almost expected to be curtsied to.'[15]

Other old friends entertained them too. They lunched with the Kenneth Clarks, with Lady Zia Wernher and with the Vansittarts; they dined with Emerald Cunard and with Sir Philip Sassoon and sometimes they dropped in at No. 5 Belgrave Square to have tea with Chips and Honor Channon. During the day much of Olga's time was spent with her family— shopping with her mother and visiting Marina who was still confined to bed. Paul used this time to move about with his old friends, especially with Archie, Chips and Georgie Kent, and to visit exhibitions and galleries. He managed to keep official engagements to a minimum and the only official record of his visit is a brief note by Sir Robert Vansittart, written at the request of the Foreign Office: 'I do not think that Prince Paul said anything of particular note. But he is—still—very clearly and warmly Anglophile. And I think it is clear that he has no intention of committing himself to Germany. He is more critical of France than the last time we met—comprehensibly, but without bitterness. I think he clearly intends to keep his country on a middle course.'[16]

On 2nd November Olga entered in her diary: 'Pacey and Mummy left for Paris at 11 this morning. They were both sorry to leave, especially Pacey who must return to his hard labours and loved every moment here.' Olga did not exaggerate, for immediately after his return to Belgrade, on 15th November, Paul dashed off an ecstatic letter to Berenson:

I had a lovely 3 weeks' holiday in Paris and London where I went to consult doctors about my arm which seems to develop a curious and unpleasant illness—ossification of the muscle. I had the good fortune, in London, to fall on a remarkable German doctor (émigré) Prof. Landau. But enough on that unpleasant subject. I gave way completely to my craving for art and rushed from one gallery to another and visited all my old haunts and shops over again. I bought the Titian portrait after keeping it for 3 days in my bedroom and realizing that it was a picture I would like to spend my life with. I also found a delightful Rubens sketch. By the way, I saw a fine Piero di Cosimo which has just come to light and which must be the picture mentioned in Vasari representing Silenus riding an ass and escorted by children and bacchantes. The landscape is beautiful and almost Venetian. I've asked for a photo which I will forward on to you. K. Clark I saw a lot of and mentioned my scheme about your book . . .[17]

Exactly one month after Paul had returned to Yugoslavia Kenneth Clark wrote to inform him that he had acquired for Paul a Claude for practically nothing and that at last Paul's pride and joy, El Greco's *Laocöon*, was on its way to Belgrade:

I was away in Paris when your first telegram came, but fortunately I was able to come home in time to have a good look at the Claude. I remembered seeing it in the Yarborough sale and being very much taken with it and a second view confirmed my opinion. It is unquestionably genuine and very beautiful of its kind—far better than either of those at Colnaghi's. It had fetched £750 at the Yarborough sale and I believe Innes gave about £1,200 for it, but that was in 1929; so I felt that it would be cheap at anything up to £500. I never expected to get it for as little as £220, but it seems that those dirty dealers made a ring against the sale because the unfortunate Innes had bought on his own judgement and not through Bond St. As soon as I had got the picture I had it sent to the gallery and looked it over carefully. It really is a beauty and in quite good condition, and I think you have got a real bargain. I will have it packed tomorrow and sent out with the Greco. The latter I have seen in its case and it looks very snug and solid . . .[18]

Paul was delighted with this news, but his ambitions were

far from satisfied. Towards the end of January 1936, he was angling not only for the Piero di Cosimo but also for an Antonello by which he had been much struck in the Jahrbuch sale in Vienna. In addition he was investigating a Bellini, which he believed to be an original, and working on a theory that he had picked up in London: that El Greco had been influenced by Hieronymus Bosch.

Although there was no dramatic change in the pattern of their lives, 1936 was a much happier year for both Paul and Olga. It began with a jolly family Christmas and New Year for which the Toerrings came to stay. Immediately afterwards, Paul made an unexpected trip to London, the reason for which was the death of King George V on 20th January. Paul and Olga had known for some days that he was seriously ill so the telegram that they received from the Duke of Kent came as no great surprise.

King George's funeral was a magnificent occasion. The ceremony took place at Windsor but beforehand the cortège processed through the London streets from Westminster Hall, where the King had lain in state, to Paddington. At the head of the procession the coffin, draped in a Union Jack, was drawn on a gun carriage by the Royal Marines. Behind them walked the men: first came Edward VIII, then his brothers and then a group of foreign royalty, all in uniform. Amongst these, with the Prince of Piedmont, King Boris of Bulgaria, King Carol of Rumania, the Kings of Denmark and of Norway and many others, walked the Prince Regent of Yugoslavia. The Queen's coach followed, carrying Queen Mary and her sister-in-law, the Queen of Norway. It was a misty, damp London day and the procession moved very slowly, and as it passed the crowds were silent. Chips, who had been watching from a window in St James's Street, wrote that night: 'Paul looked well but shuffled in his long coat and ugly uniform. Fritzi of Prussia looked very handsome in a white uniform and the King of Rumania, as ever, looked ridiculous.'[19]

Paul had arrived in London a few days before the funeral and remained for only a few days afterwards. He stayed with the Kents at Belgrave Square and spent much of his time with Queen Mary who, despite her own grief and loneliness, was especially sweet to him.

Paul returned to Yugoslavia on 10th February to find that all was well and that the trip to London had given an enormous boost to his prestige in the country. On the domestic side the new house in Belgrade, Beli Dvor, was almost completed. Paul and Olga had waited a year and a half for this house and Paul had supervised every step of its progress. In the last months of 1935 and the first of 1936 one or other of them had visited it every day. Finally, on 15th March 1936, they moved in. In contrast to their quarters at the Old Palace, Beli Dvor was spacious and beautifully proportioned. Paul adored it. It was a perfect setting for all the art treasures, books, china and other exquisite objects that he had collected or been given. It was comfortable too. In all, it housed about twenty-six staff, including an English nanny and governess and two French chefs. Paul was a gourmet and even during the regency he retained complete control of the kitchen. Each morning, after his massage and before work began, he would go downstairs to consult with whichever chef was on duty and plan the menus for the day. If he chose fish they would be taken live from a well stocked pool.

Living at Beli Dvor made entertaining easier and more enjoyable. The guests fell broadly into two categories. In one came most of the Yugoslav officials: politicians, diplomats, fellow regents and military men. In the other, the people with whom Paul and Olga could relax. This group now included the Balfours,* the Parrotts† (usually with King Peter), the Strandtmans,‡ Queen Marie and the Campbells. Sir Ronald Campbell had arrived in December 1935 as the new British Minister. He was more intelligent than his predecessor, who had played the rôle of a kind uncle and had really been happiest when shooting with Paul or playing Lexicon with Olga. Paul liked Sir Ronald from the start and was to become extremely fond of him.

In 1936 the summer months were brighter too. Olga, who

* Jock Balfour had been posted to Yugoslavia as First Secretary at the British Legation.

† Cecil Parrott, King Peter's tutor, had come to Yugoslavia straight from Cambridge. In 1935 he had married a Norwegian, a former nurse to King Peter and his brothers.

‡ Yugoslavia did not recognize the U.S.S.R. Mr Strandtman was the representative of Czarist Russia in Belgrade.

had given birth to a daughter in April, was blissfully happy. With two sons already, she had been longing for a girl. Paul was healthy and more confident about politics. Although he still had to cope with a vast amount of work and the usual rounds of official entertaining, he was surer of himself and happier about his lot. Apart from his official duties there was a lot to occupy his mind and all of it was pleasurable.

First of all, there were the plans for his new house in Slovenia. Since going through his cousin's papers and discovering that Alexander had never officially made over Bohinj to him, Paul had been looking for a house to buy near Bled. He found Brdo,* an old German castle set in a huge park. Brdo was square in shape, built round an open courtyard and with an enormous circular turret at each corner. As with Beli Dvor*, Paul spared no effort to make the house beautiful. He brought from Florence the famous English landscape architect, Cecil Pinsent, to match the colours and to design the fountain and steps.

Then there were their guests—and there were many friends who visited Yugoslavia in 1936. Olga's parents had been in residence since the arrival of the baby, Elizabeth, in April and the Kents came in June. One of Paul's favourite pastimes was clearing trees on the estate and he and Georgie Kent would spend hours chopping. They would appear for tea on the terrace dripping with sweat and wearing nothing but their shorts, much to the horror of Miss Ede, the diminutive and ferocious English nanny. The Infante Alfonso, and his wife Beatrice, came too and so also did Chips with a motley group of friends.

The visit to which, after the departure of Georgie and Marina, Paul looked forward with the greatest anticipation was that of Bernard Berenson. The elderly and frail historian was planning an expedition to the churches and monasteries of southern Yugoslavia. Paul was fearful lest his friend should find the going too rough and went out of his way to make arrangements for his safety and comfort. Berenson was due to set foot on Yugoslav soil on 19th July and two days before Paul wrote a note of welcome from the royal palace in Bled: 'This is

* The late President Tito made Brdo his official summer residence, and Beli Dvor his home in Belgrade.

just one line to welcome you to this land—to say that my thoughts are much with you and that I hope all goes well. Please let me know if anything isn't right or if they bother you too much which may easily be the case through "excès de zèle", for this is the east! I regret that you are not going to Ohrida and feel it my duty to discourage you from going to Žicá. Le jeu ne vaut pas la chandelle and the discomforts of the journey will not be repaid by all the "restorations", and bad ones too, of the church. We are still at Bled and am unable to say yet when we can move into our new abode. In any case this time we shall meet and to that I'm looking forward more than I can say.'[20] As it turned out the journey passed without mishap and Berenson was impressed with the Serbo-Byzantine frescoes and icons that he saw.

In August 1936 Edward VIII also paid a fleeting visit to Yugoslavia. The King of England had decided to spend a month cruising off the Adriatic coast in the company of some friends. Because the imposition of sanctions had caused considerable anti-British feeling in Italy, his original plan of boarding his yacht, the *Nahlin*, at Venice had been abandoned. Instead he had decided to join the boat at Sibenić on the Dalmatian coast. The change of plan caused a certain amount of panic in Slovenia. Olga was worried that she might be obliged to send her parents away to make room for the King, should he decide to stay in their house. Paul was concerned about security and neither of them were pleased at the prospect of entertaining Mrs Simpson. By this time the press had caught on to the fact that she was a member of the King's party and, like the royal family in Britain, Paul and Olga did not approve.

Over the security arrangements Paul took matters firmly into his own hands. The King had intended to travel from Paris to Zagreb, where his private coach was to be shunted over to be coupled on to a local train that would take it on to Sibenić. Paul considered this manoeuvre, in the capital of Croatia, highly dangerous. He therefore asked Jock Balfour to contact the Foreign Office, explain the position and offer his own royal train for the entire journey across Yugoslavia. Jock received a laconic reply to the effect that the King had already completed the arrangements for his journey and was unable, at this stage, to alter them. Paul disregarded this. On 9th August he drove to the small frontier station of Jesenicé to greet the King. Whilst they were talking on the platform a railwayman swiftly uncoupled the King's coach and shunted it round to join the Yugoslav royal train. When the King turned to climb back into his coach he found that it had disappeared. A smug Prince Regent then proceeded to escort him to the royal train on the other side of the station.

King Edward's return trip through Yugoslavia, some three weeks later, from Turkey to Vienna, in the Ghazi Ataturk's special train, was briefly interrupted at Belgrade where the royal party stopped long enough to visit, in the late evening, the royal palaces at Dedinje and Beli Dvor. The British Ambassador being on leave, Jock Balfour was at Belgrade Railway Station to meet the royal party:

Flanked by the Yugoslav Prime Minister and the Turkish Minister at Belgrade—both rotund top hat-crowned barrels, the former large sized and the latter squat—and with the Legation staff lined up in the rear I was waiting on the platform as the train drew to a halt at about 9 p.m. At a station down the line Prince Paul had joined the royal party which was accompanied by Sir Percy Loraine, our Ambassador in Turkey, now bound for a race meeting in Vienna. Dinner was finishing in the dining-car opposite us, at the door of which Sir Percy appeared for a moment to cast a disdainful glance in our direction.

Five minutes or so later I saw the King framed in the exit— a lighted cigar in his hand and looking slightly flushed. 'Who are you?' he curtly enquired as I came forward. 'Balfour, Sir, the Chargé d'Affaires whom Prince Paul presented to Your Majesty at the frontier station.' 'Of course,' said H.M. clambering down unsteadily from the train. I propelled him towards the waiting group, putting my arm to his shoulder. ('You must be an old friend of his,' said one of the Legation staff afterwards!) Having presented Stoyadinovitch the turn came for the Turkish Minister: 'Le train de votre Ghazi est, est . . .' 'What the hell is the right word?', hissed the King. 'Magnifique,' I whispered back. 'Yes, yes, magnifick,' exclaimed the King with the most British of accents. Next came the Junior Secretary of the Legation, a dapper little man with an eyeglass named Greiffenhagen. 'I had a ship-mate of your name before the war,' said H.M. 'That would be my brother,' answered Greiffenhagen. 'And what became of him?' 'He was killed at Jutland, Sir.' This news had a sobering effect on the King who from that moment became a Prince Charming in his talk with the other members of the staff.[21]

It is difficult to say whether the King of England's trips through Yugoslavia were disliked most by Paul, the British Legation, the King, or Mrs Simpson. The relationship between Paul and the King was inevitably strained. Paul opposed his friend's liaison with Mrs Simpson and on the outward journey, when the party had stopped briefly at Brdo, Olga had made a point of not receiving her as the King's lady. Wallis Simpson, who was on holiday with the man she loved, resented these interludes, for they served as reminders of official Court attitudes in London.* For the British Legation, the arrival of their King had a profoundly demoralizing effect, not least for the fact that he seemed at the time to be successfully flouting the very conventions by which they as diplomats, supposedly like their royal masters, could expect themselves to be judged. As one Balkan diplomat at Bled slyly put it to Jock: 'Comme monarque d'un grand pays, votre Roi, lorsqu'il part en vacance, peut evidemment se permettre le plaisir de voyager ensemble avec sa maîtresse. Ce qui n'est point possible pour le roi de la Roumanie.'†[22]

When, after the funeral of George V, Paul had returned to Yugoslavia, the political situation had been encouraging. Stojadinović had established the J.R.Z. as the major force in the Skupština and he had effectively silenced his two rivals, General Živković and Mr Jevtić. He had, moreover, already begun to turn his mind to international affairs. This was a subject which Paul understood and liked and soon he and Stojadinović were working happily together. Of their close partnership the

* Later, as Duchess of Windsor, she would write disparagingly, in her biography *The Heart has its Reasons*, of the hospitality which she and King Edward were shown by the Prince Regent.

† Having deserted his wife Helen, King Carol of Rumania was at all times prevented, by official diplomatic pressure, from travelling openly with his mistress, Mme Lupescu.

7. The official wedding photograph of Prince and Princess Paul of Serbia.

8. At the christening of Crown Prince Peter of Serbia, October 1923,
l to r: King Alexander of Serbia, Queen Elisabetta of Greece,
Queen Marie (Missie) of Rumania, King Ferdinand of Rumania
and the Duke and Duchess of York.

9. October 1934: King Alexander's assassin cut down by a guardsman's
sabre.

British Minister wrote: 'Which of them is the dominant partner is a question to which I have not yet found the answer. Though Prince Paul is generally credited with being the source of inspiration, I have the impression that Mr Stojadinović's practical common sense not only acts as a brake on H.R.H.'s impulsiveness, but does more to shape his mind than he realizes.'[23]

The overall aim of their foreign policy was to create a strong and independent Yugoslavia. In the past, Yugoslavia had looked to the Great Powers for protection and in particular to France. But France was no longer a reliable friend: she had behaved badly over Abyssinia and she had signed a pact with the U.S.S.R. By the beginning of 1936, Europe was rapidly dividing into fascist and anti-fascist blocs and in order to avoid the danger of Yugoslavia being torn apart in a struggle between the two sides, Stojadinović determined on establishing a solid Balkan bloc with which the Great Powers would hesitate to interfere. He took, as a basis for his plan, the Balkan Entente. The signatories to this agreement were Yugoslavia, Greece, Rumania and Turkey. For any bloc to be effective, Bulgaria would also have to be a member, but here there were problems. The very existence of the Balkan Entente was evidence of the need which the member countries felt, to protect themselves from Bulgaria's territorial ambitions. Although Bulgarian relations with Turkey and Yugoslavia had been improving, both Greece and Rumania were still wary of rapprochement. During the early months of 1936 Paul and Stojadinović started to collaborate with the Turkish Foreign Minister on plans for the future of the Balkans.

Meanwhile Hitler had made his first aggressive move. In March he had occupied the demilitarized Rhineland. This was a breach of the Treaty of Versailles and a 'casus foederis' under the Locarno Pact, but neither Britain nor France took action. In Yugoslavia Paul and Stojadinović feared that there might be repercussions. Other countries might fail to honour their peace treaties. If the Little Entente broke down, Yugoslavia would once again be exposed to the threat of a Hapsburg restoration and this eventuality was dreaded in Belgrade not least for the opportunities it would give Mussolini to meddle directly in Balkan politics. As a result of the conquest of Abyssinia, Paul saw Yugoslavia more than ever exposed to invasion by Italy. His anxiety was all the more acute in the light of the hollow pretence behind the system of collective security when invoked as a remedy against aggression by leading members of the League of Nations. As was obvious from Abyssinia and the affairs in the Rhineland, these nations were themselves unwilling to practise what they preached.

The Yugoslavs were unhappy about the drift of French policy, and thoroughly muddled by the lack of direction of British policy. In Britain, Baldwin's leadership was weak, there were divisions within as well as between the major parties, and opinions were sharply divided about whether or not the Germans posed a threat to European security. In an attempt to understand the British viewpoint, and to urge Britain and France to join forces against Mussolini, the Yugoslav Ambassador to the League of Nations, Mr Purić, invited Eden for a drink in the Carlton Hotel, next door to the new League of Nations building. In an hour and a half of conversation Purić learnt nothing at all. Eden was vague and seemed hardly to realize what an adverse effect British indecision was having on European affairs. When he concluded complacently, 'England is slow but she always wakes up in time', Purić could hardly contain himself. Speaking in plain terms he told Eden that 'if England could afford to be indecisive and undetermined for a relatively long time, other countries, even against their will, could find themselves forced to reach agreements without England and possibly even against her'.[24]

The only country which appeared to have a clearly established foreign policy and which showed interest in the fate of Yugoslavia, was Germany. In June 1936, Dr Hjalmar Schacht, president of the Reichsbank, had arrived in Belgrade. He had come to speak to the Yugoslav leaders about the possibility of German economic aid. Yugoslavia, though basically an agricultural economy, was rich in minerals and for some time the Germans had been aware of her valuable source of iron ore. The purpose of Schacht's visit was to prepare the way for economic aid and to enhance, thereby, Berlin's political influence in Belgrade. They had chosen their moment with care. Yugoslavia was suffering the effects of its adherence to the League of Nations' sanctions against Italy.

According to the German minister in Belgrade, Stojadinović paid the liveliest attention to Dr Schacht's suggestions, and in a conversation afterwards agreed that German experts should come to inspect their iron ore deposits. In fact the conversations covered more than economic relations, for a note in Stojadinović's hand reveals that political and military questions were discussed as well. It appears too that Schacht had been entrusted with a message from Field-Marshal Goering and on 12th June, Stojadinović passed on this message to the Prince Regent: 'Germany is willing to furnish us complete security against Hungary and Italy. At the present time this offer appears unusually important for us. For peace in our country and to secure Yugoslavia's future, we must as soon as possible obtain insurance against Italy.'[25]

How much Paul knew about the nature of his Prime Minister's talks with Dr Schacht is uncertain. Stojadinović's own enthusiasm for the economic package was understandable. He was an astute businessman and the Germans were offering Yugoslavia excellent terms. There was little in the economic programme to alarm the government from an immediate political point of view, though the British Ambassador was quick to note the possibility of a future stranglehold:

> The danger, of course, is that Yugoslavia may end by becoming so bound to Germany economically that in any crisis she would have no alternative but to do her bidding. I have not hitherto taken an alarmist view of the German economic penetration of this country. The United Kingdom is not in a position which obliges her to compete seriously on the Danubian basin, which is a natural outlet for Germany, who must find markets somewhere. There is a certain safeguard moreover, in the fact that Yugoslavia is not anxious if she can avoid it, to put too many eggs in one basket. Also, until recently, she had not purchased armaments from Germany, whom she regards, so the Minister of War told the military attaché, as a potential enemy. In the last few days, however, I have learnt that an order has just been placed in Germany for one Dornier bomber of a modern type, to be followed later, if satisfactory, by 19 others, and that a similar purchase is contemplated for the Navy. This is the

more regrettable in that the air force would much prefer British machines. So long however as British firms are unwilling to give easy payment facilities, and the most modern types of machine are (quite rightly) not allowed to be sold to foreign governments, we must expect Yugoslavia to turn more and more to Germany for the development of her air arm. Once the principle of not buying war material in Germany has been violated, there is no knowing to what extent the tendency may develop. If it went far, it could only end by further fettering Yugoslavia's liberty of action in any crisis threatening to involve her in hostilities.[26]

The assurances that Dr Schacht brought from Goering were welcome in Belgrade. However, the German plan was not merely to protect Yugoslavia against Italian aggression. It was designed to forge a closer understanding between the two countries. Hitler's relations with Mussolini had been improving throughout 1936 and in October Count Ciano, the Italian Foreign Minister, visited Berchtesgaden. Hitler and he discussed many subjects, including Yugoslavia. Hitler impressed upon Ciano the importance of a rapprochement between Italy and Yugoslavia, which, he considered, would help to draw Yugoslavia away from British influence. When sanctions had been dropped in June, Italy and Yugoslavia had signed an economic and commercial agreement. On 1st November, Mussolini made a speech in Milan, in the course of which he hinted at the possibility of a firm friendship between the two countries and, incidentally, used the word 'axis' for the first time in his life.

Paul responded to Mussolini's gesture immediately. Yugoslavia had been seeking peaceful coexistence with Italy for years. A new basis of understanding would not only relieve Yugoslavia of an ever present threat to her borders, it might help resolve internal difficulties as well. The Croat problem was troubling Paul. Stojadinović paid little attention to it and when Paul and Maček met at Brdo on 7th November 1936, their discussions came to nothing. Maček's position had not changed and Paul was not prepared to give way. If relations with Italy improved, the Italians would have to stop supporting the Croat movement from abroad. This, Paul hoped, might make Maček less uncompromising.

For all their outward show of enthusiasm, both Stojadinović and Paul were suspicious of Mussolini's advances. He had double-crossed them before and they had no explanation for his sudden burst of friendliness. They knew nothing of the talks that Hitler had had with Ciano in October and when Paul visited London in mid-November he discussed the whole affair with Eden: 'His [Prince Paul's] own inclination was to show friendliness but wariness. Neither he nor his government had any confidence whatever in the assurances of Signor Mussolini. The Prince Regent could not so easily forget his cousin's murder. At the same time he thought it would be foolish to repulse these advances. He would therefore take them up and be willing to make some progress with them, perhaps even to the point of signing some non-aggression pact, or other harmless if somewhat ineffective declaration. Further than that, however, he would not go. He had no intention of allying himself with Italy. Did I think this course right?'[27] Eden replied that he thought Prince Paul was right in not contemplating an alliance and went on to explain the British view of the importance of maintaining some rivalry between Italy and Germany. In the same conversation Paul brought up the subjects of trade and armaments. He was pleased by Eden's attitude which was considerably more responsive than Sir John Simon's, and noted 'most friendly towards us and promises every support as considers economic questions from political angle'.[28]

In the following months Eden managed to increase British trade with Yugoslavia, but not enough to catch up with the German lead. As for armaments, the British rearmament programme was taking all that the industry could produce.

Paul and Olga's visit to England in November 1936 did not turn out to be as pleasant as the one the previous year, although it started well. They stayed, again, at Belgrave Square and spent week-ends at Coppins, the country house that the Duke of Kent had bought in Buckinghamshire. The Duke cared almost as much about Coppins as Paul did about Beli Dvor and he and Marina were very happy with their new house and their young son, Edward.

As always, in London, Paul and Olga found themselves caught up in a mass of social engagements. Besides the family, they saw many old friends and they met Rex Whistler who had recently designed the costumes and scenery for a production of *Pride and Prejudice* which was playing in the West End. But as their visit was not a private one, Paul and Olga were obliged to attend a number of official functions. One of these was a concert at the Yugoslav Legation. Chips Channon who was in the audience described the arrival of the royal party: 'Paul dark and distinguished and Princess Paul angular and handsome under her vast tiara, followed by the Infanta Beatrix and the Duke of Kent.'[29] Of the occasion Olga herself wrote: 'Crowds and heat and my tiara was agony.'[30]

However, it was not the official business that upset their visit. In November two issues which had been simmering in the background of their lives finally came to the boil. One was the Spanish Civil War, the other King Edward VIII's relationship with Wallis Simpson. When Paul and Olga had been in England the previous autumn, Wallis Simpson had been in evidence but nobody was taking the liaison very seriously. In Slovenia too, when the King passed through, the matter had not been given much importance. But now, the main topic of conversation in London society was 'will the King marry Mrs Simpson'? On 14th November Paul spent the whole day with Chips and was amazed to hear that there was open talk of abdication in the House of Commons. He and Chips naïvely decided that a substitute would have to be found and they discussed all the eligible princesses in Europe, but failed to find one that would do. On 17th November Paul had an audience with Mr Baldwin and found the ageing Prime Minister totally preoccupied with the fate of the Crown. In his diary Paul entered a short account of their conversation: '*Baldwin*: Relies on Eden for foreign policy which he himself little understands. A tired man who thought of giving up his place to younger people after he had seen crown firmly established. But now he won't do so. Great trouble between now and Xmas. Long talk with David [Prince of Wales] night before, tears in his eyes . . . but where "she" is concerned adamant. Wishes to marry her. Bruce [Prime Minister of Australia] tells Baldwin that Australia would leave Empire. Queen hurt by David taking her to Gallipoli. He doesn't yet know what prompted Laval-Hoare pact. Hoare left without mentioning anything.'[31]

Three days later, on 20th November, King Edward VIII

announced, to his mother and brothers, his desire to marry Mrs Simpson. From that day onwards this news, and the fact that Alonso, the second of Infanta Beatrice's sons, had been killed in action in Spain, dominated Paul and Olga's stay. The Infanta, who was then in her seventy-ninth year and who had always been particularly close to both Paul and Olga, was desperately upset at the death of her son. She was staying at Claridges and, utterly grief-stricken, was unable to eat. Olga visited her daily. Meanwhile the tension surrounding King Edward mounted quickly.

After the initial announcement to the family on 19th November, there was a lull, at least as far as Paul and Olga were concerned, until the storm finally broke on 3rd December. On the morning of 3rd December all the newspapers carried the story of the King's wish to marry Mrs Simpson. At last, restraint was thrown to the wind and no questions were ignored: should the King abdicate? Would the Empire fall to pieces? Would there be a morganatic compromise? Paul, Olga, the Kents and the Yorks cancelled all their engagements and No. 3 Belgrave Square became a place of frenzied telephone calls and interminable waiting.

Paul was in a strange position. Of the three royal brothers, David had been his friend first, when Paul had gone up to Oxford. Then he had got to know Bertie, largely through his marriage to Elizabeth Bowes-Lyon, and Bertie had been his own best man. Finally Georgie had become a close friend through his marriage to Marina. Paul must have known, better than almost anybody, what agonies each of the three brothers was going through. David determined to marry, sick of the advice and remonstrances of politicians; Bertie, dreading the position that he saw coming to him and for which he felt unsuited; and Georgie heartbroken to see the brother whom he adored giving up his country for a woman whose character and worth he could not judge.

On the days leading up to the abdication, Olga recorded the significant events in her diary:

Dec. 4th: Day of uncertainty. Georgie and Atinse [Marina] went to see Aunt May at 12—walked in the garden with her —very upset and angry with David. Meanwhile Mrs S. has gone secretly to Paris then Cannes—will he follow her? He sits alone, almost mad without her, to think it all out. So awful to see their names on posters in the street. . . . Tea at home. The Yorks came for a wander, he mute and broken. . . . Bertie rang up to ask Pacey to go round and see them—he stayed nearly 2 hours—he put off leaving till Tuesday.

Dec. 5th: Nothing decided. Many don't want an abdication yet. Others feel, like the family, that he had better go as he can't be trusted to play the game. The Dominions won't hear of the marriage. Georgie rang David up last night—said he would love to help him and see him. David said perhaps today but didn't let him come. . . . Aunt May, Mary and the Athlones came to tea. Former very upset, tried to appeal to him in vain.

Dec. 6th: Nothing new. The Cabinet met twice today and Baldwin has been back and forth to the Fort. David has let nothing out of his intentions. We four drove to Royal Lodge to tea with the Yorks, found Harry and Alice* there also. Bertie in an awful state of worry as David won't see him or telephone.

Dec. 7th: Same suspense. Two parties are beginning to form —for and against abdication. We hear that she says she will give him up—no doubt to get him back after. Georgie tried to see him in vain. May tomorrow. Bertie was there tonight.

Dec. 8th: Still nothing decided. Hopes a bit risen because she announced today that she is willing to give him up for the country's good but he must decide. Georgie went to the Fort at 11 and stayed there all day. . . . He is sleeping at the Fort. Has been with David for hours on end. He is calm and quite decided to go. What a calamity and what an inheritance for Bertie! How can he let down the Empire like this and not mind? . . . Saw Pacey off at 2—very heavy hearted to leave now.

Paul was on his way back to Belgrade when the abdication was finally announced on 10th December. Olga stayed in London for a few days and then joined him.

The Duke of Kent, who had seen the final dénouement from close quarters, immediately wrote to Paul: 'Just one line to say

* The Duke and Duchess of Gloucester.

how sorry I was not to see you again before you left. It was lovely having you and I miss you now . . . and wish you could have stayed longer. I'm afraid it wasn't a very happy visit with all that was going on here. I was glad I was able to be with David a little and try to be a little help but there was nothing to be done and he had made up his mind. He was very calm about it all—except about her. But he never broke down and wouldn't think either of the future or of what he was giving up—only of her. One can only pray for his future happiness which one doubts of. It's all been horrible and I'm so miserable about it all. I feel rotten, cold and nervy and altogether bloody. I wish Olga wasn't going as she's been an enormous help to Marina, but luckily Lilia is coming to stop for a little. Mummie hasn't yet made up her mind as to what she's going to do. They are extraordinary people and never bother about anyone except themselves!'[32]

The Duke of York was hailed as George VI and the public soon forgot about the abdication. But for those who had been closely involved the wounds took a long time healing. People who had been intimate with Wallis Simpson became social outcasts; and King Edward VIII's courtiers did not become King George VI's. Queen Mary especially was involved in the purge. To Paul she wrote a long and uncompromising letter full of bitterness about Wallis Simpson and the harm which she had done her son. In it she begged Paul and Olga never to see or speak to Lady Cunard again, for she felt that Emerald, along with the others who had made a fuss of Mrs Simpson, was in large measure to blame for what had come to pass.

Meanwhile, the subject of this letter, Emerald Cunard, was so worried about her social position that on the eve of the abdication she approached Maggie Greville and said, 'Maggie darling, do tell me about this Mrs Simpson—I have only just met her.'[33] Others were also quick to betray Wallis Simpson. They became known as the 'Rats' and Osbert Sitwell wrote a poem about them entitled 'Rat Week', a copy of which was sent to Paul by Chips.

After the abdication Paul heard little more from David. The Duke of Windsor, as he had by then become, wrote once, a sad letter from Austria, thanking Paul for his Christmas card. 'I do thank you and Olga very much for thinking of me; I had no card this year as I left England in such a hurry and anyway did not somehow catch the spirit of Christmas, alone and isolated here.'[34]

From Godfrey Thomas, who had been King Edward's private secretary, Paul received a letter some time later which reveals at least a little of the misery the King's abdication caused to those in his immediate circle:

It was nice of Your Royal Highness to write to me as you did. I knew that you would understand what we were all going through last December, and I think I can claim to have felt it as much as anyone, having been with him for so long.

It was heartbreaking to see 17 years' work, helping him to keep his flag flying, crumbling into dust—the humiliating way it did—but there was *nothing* to be done: he wouldn't listen; wouldn't let anyone help him in his sorry affair. One merely sat there, helplessly, watching him insisting on playing a lone hand, and playing his cards so badly into the bargain.

But it was the greatest of tragedies. He had so many good qualities tucked away in that strange and complicated make-up of his, that it only needed the fraction of a turn to make him into a first class king in the modern sense.

But we couldn't find the key, and even if we had, I doubt whether he would have let us use it.

I wouldn't mind so much could I convince myself that the step which he has seen fit to take were likely to lead to his real and eventual happiness. But I view the future with considerable misgiving.

I found H.R.H., in Austria, in the best of health. He was perfectly charming, considerate and easy to deal with—right back to his old form of 10 to 15 years ago. To me there was something pathetic about it. This frame of mind was, I think, *partly* due to a feeling of temporary relief at having cast off a burden, but to a great extent I should say that his spirits were rising in proportion as the day approaches when he can see the lady again. He at any rate seems to have no regrets for the past and he certainly has no qualms about the future. He is certain, in his mind, that he is booked, from now on, for a life of perpetual married bliss.

138

Long may it last, is all one can hope for him.

I am one of those who, making *all* allowances for the difficult position in which she was placed, could gladly throttle the lady for the wreckage of which she has been the cause. But countless people will be ready to lynch her if she doesn't make him happy now. I think she *can* do it, if she plays the game. It's up to her now, and as you rightly say, the chance of happiness is the only thing he has got left.[35]

CHAPTER VIII

1937–1938

Regency II

When Paul returned from England in December 1936 he found that the first moves towards an official agreement with Italy had already been made. Count Ciano had approached Mr Dučić, the Yugoslav Minister in Rome, to suggest a meeting with Stojadinović. The latter had lost no time in drafting a reply, 'couched' as he related to Paul 'in a great many nice words'.[1]

The Italians accepted the suggestion that representatives from each country should conduct the preliminary negotiations and Paul and Stojadinović selected Dr Ivan Subbotić for this purpose: he was an experienced diplomat and had been Yugoslavia's representative at the League of Nations and later Minister to the Court of St James. Subbotić's negotiations began formally in February but such was the suspicion in Yugoslavia that he was obliged to visit Italy twice before they started: once in December 1936 to check that an agreement really might be possible, and once in January 1937 ostensibly for a ski-ing holiday.

When Subbotić finally arrived in Rome at the end of February he carried with him the following brief from his Prime Minister: 'no concessions should be made simultaneously on all points of disagreement. Yielding should be linked with concessions made by the Italians on other points . . . there are four fundamental questions so far as you are concerned, the pact, Albania, the terrorists and the minorities.'[2] Subbotić kept to these instructions, and, using a subtle mixture of firmness and flattery, negotiated an agreement which undoubtedly favoured Yugoslavia.

Most important of all, Subbotić avoided a purely bilateral treaty by forcing the Italians to recognize all Yugoslavia's existing alliances. On the subject of terrorists he exacted both a formal statement, that terrorists working against Yugoslavia would no longer be tolerated in Italy, and a secret agreement covering more specific matters such as co-operation between the two police forces and the internment of Pavelić and other Ustaše ringleaders. For the Yugoslav minorities Subbotić obtained further valuable concessions, and when it came to the economic pact the balance appeared to be so much in Yugoslavia's favour that even Stojadinović was surprised. Italy not only agreed to import more Yugoslav products, but also promised to treat Yugoslavia as a favoured nation in all commercial relations.

The only topic over which Ciano had stood firm was Albania. Subbotić had hoped to force on the Italians a declaration which would have checked or even reversed their growing influence in Albania, but he failed and was obliged to accept a declaration which virtually recognized Italy's position. For Yugoslavia, this was a relatively small price to pay.

On 25th March Ciano arrived in Belgrade and he and Stojadinović put their signatures to the political agreement. They also talked at length about world affairs and about their own personal positions. Of Stojadinović, Ciano noted: 'A fascist. If he is not one by virtue of an open declaration he is certainly one by virtue of his conception of authority, of the state and of life.'[3] Ciano was particularly impressed by the freedom which Prince Paul gave to his Prime Minister. In one sense he overestimated it. Stojadinović was not a modest man and he was inclined to exaggerate his own authority. Certainly all his policies were subject to Paul's approval, and his communications during March suggest that the Regent was playing an active part in directing Subbotić's negotiations.

But in another sense Ciano was right. Stojadinović was allowed to operate the political machine with surprising freedom of action. There was no effective parliamentary opposition to his party and, more important, there was nobody of sufficient calibre to fill his place. Paul had overall control, but he had no wish to be a dictator and thus had to go along, at least part of the way, with Stojadinović's policies. At the time of the Italo-Yugoslav pact, they were in agreement over most points, but later on Paul was to become increasingly unhappy about some of the ideas and personal ambitions of his Prime Minister.

Soon after the conclusion of the agreement Paul travelled to England for King George VI's Coronation. In Europe reactions to the pact had been mixed. The French press had launched a bitter campaign against Yugoslavia, but the English, whose government had signed a Gentleman's Agreement with Italy only two months before, were non-committal. From some quarters, Paul even received praise. Sir Nevile Henderson, who in 1935 had urged Paul to 'make a step forwards as regards Italy',[4] wrote to congratulate him:

At the risk of being regarded as presumptuous I feel I must write and tell you what real pleasure and satisfaction it gives me to see how successfully Y.R.H. is running the policy of Yugoslavia. As you may remember even before you took the leading part out there, I always told you that you were a marvellous diplomat. So naturally I pat myself on the back and say how clever I was to recognize at once, as I always did, your talents and abilities in that line. I admit that there is that much of self satisfaction about it, but that is only the superficial side of it. The feeling is much deeper than that as regards your personal self and the fortunes of Yugoslavia which (need I repeat it?) will always be a matter of intense interest to me. So it is an immense joy to me to watch Yugoslavia, under your guidance, going from strength to strength and playing with increasing assurance the vital part which she should in keeping the peace of Europe.

I got back from exile (Buenos Aires) some ten days ago and proceed to my new post (Berlin) on April 30. There is no job in the world today which I would rather have, difficult though it may be and strewn with pitfalls, for Europe generally and myself personally. Honestly I don't care much so far as the personal risk is concerned so long as, if I do fail and crash as I may well do, it is on a point of policy and not over some personal bêtise or stupidity. The latter would be humiliating and disagreeable but I am quite ready to fail if I am not allowed to follow the policy I want. That we shall see. Anyway the curtain rises for me on April 30th and what the play will be like remains in the lap of the Gods. I wish I could have stayed over the Coronation here and have had thus an opportunity to see and talk with you—But anyway

Berlin (my third B in succession) is not so far away as Buenos Aires.[5]

Paul was in England for about a fortnight and divided his time between old friends, court functions and official audiences. As was his custom when abroad, he kept a brief record in his diary:

Sun. 9th May: Arrive in London. Met by Georgie. Family dinner: Buckingham Palace.

Mon. 10th May: Lunch B.P. Banquet B.P. Blomberg* introduced to me. Tells me how pleased he is that our relations are good. Expresses his particular delight that we are friends with Boris 'er ist uns sehr nahe' [he is very close].

Tues. 11th May: Lunch: Oxford. Dinner: Gloucesters.

Wed. 12th May: Coronation of Bertie and Elizabeth.

Thurs. 13th May: Lunch: Georgie. Banquet B.P. Delbos† *gushing* and delighted that I accepted to go to Paris.

Friday 14th May: Lunch: B.P. Dinner: F.O. Court Ball. Delbos told Blum‡ whom he admires very much 'Quel dommage que vous soyez marxiste' 'Et il l'est!' Confident in France. Seems worried about Italy. 'En Russie il y a de grands changements. Stalin devient dictateur' (this said with satisfaction and approval). After my explaining our Italian pact and the unjustified attacks of the French press he said 'C'est une scène de jalousie à la femme qu'on aime' . . .

Sat. 15th May: Lunch: B.P. Go to Coppins.

Tues. 25th May: Leave London for Paris heavily guarded.[6]

The cause for the heavy guard with which Paul left London on 25th May 1937, was an urgent telegram from Sir Eric Phipps, the British Ambassador in Paris, which had arrived at the Foreign Office on 15th May: 'A member of my staff learns from an informant who has proved reliable in the past that at a

* German War Minister.
† French Embassy Official.
‡ Prime Minister of France.

meeting in Paris of Third International it was decided to initiate a new terrorist campaign scene of which would be Yugoslavia and first victim Prince Regent. Informant stated that he believed that advantage would be taken of Prince Regent's presence in Paris next week to attempt his life, and added that M. Daladier had been given extraordinary powers to deal with the situation.'[7]

The Foreign Office was not unduly alarmed by this rumour, and nor was Paul. As it turned out, his stay in Paris passed without incident. Paul's purpose, in going to France, was to dispel some of the anger and suspicion that had resulted from the Italo-Yugoslav pact. The French were reluctant to see their influence in Yugoslavia declining and could not readily accept the independent foreign policy that she was pursuing. Paul was reasonably successful in his mission. He talked with a number of ministers and met Léon Blum who in May of the preceding year had become Prime Minister. Paul, who had not trusted Laval, was favourably impressed with Blum: 'Blum came to tea with me at the Ritz. He's got a most agreeable voice. We discussed many subjects and he seemed struck that I took milk in my tea 'comme un anglais et pas à la façon des Russes'.[8] In making this remark, the Frenchman had been more tactful than he realized.

The summer of 1937 Paul spent at Brdo in Slovenia. As well as the usual contingent of family, the Channons, and later Bernard Berenson came to stay. Although Paul was inclined to flatter Berenson he was particularly pleased to see him this time for it was on Berenson's advice that he had just acquired a beautiful Mantegna.* Paul was thrilled with the painting and delighted to have a chance to show it off. It was a rare opportunity for him to enjoy the company of his much admired friend.

Chips' visit was, by contrast, an excuse for more light-hearted entertainment. Paul laid on an elaborate shoot of driven chamois as well as various outdoor expeditions and there was, as always, plenty of tennis. In the evenings Paul had time to talk, and with Chips he was able to let off steam: 'Paul is indignant and indeed apprehensive of what he calls our "footling" foreign policy which he thinks is far too weak, too

* Head of St Jerome.

pink and too pro-French and he is right. The English seem to want, at least to countenance, Communism everywhere except in England. Perhaps with his Slav perspective he sees things too dramatically, and yet he is usually right. He fears that England will go Socialist one day but there I think he is only half right, for it will never be more than half Socialist. In fact it is almost that already.'[9] Chips was in his element at Brdo. Royalty itself was a constant source of fascination to him and with Paul he felt almost part of the family. Yet he was not insensitive to the pressures and restrictions which lay behind the glamour and after only two days in the country he noted in his diary 'all is not well in Yugoslavia'.[10]

When Chips arrived at the end of August Paul was still recovering from the strain of a series of religious battles which, throughout the summer months, had been threatening to tear the country apart. In Yugoslavia there were three main religious groups: the Eastern Orthodox in Serbia and Macedonia, the Roman Catholics in Croatia and Slovenia and the Moslems in Bosnia and Hercegovina. Although the majority of the population was Orthodox the Roman Catholic minority was considerable, amounting to about six million people, and for some time the question of a Concordat with the Vatican had been at issue.

Paul supported the Concordat. He saw it as yet another step towards a true Yugoslav state, and he and Stojadinović endeavoured to get the measure through Parliament. However, the right wing, ultra-Serbian, elements in the government seized upon the Concordat as their chance to bring down Stojadinović. Jevtić made a mysterious trip to Paris, where he had always had a following, whilst General Živković stirred up trouble at home. The General and his followers were able to enlist the support of some powerful members of the Orthodox Church and as the summer heat increased so did political feelings in the country. Pamphlets claiming that Prince Paul stood to gain financially by the enactment of the Concordat were discovered on premises connected with the Orthodox Church. Then, on July 19th, members of the Orthodox Church defied government rulings and held a procession in Belgrade: rioting broke out and the Bishop of Shabatz was injured in the fray.

Paul, judging that crisis point had been reached, stopped his Prime Minister as he was about to defend the Concordat in the Skupština. Gradually the country quietened down as Paul did all he could to humour the ecclesiastical authorities. But the affair had brought home to him the frictions that still existed within his country. In a conversation with Terence Shone, First Secretary at the British Legation in Belgrade and also a friend, Paul spoke openly about his difficulties: 'He confessed that he had been scarcely less anxious than at the time of King Alexander's death and complained that his Prime Minister had been over-optimistic and shown a remarkable lack of foresight. He then went on to rail against Serbian politicians in general, maintaining that they were hidebound and tactless and that but for them he could have reached agreement long ago with Dr Maček on the Croat question. But, he asked, what should he do if he did dispense with Stojadinović? If he did charge someone else with the formation of a government, might it not be that some other clique or body of opinion would then demand another change? What would be the attitude of the Army in such chaotic conditions? And who, in any case, was there to take Stojadinović's place?'[11]

Paul resolved not to dismiss Stojadinović, but to let him conduct the foreign policy while he himself endeavoured to re-establish contact with the Croats. By late summer Paul had two channels of communication with Maček. The first of these was through an intermediary, Dr Šubašić, who reported either directly to Prince Paul or through Father Korošec. In this way Paul received assurances of Maček's continuing goodwill and personal devotion to himself.[12] The second was opened as a result of the efforts of Dr Cvetković. Cvetković was Minister of Social Policy and Public Health in Stojadinović's government and as such had become involved in internal politics. In addition he was a popular man with a great many friends, and he was aware that most people were sick of the feud between the Serbs and the Croats. In early August Cvetković informed Prince Paul that he had been to Zagreb and had had talks with men who were close to Maček. As they had appeared optimistic about a 'Sporazum'* he had engaged them to look into the matter further and to transmit messages to Maček. By November,

* General agreement or understanding.

Cvetković's negotiations had reached a point where Maček was requesting an audience with the Prince Regent.[13]

Meanwhile, Stojadinović had embarked on a tour of the European capitals. He visited London and Paris, but it was not until he reached Rome and later Berlin that he was received with undivided attention. In Rome Mussolini and Ciano pandered to his tastes and entertained him with the beauties of Rome society. In Berlin no effort was spared. He was met at the railway station by Goering, Neurath and five ministers of state and was taken to shoots and to banquets and to an impressive selection of industrial and military establishments. Stojadinović did not commit his country to any particular course of action during these visits, but he established close and amicable relations with both Mussolini and Hitler. His policy was the characteristically cynical one of saying to each exactly what he wished to hear. However, the visits had a considerable influence on the Serbian leader himself: he was greatly impressed by the Fascist system. He told Mussolini that he was going back to Belgrade to build up his party on the basis of a dictatorship[14] and he confided to Hitler that his aim was to win over the youth of his country, as Hitler had done in Germany.[15]

In the world beyond Yugoslavia the main focus of attention in 1937 was the Civil War in Spain. From the beginning, both Mussolini and Hitler had been sending aid to General Franco. Despite this obvious fascist involvement, Britain and France had persevered in a futile attempt to remain aloof. Although they were officially neutral, both were divided by the struggle and in France the rift was particularly acute. The majority of Frenchmen supported the communists, as they did not want a third fascist state on their borders. However, the left-wing government of Léon Blum was unpopular amongst certain groups and these saw support for General Franco's government as a means of hitting back against their own.

Paul received first-hand news of the struggle from the Infante Alfonso, who was based in England canvassing support for Franco. Alfonso and Franco had been cadets together in Toledo and had subsequently seen active service together in Morocco, but friendship was not the driving force behind Alfonso's efforts. Like Paul, he loathed and feared communism and having just returned from a trip to Spain in March, he wrote to give Paul a graphic account of the latest atrocities:

> The Military Governor of the province of Badajoz told me that in his province alone they have exact evidence of about 14,000 people murdered and about as many 'disappeared'. The latter may be either dead or alive in red territory, having been carried off by the Bolshies. Terrible atrocities have been committed on the usual Soviet lines. I need not tell you about them but I fear they are just as bad as in Russia.
> A great barter trade is being organized with countries of the anti-communist bloc. Chiefly Portugal, Germany and Italy. The whole war would have been over in 3 months if it had not been for France.
> Even as late as the 5th of March (the day before yesterday) supplies and men keep pouring across to Barcelona. The non-intervention regulations about volunteers have been circumvented now by the simple method of supplying Frenchmen, Russians and other foreigners with Spanish passports in France, and as only 'foreign' volunteers are banned the French authorities let these 'Spanish' refugees return home . . .[16]

In sending aid to Franco, Hitler was far less genuine in his desire to help than Mussolini. Hitler's aim was to prolong the war as it offered an obvious breathing space for Germany and a distraction to others. Spain was an ideal training ground for German airmen, a good place to test equipment and a valuable source of minerals. But over and above these practical considerations came the political rewards: the weakening of France and the strengthening of the bond with Italy. For Hitler, 1937 was the year of consolidation of the Rome-Berlin Axis. In January Goering visited Rome, in May Neurath, and in June von Blomberg. In September, Mussolini himself met Hitler at Berchtesgaden, but discussions did not go smoothly as Mussolini's attitude to Hitler wavered, from one moment to the next, between admiration and jealousy. In particular, Mussolini resented the German attitude that the Anschluss was inevitable. He was motivated by a sense of rivalry and by a basic fear that the Germans might not rest content with

Austria, but would drive on down to the Adriatic via Trieste. The Italians saw their pact with Yugoslavia as a barrier against precisely such an eventuality.

By the end of 1937, however, relations between the two dictators were good. This was important to Hitler for already, at a meeting in the Reichs Chancellery with five of his most senior men, he had disclosed his plans for Austria and Czechoslovakia.* On 11th March 1938 Hitler ordered the march into Austria, but before doing so he sent Philip of Hesse, as special envoy, to obtain Mussolini's agreement. At 10.25 p.m. Hitler received a telephone call from Philip of Hesse with the message he had been counting on, and at daybreak on the 12th March German troops crossed the frontier into Austria. As Hitler had planned, the occupation was an entirely peaceful one and when he entered Vienna on 14th March crowds were waiting in the streets to welcome him. It was not until later that the Austrians, and the rest of Europe, became aware of the brutality and persecution which the Nazi occupying force brought in its wake.

Neither France nor Britain reacted strongly to the Anschluss. British policy was fashioned by three people: Neville Chamberlain, Lord Halifax and Sir Nevile Henderson. Chamberlain had replaced Baldwin as Prime Minister in May 1937, and was determined to be a great peacemaker. His views were so at variance with those of Anthony Eden that the latter resigned from his post as Foreign Secretary in February 1938, to be replaced by Lord Halifax. Sir Nevile Henderson, the recently-appointed Ambassador at Berlin was an admirer of Chamberlain and a strong supporter of the policy which came to be labelled 'appeasement'. Writing to Paul in June 1937 he had made this clear: 'One thing I am convinced of. These people want to be friends with us and for the life of me I cannot see why we should not be friends.'[17]

On the night of 11th March 1938, Sir Nevile Henderson had been invited by Goering to a reception in the 'Haus der Flieger' followed by a performance of the State Opera Company. He attended the function in order to see the Field-Marshal. On his arrival he greeted Goering coldly, and immediately the

* According to the Hossbach Minutes this meeting took place on 5.11.37.

latter scribbled a note on the back of his opera programme. It read: 'As soon as the music is over I should like to talk to you and will explain everything to you.' The last five words were underlined three times. In the conversation which followed Goering gave his explanation and Sir Nevile delivered on behalf of his government a protest 'in the strongest terms'.[18] But neither government nor ambassador believed that this protest would have any effect. Only three days before Sir Nevile had posted a letter to Paul: 'Poor Austria: I was not surprised and had warned the F.O. a week or two before that I anticipated something even worse. How long Schuschnigg can hold the fort remains to be seen. The most I hope for, or have ever hoped for, is that Austria keeps her soi disant independence on the lines of a pre-war Bavaria. But if the bell rings at Berlin, Vienna will in future have to answer it. That, I fear, is inevitable. It is useless to bolster Schuschnigg up, if one is not prepared to fight to do so. Fair words at Vienna and protests at Berlin are quite useless without cannon and aeroplanes behind them.'[19] By this stage even Sir Nevile was beginning to see through his German friends.

In Yugoslavia the Anschluss came as no surprise. Paul had heard that it was imminent on March 10th, and on the 12th the rumour was confirmed. On receiving the news, the Yugoslav government took the only course open to them. They sent orders to their frontier guards to co-operate with the Germans along the Austrian border. They then sent a request to the German government for a guarantee of the Yugoslav frontier.* It was some time before reports of the expulsion of Jews began to filter through, but even then the events in Austria appeared no more savage than those which had been going on in Soviet Russia for a long time, and which had been largely ignored by the Western powers.

Well pleased with his success in Austria, Hitler next turned his attention towards Czechoslovakia. Although his ultimate goal was complete occupation, his excuse for interference was the German minority in the Sudetenland.

In April 1937 President Beneš of Czechoslovakia had visited Belgrade. In his memoirs Beneš subsequently claimed

* This was received three weeks later when the Anschluss had been successfully completed.

that this visit had been made because 'world peace was at stake' and because he believed that Prince Paul was about to join the Rome-Berlin axis.[20] A note of the conversation, which Paul took at the time, does not support this claim. It does, however, shed an interesting light on Beneš' assessment of Germany: 'He doesn't believe in the German danger, German strength or German designs on Tcheckoslovakia. Hitler doesn't really want the Sudeten Deutschen who were always the most radical element in the late Hapsburg monarchy. The internal conditions of Germany are terrible and there are several factions. Neurath is getting stronger daily. Hitler is 'une marionette' in the hands of the army who'll get rid of him as soon as they no longer need him.'[21]

Exactly one year later Hitler was pre-eminent in Germany. He had sacked Neurath and carried out a purge of the army, replacing the old generals with either puppets or members of the S.S. Furthermore, he had taken Austria and was thus able to exert pressure on Czechoslovakia from three sides. President Beneš was in an impossible position. Of Czechoslovakia's allies, France was unreliable and Russia was powerless to help so long as she was unable to send troops through Rumania or Poland. Rumania was anti-Russian and Hitler had spent the previous year working on Colonel Beck to ensure Polish neutrality in 1938. Nor was the combined effort of Britain and France much comfort. Chamberlain took Hitler at his word and restricted his discussions to the question of 'home rule' for the Sudeten Germans. He and Daladier, who had replaced Blum as Prime Minister of France, concentrated on trying to make the Czech government come to terms with the Sudeten Germans whilst Hitler, who was in complete control of the Sudeten Nazi party, remained quiet.

For the Yugoslavs, the situation in Czechoslovakia posed a greater threat than that in Austria, for Czechoslovakia was a member of the Little Entente. Although Yugoslavia was not bound to defend her if Germany alone invaded, she was certainly bound if Hungary, either alone or with Germany, attempted to regain territory lost after the First World War. Herein the danger was compounded. In 1919 Hungary had not only lost the whole of Slovakia to the new Czechoslovak state, but also considerable territory to the new Yugoslav state.

Encouraged now by success in Czechoslovakia she might well extend her claims southwards against Yugoslavia. Stojadinović spent the summer of 1938 trying to keep the peace between Hungary and Czechoslovakia. At the same time Hitler was urging the Hungarians to press their claims with greater force. But Hungary dithered, on the one hand anxious to benefit from the division of Czechoslovakia, on the other fearful of a war with the Little Entente.

By September 1938 the Hungarians had still not come to a decision and Stojadinović had agreed to the suggestion of his Minister of War that Yugoslavia should partially mobilize. By this time, also, Chamberlain had reached the final stages of his attempted peace negotiations, which culminated, on the 29th, in the Munich Conference. Here, Italy, Germany, Britain and France agreed on plans for the division of Czechoslovakia. One thing at least was clear: it was pointless for Yugoslavia to worry about her obligations to her ally. On 1st October Hitler marched into the Sudetenland backed by the Munich Agreement. Czechoslovakia lost her fortifications and 11,000 square miles of territory and President Beneš was forced into exile. In Britain, the reaction was twofold. For some, Chamberlain was a peacemaker and a hero, for others he was a blind and gullible fool.

For Paul and Olga's family, 1938 was a sad year. It brought three deaths: Prince Nicholas of Greece, Queen Marie of Rumania and Prince Arsène. Of these the one which brought the deepest sense of loss, for Paul as well as Olga, was that of Olga's father, Prince Nicholas.

The gentle and good-humoured Prince Nicholas, who from the start had got on well with Paul, had spent most of his last twelve summers at Bohinj and at Brdo. There he had fished and painted and whiled away long hours sitting with his son-in-law, telling amusing and scurrilous stories and providing the companionship for which Paul had felt so great a need.

In November 1936, Prince Nicholas and his wife had gone back to Athens after fourteen years in exile.* But they had barely settled in when Prince Nicholas was taken ill. Paul and Olga had found him drawn and aged when they went to Athens for the marriage of Prince Paul to Princess Frederika in early

* The Monarchy had been restored in Greece in November 1935.

January 1938, and after their return to Belgrade Olga had remained in constant touch with her unhappy mother. On 29th January she left again for Athens and was with her father when he died on 8th February.

For the next six months, Olga devoted almost all her time to looking after her mother. Of the three sisters she was the most readily available. Elizabeth found it difficult to leave home and Marina was becoming increasingly involved in British affairs and had countless royal engagements. Olga stayed with her mother in Athens for most of February and March, before bringing her to Belgrade where she remained till May. They both then left again for Paris to undertake the painful task of clearing the flat of all Prince Nicholas' possessions. It was a lonely time for Paul in Belgrade, especially in the winter months which he detested with such vehemence.

Soon after Olga and her mother had returned from Paris they received a wire from King Carol with the news of his mother's death. Paul had been particularly fond of 'aunt Missy'. A granddaughter of Queen Victoria, half English and half Russian, Queen Marie of Rumania had had some of the best characteristics of both races. She had been beautiful, energetic, eccentric and romantic. Her great interests had been writing books and collecting beautiful things. It was this which had brought her close to Paul, whom she remembered in her will:

For Paul of Serbia:

1. Two carved gilt vitrines with fine old fans.
2. Two old Battersea enamel candlesticks.
3. Italian painting in black frame on amethyst background. God looking down out of the clouds.

I leave him these souvenirs because we were always great friends and because he has an artistic feeling for lovely things.[22]

Two uninterrupted months at Brdo followed Queen Marie's funeral. Then Olga's mother heard that her eldest brother was ill in Paris and almost simultaneously Paul learnt that his father was dying. Paul felt little affection for Arsène, who had become a gambler and a drunkard in old age. Something, however, had to be done for him so Olga decided to accompany her mother back to Paris and look after both her uncle and her father-in-law. She found Arsène in a sorry state. Paul had arranged for a monthly allowance to be paid to him but the last few cheques were littered around the flat, uncashed, for the old man had been too weak to cope.

Unable to eat or speak, his life dragged on. Eventually, Olga was obliged to leave—to attend her uncle's funeral in Coburg. No sooner had she and her mother reached Germany than they received the news from Paul that the pathetic old man had died. His body was brought to Yugoslavia and the funeral was held at Topola on 23rd October.

Throughout these gloomy months attention also focused on the fifteen-year-old King. Peter was having a strange upbringing, being all at once everybody's and nobody's responsibility. After King Alexander's death he had remained at Dedinje with his mother and younger brothers. In 1937, Queen Marie had had to go to London for an operation and from then onwards she, and the two youngest boys, had spent a lot of time abroad. In a way this was fortunate for Paul, as there had always been a danger that the opposition parties might try to centre round her. But it also meant that Peter was left very much alone. Both of Paul's sons were at school in England: Nicky at preparatory school and Alexander at Eton. Though Alexander and Peter had not got on particularly well as children, by 1938 the differences had evened out a little and during the school holidays Alexander and Peter spent a considerable amount of time together.* But the holidays were relatively short and for most of the time the young King's main companion was Mr Parrott. Parrott did his best to amuse and interest the boy and tried to get him used to the company of children of his own age, but the restrictions were inhibiting.

Intellectually, King Peter was not bright. His early education had been neglected and the attempt to educate him privately was not proving satisfactory. In March 1938, Parrott was so

* This was a relief to Princess Olga, who had been watching her nephew's development with much concern: 'Peter came along to lunch: we found him much improved and more talkative and at his ease, poor child. I feel so sorry for him as his life is so unnatural.' Princess Olga's diaries, 10th March 1938.

worried that he wrote in the strongest terms to Paul, opening his letter with the following paragraph: 'Sir, Peter gives such evident signs of an improperly developed mentality that it is absolutely imperative to consider a radical change in the present system of education.' Parrott went on to enumerate the problems: King Peter could barely speak or write Serbian, his French and German grammar were almost non-existent; his knowledge of Latin was so superficial that it had no value as a training in logical thought. And so the list continued. Parrott put the blame in part on the timetable which, he said, included far too many unimportant subjects, but mainly on the Serbian teaching staff. 'These masters rush through the lengthy programme of the school curriculum like giants in seven league boots, sometimes taking two classes at once in their stride, without heeding Peter's mental development which is left shambling far behind. Speed and achievement, reckoned by the number of classes nominally passed, is the only important factor in this breathless chase. Peter is a slow worker—he thinks slowly, talks slowly and writes slowly. . . . The only possible way that they can even make a show of covering the ground is by allowing Peter to be an utterly passive factor in the system. The master speaks for Peter, the master writes for Peter, the master even thinks for Peter.'[23] Mr Parrott advocated a number of reforms, most of which Paul implemented. However, the one really important one, a change of professor for Serbian, was left out.

King Peter was fourteen and a half years old at the time of this report. He had three and a half years to go before he reached majority and became King. It must have been disheartening for Paul to think that the kingdom for which he was working so hard was to fall so soon into such unprepared hands. But in part Paul was himself to blame. Although he and Olga had Peter and Mr Parrott to lunch at Beli Dvor, he did little to encourage his nephew to overcome his shyness and he made no attempt to teach him about politics. Some of Paul's behaviour was probably intentional, some was not. It would have been unwise to involve the boy in the political world when he was still too young to understand it fully, as he might well have come under the influence of intriguing and unscrupulous politicians. On the other hand, it would have been of enormous

155

benefit if Paul had been able, or known how, to give Peter more confidence. It is quite possible that Paul simply didn't know how to set about it. For much of his own childhood he had himself been completely neglected, and it was not until he reached Oxford that he had begun to feel some sense of his own worth. With Alexander and Nicholas he had had no problem as they were both straightforward, easy-going children. Peter was diffident and complicated and Paul probably found it easier to dismiss this extra worry from his mind, rather than to try to find an answer to it.

By the start of 1938, Paul had been Regent for more than three full years. He was more relaxed about his duties and in the first months of the year even found the time to organize two concerts and an exhibition of Italian art. The latter, for which he had had the paintings shipped over from Italy, attracted 82,000 visitors in a period of six weeks. For a city with a population of only 241,000 this was a considerable figure, and Paul, as a letter to Berenson indicates, was justifiably proud: 'The weather has been foul; two days ago we were under snow and I have not seen the sun for weeks. The exhibition is a bright spot though. Till tonight, 37,836 people saw it and left 639,000 dinars. I had also the satisfaction to have organized two concerts . . . with 5,000 seats and . . . 200 musicians. It is pleasant to see how the public responded. One feels that they were craving for something to be given them outside the political circus.'[24]

Although the summer was disrupted by Olga's travels, it was on the whole an enjoyable one for Paul. The family, Chips Channon and other friends visited Brdo—which was becoming an idyllic place—and Paul, who was feeling well and active for the first time in three years, played tennis with Olga and, during the school summer holidays, squash with Alexander. Most surprising of all, Paul took to swimming in the river with Georgie Kent. Ever since his half demented cousin, George, had tried to drown him in Lake Geneva, Paul had avoided swimming at all costs.

It was as Paul gained greater confidence and stature as Regent that his sense of isolation and imprisonment began to fade. Where before an excursion over the border had been a major operation, involving early morning starts and dodging of detectives, Paul now made frequent trips abroad. Sometimes it was to shop in Munich with Georgie, sometimes it was to spend a few days shooting with King Carol in Rumania. On one occasion he drove with Olga into Italy to see their old friend the Duke of Aosta, who had just been appointed Governor of Abyssinia. On another, they and all the children, drove to the Toerrings' country house in Bavaria, where Georgie and Marina were also staying for a wine festival.

But whereas these were short distractions, Paul's main holiday was always spent with Olga in London and in 1938 they had been invited to stay at Buckingham Palace. In comparison with some of their former visits this one was relatively quiet. In part this was because of the children, who were no longer all confined to the nursery. At Buckingham Palace the two princesses, Elizabeth who was twelve and Margaret who was eight, were frequently allowed to lunch with the adults. In addition, both Nicky and Alexander had to be visited and taken out from school. Nicky was, as always, doing well but Alexander was posing something of a problem. He had already experienced his first beating and the master's report was not encouraging: 'he is far from stupid but makes no effort!' Paul, who had himself been naturally diligent at school, found the exuberance and lack of application of his firstborn difficult to accept.

Despite the children Paul and Olga had plenty of time to see their friends. The King and Queen gave a huge party for them and Paul made his customary pilgrimage to the National Gallery where he amazed his wife with his encyclopaedic knowledge of its contents. Of his official talks by far the most important was that with Chamberlain. The Prime Minister was not optimistic about affairs in Europe and after discussing a number of hopeless alternatives, confessed to Paul that his only hope was that 'something might happen in Germany (?!)'[25] The punctuation was Paul's addition. He could not share Chamberlain's faith that everything would come right in the end, nor could he understand what the Prime Minister thought might happen.

During his time in London Paul took the opportunity to plead once more for British aid. In October Dr Funk, the new German minister of economic affairs, had visited Yugoslavia and had proposed a contract by which Germany guaranteed to take 50 per cent of all Yugoslav exports, and to give technical expertise for her mining operations and money for her export of ores. In return, the Yugoslavs only had to buy more German products. The Yugoslav government refused. They were unwilling to let the Germans invade their economy more than they had done already. But their refusal was only a delaying tactic, for unless they could find markets elsewhere, they would eventually be forced to give in to the German offer. Paul begged the British to increase their trade with Yugoslavia. Sir Ronald Campbell backed up his plea with a memorandum to the Foreign Office explaining the Yugoslav predicament, and outlining the ways in which the British government could help: by increasing Anglo-Yugoslav trade, by encouraging British investment in Yugoslavia, and by supplying aircraft.[26] The Foreign Office response was sympathetic but not particularly helpful. The Air Ministry could provide some of the aircraft Yugoslavia needed but 'was not in a position to make rash promises'. As for trade, there were problems. To compete with the German system of bulk purchasing British firms would have to be given government subsidies and this was contrary to the British principle of free trade. It was, furthermore, a plan which Chamberlain considered unnecessary. He did not understand the relationship between economics and politics and when he spoke in the House of Commons on the subject of Dr Funk's tour of the Balkans he denied that it had had any political significance.[27]

All too soon, on 6th December, Paul had to leave London. As always he had enjoyed every moment of his visit. It had been a change staying at Buckingham Palace, and he had been touched by the affection of his hosts and especially by the effort the King had made to inquire into and understand the political situation abroad. He left alone, this time amidst rumours of terrorists arriving from the U.S.A. Olga moved to No. 3 Belgrave Square where she stayed on with the Kents for another fortnight.

When Olga finally returned home on 24th December, she found her husband low and depressed, in the middle of a ministerial crisis. His problem was, quite simply, his Prime Minister.

Paul had long given up hope that Stojadinović would make any real effort to solve the Croat problem. But in 1937 he had taken this task out of the Prime Minister's hands, and for the past year he and Cvetković had been running the negotiations. These were going remarkably well. Both Paul and Cvetković had been meeting Maček, and at last it seemed that an agreement might be within sight.

Paul had other reasons for mistrusting Stojadinović. He had great respect for Stojadinović's brain and ability but he knew that there was a bad side too. Stojadinović was unscrupulous and it was natural for him to gravitate towards the most powerful side. What really worried Paul were the reports that he had begun to receive of Stojadinović's personal ambitions and fascist leanings. These first reached him in November via the Chief of Police, Milan Acimović. It appeared that Stojadinović had been reorganizing his party, the J.R.Z., along the usual fascist lines: they were parading in green shirts, using the fascist salute and referring to Stojadinović as 'vodja' or 'leader'.[28] In fact Stojadinović was by this time so sure of his own power that he failed to notice a slight change in emphasis on the word 'vodja'. Many of those who turned out in the streets to hail him were not shouting 'vodja' at all but 'djavol' or 'devil'.

Stojadinović's reputation for being pro-German was making him unpopular in Serbia and this was beginning to rub off on Paul. Paul determined, therefore, to take action and instructed Acimović to conduct a discreet investigation. The choice of Acimović for this task was unwise. Admittedly he was Chief of Police but he was also either in league with Stojadinović or highly susceptible to bribery. Thus, when Paul came back from his holiday in England, he found waiting for him a report which was far from satisfactory. Instead of carrying out his inquiries in secret, Acimović had approached Stojadinović directly and had returned with a series of feeble and unconvincing explanations. The word vodja, for instance, simply referred to Stojadinović's position in the party, and the J.R.Z. salute was quite different from the Roman salute, especially when seen 'from the time of raising the arm until the time of lowering it'.[29]

Paul was certainly not fooled, but he could not peremptorily dismiss his Prime Minister on the grounds of mere suspicion of disloyalty. Stojadinović held office by constitutional right and could only be removed by constitutional means. Furthermore, elections were due in mid-December anyway and the country was in its usual state of pre-electoral excitement: an attempt to get rid of the Prime Minister would only have added to the turmoil.

It was the aftermath of this election which brought about the depression in which Olga found her husband on 24th December.

The system of voting was by lists. The government list included the J.R.Z., Father Korošeć's Slovene Populist Party and Mehmed Spaho's Yugoslav Moslem Organization. The United Opposition list, led by Dr Maček, was made up of the Croat Peasant Party with various dissident Serb elements that had been excluded from the government. To Stojadinović's surprise and fury the United Opposition took a large number of votes from the government and obtained 41 per cent of the total. Stojadinović had considered his popularity to be at a peak, and unwilling to believe that it was not, set out to find a scapegoat. His baleful eye settled on the ageing Father Korošeć. He had already complained to the Prince Regent about the Minister of the Interior's liberal views. Now he blamed him for the loss of votes. He had become so sure of himself that in an explanatory letter to Prince Paul, he numbered, amongst his accusations, the fact that Father Korošeć had had the temerity to permit government employees to vote precisely as they wished.[30]

On 22nd December Father Korošeć resigned and his place was filled by the Chief of Police, Acimović. But for Stojadinović, things were not going as well as he thought. Ultimately, his fate was in the hands of the Prince Regent and at that moment three factors were uppermost in the Prince Regent's mind. First, the Prime Minister's megalomania, secondly, the fact that Maček, disappointed by the election results, was keener than ever to work on an agreement, and thirdly the treatment of Father Korošeć. The old Slovene had been in disgrace at the end of King Alexander's reign because of his opposition to the dictatorship, but besides this he had been faithful to the crown and, since its creation, to the Yugoslav state. He had known Prince Paul for a long time and had frequently acted as his confidant and adviser. When he handed in his resignation on

10. At a public display. The young King Peter to the fore, the Prince Regent Paul standing behind, c.1935.

11. Princess Olga.

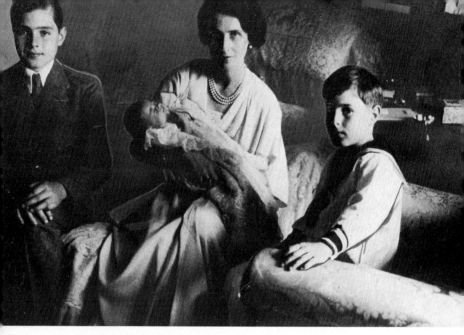

12. Princess Olga with her three children, Alexander, Elizabeth and Nicholas in 1936.

13. Prince Paul's Belgrade Palace, Beli Dvor.

22nd December, supposedly on the grounds of advancing years and declining health, he told Prince Paul the real reason. All things considered Paul had too much against Stojadinović to leave him, for much longer, in a position of power.

CHAPTER IX

1939

Regency III
The Sporazum and World War II

For Paul 1939 began with the realization that Milan Stojad-inović would have to go. By mid-January, Stojadinović was himself aware that he could neither afford to lose the support of the Slovene Populist Party nor have Father Korošeć working against his coalition. He therefore decided to offer Korošeć the post of President of Senate. This, he reasoned, would keep the Slovene in the Government, but in a neutral position from which he would be unable to interfere with the growth of the J.R.Z. Father Korošeć, urged by Paul, accepted the post. It had one advantage, the full importance of which Stojadinović had failed to take into account: at times of ministerial crisis the President of the Senate was traditionally called upon to advise the crown. Unwittingly, Stojadinović had engineered the means of his own removal.

Although Paul had ample evidence of his Prime Minister's malpractices he had to tread warily, for Stojadinović still had a considerable following amongst the Serbs and the Serb politicians. But at the end of January an event occurred which finally prompted Paul to take decisive action. Ciano had arrived for talks with Stojadinović, with whom he was on extremely friendly terms. Ciano's main concern was to secure the Yugo-slav's approval of the Italian plans for an occupation of Albania. The topic was not a new one as it had been under discussion, at intervals, since the previous May. The Italians wanted an assurance that the Yugoslavs would not hinder their proposed invasion whilst the Yugoslavs required a guarantee of their own frontier. In the event, the conversation between Ciano and Stojadinović went considerably beyond these policy objectives and ended in a somewhat hazy agreement that Albania should be partitioned between Yugoslavia and Italy. Stojadinović failed to mention this in his report to the Prince Regent and when Count Ciano, unaware that Stojadinović had not passed on this part of their conversation, made several allusions to the possibility of territorial changes in Albania, Paul was outraged. Not only had his Prime Minister gone behind his back, and that of the other regents and the government; he had attempted to strike a private deal which would have placed Yugoslavia in the category of unprovoked aggressor. The plan for Stojadinović's dismissal was set in motion on 3rd February. It was an almost identical repetition of the scheme by which, in 1935, Stojadinović had himself come to power. It began with a violently anti-Croat speech in Parliament which Stojadinović failed to answer. The same evening Father Korošeć, acting on Paul's instructions, called a private meeting of five government ministers. After the meeting, the five ministers handed in their resignations to the Prime Minister on the grounds of the government's attitude to the Croat question. Under normal circumstances the Prime Minister would have been allowed to choose replacements and to take them to Prince Paul for approval. But this time the Prince Regent refused to let Stojadinović form a new cabinet and on 4th February he had no alternative but to resign.

To those outside Paul's immediate circle the fall of Stojadinović came as a complete surprise. Only five days previously he had been telling party members of his plans for the next four years, and Ciano is recorded as having described Stojadinović as 'miles ahead' of other Yugoslav politicians. But if his removal was a shock for the Yugoslavs it was a disaster for the Italians and the Germans, both of whom had spent a great deal of time, and effort, in establishing good relations with the powerful and versatile Serb.

Paul immediately appointed Cvetković as the new Prime Minister and Cincar-Marković as Foreign Minister. The latter had been ambassador in Berlin and was probably chosen in an attempt to mollify the Germans. Cvetković, on the other hand, was chosen for a very specific reason. Of all his ministers, Paul considered Cvetković the one most likely to be able to settle the Croat question.

More than ever before it was imperative that a settlement should be reached. Paul was worried that Hitler might make use of Croat separatism, as he had made use, elsewhere, of the Sudeten German minority and the Slovak separatists. Unlike the Serbs, the Croats had no reason to dislike the Germans and as their impatience with the centralist government in Belgrade increased so did the probability that they might look to Germany for help. Throughout the winter months warnings that this might be the case had been filtering through to Belgrade.

In February Maček was still optimistic about an agreement. The day before the fall of the Stojadinović government he had sent word to Cvetković approving the formation of a joint Serb-Croat committee to work on the agreement and again reaffirming his loyalty, above all, to Prince Paul, 'of whom', the intermediary had reported, 'he speaks only in the highest terms, and in whom he has a great deal of faith'.[1]

As soon as Cvetković had organized his cabinet he informed parliament that the Croat problem was to have priority, and detailed negotiations on the nature of the agreement began. But all did not go smoothly. The legal basis of the constitution was a complex matter and, in addition, Maček and Cvetković had to face objections from other interested parties. On one occasion, the Serbian members of the United Opposition refused to approve a draft and on another Paul stood firm. Each time proceedings reached a stalemate the danger of outside interference grew. At one point in mid-March Maček's closest collaborator, Košutić, travelled to Prague for 'personal reasons'. It was widely rumoured that he had gone to find out the steps by which Croatia could become a German protectorate. Maček himself was not above suspicion. His aim was to achieve autonomy for Croatia at all costs, preferably within the Yugoslav State but, if this turned out to be impossible, outside it. On the occasions when negotiations broke down he was quick to pick up the threads of the Croats' longstanding flirtation with the Italians.

The sheer uncertainty of these long negotiations had a

depressing effect on Paul. And they were not his only worry, for though he had breathed a sigh of relief immediately after dismissing Stojadinović, he had then had to face the task of working with a new and less experienced team. Stojadinović had been an extremely competent Foreign Minister, and in character had been a perfect match for Paul. His unbounded optimism had balanced Paul's instinctive pessimism and his common sense had been a comfort in times of stress. In the first few months after his departure, therefore, Paul felt very much alone at the helm.

It was at this sensitive moment that Cecil Parrott handed in his resignation. In his letter, dated 18th February, he accused Paul of neglecting the young king:

> I have for a long time urged Your Highness to make radical changes in Peter's way of life. . . .
> Peter is being neglected. Taken as a whole, I feel Your Highness's attitude to the vital problem of his development and preparation is unaccountable. I have tried to find justification for it, but in vain. I believe that the continuance of this attitude will have disastrous results, which are bound to affect the country's future.
> If Your Highness will permit me to speak frankly; you do nothing to give Peter any adequate sense of his own position. Rather, in the fear that some autocratic ideas might manifest themselves, your attitude and actions tend to strengthen his inferiority complex. Secondly, you have postponed the solution of the question of his preparation for future duties, when it is clear that his present isolated life, remote from almost every contact, is utterly unfavourable to the development of any human being, let alone a future ruler. Thirdly, you have failed to appreciate the urgency of his education and are content to let the vital problems arising from it remain too long unsolved . . .[2]

Paul took this letter deeply to heart. When it was followed two days later by an amplification of the points mentioned above, he was not in a mood to accept further criticism. A stormy interview took place and for the next two weeks Olga found herself acting, in an unpleasant atmosphere, as intermediary. Although loyal to her husband, she was able to see that there were faults on both sides. Parrott had been outspoken but there was some truth in what he had said. Paul saw more of Peter, certainly, than most uncles see of their nephews and he probably paid more attention to the child than did Queen Marie. But he had not yet learned to treat him as an adult. Peter was neither expected nor encouraged to have views on politics or on any serious subject, and although he was often at Beli Dvor for meals with the family, he was not around when Paul and Olga entertained. Invariably he was accompanied by his tutor.

At the beginning of March Mr Parrott, who had been grievously upset by Paul's reaction to his letter, pleaded by letter for forgiveness. 'Before I wrote to Your Highness I felt a coward, because I was hiding something from you. After I wrote it, I felt I was a cad because I had wounded a friend. I had no peace of mind before. I have no peace of mind now.'[3]

Paul immediately responded to this gesture. But, although the clouds lifted, Parrott was determined to leave, and, after having put his points so bluntly, there was little chance that he would be persuaded to stay. This left Paul undecided as to what to do with Peter, who was bitterly upset at the prospect of his only companion leaving.

In the long run, Parrott's action was probably beneficial for King Peter as it forced his uncle to see him more as an individual and less as a charge. But for Paul it could scarcely have come at a worse time. At home Stojadinović was doing his level best to stir up trouble in Belgrade, whilst abroad Hitler looked stronger than ever.

Hitler's plan, in the summer of 1939, was not to destroy Poland for he looked to Polish support in the future against Russia. Rather, he wanted Poland peacefully to restore the territory she had been ceded by the Versailles settlement—especially the Danzig corridor. Since November 1938 he had been negotiating with Colonel Beck but, to his annoyance, the latter had refused to give up Danzig. Even after the occupation of Prague the Poles continued to stand their ground, and Hitler started to contemplate the use of force. It was at the end of March, when the British Prime Minister declared that Britain would support the Poles, that Hitler gave secret orders for war with Poland on 1st September. Meanwhile he directed his anger against Britain and accused her of wanting war.

In Britain Neville Chamberlain had at last begun to realize that agreements with the Führer were of little worth. Public opinion, too, had changed. Before, Hitler had been able to justify his actions on the grounds that he was reclaiming German territory. After taking Prague he could no longer do this: he had seized land which belonged to the Czechs and not Germany and in the eyes of the world he had finally shown his hand. Yet neither Britain nor France had put up any resistance to the occupation of Czechoslovakia and the resulting outcry in Britain and in the House of Commons had been so great that Neville Chamberlain had been forced to adopt a more resolute policy. When Hitler began to bully Poland, Chamberlain gave the Poles a firm commitment and the French followed his lead.

Mussolini remained an uncertain factor. He had been proud of his rôle as mediator at Munich and he resented Hitler's subsequent move into Czechoslovakia. He was particularly hurt that Hitler had failed to inform him in advance and he was worried about the Balkans, which he considered to be part of his own sphere of influence. However, he was also aware that Hitler held the balance of power and that he would have to work with him if he was to remain on the winning side. At the end of March when a personal letter from Hitler had helped to soothe his feelings, he began to prepare for a move which was designed both to increase his own prestige and to prove acceptable to Germany. On 7th April, he put into operation a plan that he had been contemplating for the best part of two years: Italy's invasion of Albania.

Although intended as an assertion of independence this action, ironically, increased the gulf between Italy and the Western powers and brought her closer to Germany. Hitler congratulated Mussolini on his campaign and seized the opportunity to press upon him a military alliance. On 21st May Italy signed the Pact of Steel with Germany. But, as he inked out his signature, Mussolini knew nothing of his ally's plan for war with Poland. Italy was not prepared for war. She had suffered considerable losses in the Spanish Civil War, which had only recently come to an end, and she needed time to recuperate. Furthermore, Mussolini was frightened by the prospect of a

167

full-scale war with France and Britain, though he was consoled, at least for the time being, by Ribbentrop's repeated reassurances that Germany was only trying to secure her 'Danzig Corridor'.

The invasion of Albania did not, of course, involve a full-scale war. Nevertheless, after the fall of Stojadinović, the Italians had felt obliged to reassess their plans. They had concluded that if the Stojadinović agreement still held with the new government, they would consider partitioning the country as discussed. If it did not they would proceed to occupy the country anyway and, if necessary, use force against Yugoslavia. To this end, they requested the Hungarians to place six of their divisions on the Yugoslav border in case they should be needed to bring pressure on Belgrade. For Paul this was the final straw. Italian occupation of Albania meant that Yugoslavia would have to share two borders with Italy. It meant also that the Italians would henceforth be able to create trouble in southern Yugoslavia by working on Albania's irredentist claims. Paul knew that, alone, his protest would carry no weight with the Duce. All that Yugoslavia could do was ask for frontier guarantees and trust that the Italians would keep their word. On Good Friday 1939, as Pope Pius XII was preparing his Easter message to the world, the Italians landed in Albania.

Paul and all his family were at Beli Dvor for Easter and the news reached them bit by bit. First they heard of the successful landings; then that the young Queen, who three days earlier had given birth to a baby boy, had appealed to Greece to send a boat for her escape. Then that Corfu, too, was threatened. The news was unreliable and much of it conflicting. On 11th April Paul decided to send his children back to England. That night, feeling isolated, helpless and frustrated, he broke down and wept.

Behind the bitter tears of the Prince Regent, brought on by Mussolini's swaggering into Albania, lay the years of struggling to preserve his country's unity and independence, and the realization of the horrors which the next few months looked certain to bring to Europe, to his country and to his family. Paul looked back on his years as Regent: on the obstinacy and corruption of the politicians; on the intransigence of the army chiefs and the deviousness of the Church leaders; on the lack of interest or assistance from his fellow regents; on the persistent intrigues and hurtful rumours; and on his own, inevitable, separation from his dearest friends. All this for a people who gave him little thanks and for a nephew who he was now accused of having neglected. Nor was it a case of mere self-pity. In his personality report on the Prince Regent that year Sir Ronald Campbell had written: 'There are those who have already been spreading the story that Prince Paul is seeking to supplant the young King. Anything more ridiculous is difficult to imagine, since, in fact, he is counting the days till he can go and settle in England on the expiry of his stewardship. Nor is this surprising, as there is nothing to endear him to his present life; his days are spent in granting audiences—most of them tedious, and many of them disagreeable—while his only relaxation is a short walk in the afternoon, with Princess Olga, on the same stretch of road, surrounded by a small army of plain clothes detectives.'[4]

Paul was indeed planning with eager anticipation to settle in England once he had established Peter firmly on the throne. He was more than ever convinced that his only spiritual home was London. Most of his friends were there and he had the greatest respect for British values and the British way of life. In fact Paul's trust of British representatives abroad was so profound that it was invariably taken for granted in official circles, and occasionally even taken advantage of by individuals—only slightly perhaps, and all in the line of duty, but nevertheless enough to colour Foreign Office files. Such was the case with Terence Shone. Shone had arrived in Belgrade in 1937 as First Secretary at the British Legation. Before leaving England he had been advised by Sir Robert Vansittart to 'cultivate Prince Paul'. This he had immediately set about doing, although the relationship was by no means an entirely false one. For instance, after a private conversation with Prince Paul in which the internal affairs of Yugoslavia had been discussed, he wrote: 'His Royal Highness's observations were so often prefaced by some such remark as "I suppose I ought not to say this, but I know I can say it to you" . . . I really believe he thinks that confidences which he gives to us here are passed on directly to the Secretary of State or Van* and are seen

* Sir Robert Vansittart, then head of the Foreign Office.

by very few people besides. If he knew that his remarks to me about, e.g., the Serb politicians or his own Prime Minister might be read by quite a large number of people, I think he would be rather put out!'[5]

It was naïve and indiscreet on Paul's part, but it was also symptomatic of his attitude to the British. Had he been the King, the reward for his efforts would have been the loyalty and love of his subjects. But Paul was not a ruler; he was a guardian. And as such he did not feel the same affection for his subjects, nor they for him. Besides, he considered himself a stranger in Yugoslavia and at home only in Britain. It is scarcely surprising then that he looked upon the British government and its representatives abroad as a force for good, or that he used his friends in the Legation to convey information which it would have been unwise for him more openly to divulge.

Normally, the information consisted of views expressed to him, or impressions he had formed—sometimes judged to be useful, sometimes not. On one occasion it was more concrete. In January 1939 Dr Stojadinović, then still Prime Minister, had shown Paul photographs of two of Sir Ronald Campbell's reports to the Foreign Office. He had been given them by Ciano. Paul summoned Campbell and told him what had happened. Fortunately, though Stojadinović had insisted on removing the photographs, Paul had memorized the code numbers and was able to quote the first sentence. Having established the authenticity of the photographs Paul sent Campbell back to London by the first train to explain things to Lord Halifax. It was about a year before the mystery was finally resolved. The culprit turned out to be a man working in the archives of the Foreign Office who had a Russian mistress. The mistress had been passing on the reports to Maisky, the Soviet Ambassador in London, who in turn had passed them to Grandi, his Italian opposite number, to make mischief with them as he pleased.

The part Paul had played in this particular episode was never acknowledged. Like most of his pro-British behaviour it was simply taken for granted. The Foreign Office were so sure of him that they paid little attention to the warnings from their ambassador in Belgrade. These came regularly and were usually much the same: 'It does not alter the fact, to which I have more than once drawn attention, that Yugoslavia's geographical position would oblige her to preserve as long as possible a neutrality which under the stress of economic considerations might even tend to favour Germany and Italy if those powers were ranged together in a future war.'[6]

Britain had failed to supply Yugoslavia with the trade and the armaments for which she had asked and in May 1939, Paul made a final attempt to remedy the situation. He instructed Dr Subbotić, the man whom he had picked to negotiate the Italo-Yugoslav pact of 1937, to call privately on Lord Halifax in Geneva. Subbotić gave the British foreign secretary a summary of Prince Paul's policies and explained to him Yugoslavia's economic and military position in detail. He informed him that Germany had absorbed 50 per cent of Yugoslav trade, and was seeking more, whilst Britain had a paltry nine per cent share. He appealed to Halifax to modify the British system of free trade, which would never compete with the Germans and to allow for bulk purchasing. As he later recounted to Prince Paul: '[I told him that] It cannot be of no importance to the English whether or not Germany gains mastery over our large sources of raw materials. The problem is not commercial but political and military-political.

'I developed the latter thesis rather exhaustively.'[7]

Halifax was most friendly and assured Subbotić that he completely understood, approved of and supported the Prince Regent's policies. As to the other matters he promised to consult his colleagues in the relevant departments in London. Subbotić declared himself ready to travel to London to follow up the discussion, but neither agreement nor visit was ever proposed.

Exactly one month later Sir Ronald Campbell sent a long report to the Foreign Office, which he concluded as follows: 'I cannot close this dispatch without making a further plea for the offer by H.M.G. of more substantial assistance to this country. I never see the Prince Regent, the President of the Council, or the Minister of Finance that they do not, at some stage in our conversation, express surprise that we do practically nothing to help. I know that the difficulties are great, and I do not press for help on a really large scale. Something comparatively modest would give immense encouragement. At the present moment we are furnishing nothing but a few aeroplanes which the Yugoslav government is paying for with great difficulty on a commercial basis.'[8] In response, the Foreign Office decided to consider increasing their offer of political credits, to arrange with the King that Paul should visit Britain as soon as possible, and to step up British propaganda in Yugoslavia. Although Paul did visit Britain, and propaganda was increased, no substantial supply of arms ever reached Yugoslavia. This was the eve of war and British arms manufacturers were already stretched to supply His Majesty's forces.

In the spring of 1939, alarmed by the fate of Czechoslovakia and by her commitment to Poland, Britain began to count her friends and, with something of a jolt, woke up to the fact that Yugoslavia was not as sure an ally as she had so complacently assumed. When Sir Ronald Campbell, on instructions from Lord Halifax, asked the standard question 'What did Yugoslavia intend to do if Germany invaded Rumania?' Prince Paul reacted furiously and asked in return what Britain intended to do. To this, Sir Ronald had no answer.

To Paul's horror, the British were beginning to behave in a clumsy and high-handed way. He was frightened that by forcing the Balkan countries to make formal declarations of this kind they would irritate Hitler. Paul knew that none of the Balkan countries were strong enough to withstand Germany for long and the chance that they would receive British aid was remote. In Yugoslavia he had to consider the proximity of Germany, the lack of arms and the fact that he could not rely on the Croats to fight against the Germans. He was in no position to make bold statements.

Sir Ronald Campbell fully understood and sympathized with Paul's position. In his report to the Foreign Office he predicted with uncanny foresight that Yugoslavia would remain neutral until the last possible moment, that under pressure from the Axis she would co-operate grudgingly with Italy and Germany and that 'in the later stages of the war if things were going well . . . the Yugoslavs might play a useful part if supplies could be gotten through to them.'[9]

But this was in the future. Of more immediate concern were the impending visits to Italy and Germany of the Prince Regent. The British were apprehensive lest Prince Paul be tempted to join some form of non-aggression pact, or worse still the Axis itself, in return for frontier guarantees.

On the last day of April 1939, Princess Olga wrote in her diary: 'April is so suddenly over and that dreaded journey to Italy looms nearer as we must leave on 9th. If only it were over. Poor Pacey dreads it even more than I do as he will have to face and speak to the Heads and each word that he utters must be so carefully weighed.'

As the day of departure approached, Paul began to show signs of the physical strain under which he was labouring. He could not sleep, he ate little and he frequently felt faint. But the Italian visit turned out to be considerably easier than he had expected. First, it lasted less than a week and, of this, only three days were spent in Rome. Secondly, he was put under very little pressure to make a firm political commitment. At the time, Mussolini was talking of peace. He himself needed four or five years more to rearm and he was trying to dissuade Hitler from precipitous action over Danzig. Paul had some experience of dealing with the Duce and knew well how to flatter him. In his conversation he encouraged Mussolini to expand on his rôle as peacemaker and reminded him of the part he had played at Munich. At this, Mussolini's face had lit up and he had replied, as if seeking confirmation, 'Yes, I think I really did play a useful part then.'

Besides the fact that he found the political discussions easy to manage, Paul had another reason for returning from Italy relatively cheerful. He had had one moment of sweet and secret enjoyment. On the second day of his visit he had had to leave Rome to attend a naval review in Naples. As he was watching the display from the Italian flagship, a Yugoslav cadet training ship had passed close by and had sent him greetings by cable. The message that he opened in the presence of the King of Italy and Mussolini was quite mundane and straightforward, but to Paul it was of special significance. The cadet training ship in question was the one on which he was secretly transporting three-quarters of his country's gold reserve to Britain.

It was with some relief that the Foreign Office received the telegram from Sir Percy Loraine, British Ambassador in Rome, on 18th May 1939: 'no further pressure to join the Axis was exerted on Prince Paul but stress was laid on the desirability

that Yugoslavia should engage herself to neutrality in event of
Axis powers being involved in war. Italians also proposed an
Italo-Yugoslav pact of non-aggression. Prince Paul avoided
committing himself on any of these points and was relieved at
having got out of the Rome visit so cheaply.'[10]

But, on the eve of the Prince Regent's visit to Berlin, the
British were uncertain of the outcome. Although Sir Ronald
Campbell had noted that Prince Paul and his Ministers 'seemed
to be throwing off the attack of nerves from which they had
been suffering', he was not entirely confident:

> I shall be easier in my mind when Prince Paul and his
> Foreign Minister have returned, if they do, with a whole
> skin. It was for this reason . . . I requested His Royal High-
> ness to receive me the evening before his departure. I
> remained with him for nearly two hours and did my best to
> stiffen him against any importunate demands that might be
> made of him. My anxiety on this score was not diminished by
> a message, which he read to me, sent by Marshal Goering
> through the Yugoslav Minister in Berlin. The theme of it
> was that Germany and Yugoslavia were complementary and
> necessary to one another; that Yugoslavia was cut out to
> play a leading role in the Balkans; that 'if anything happened
> in the Balkans' (His Royal Highness here interrupted his
> reading to say: 'This is the bit I don't like') it would be the
> duty of the Yugoslav government to decide where the true
> interests of their people lay; that if they chose the wrong
> path it would be the cause of deep personal sorrow to the
> Marshal who entertained feelings of warm sympathy and
> admiration for the Yugoslav people and its rulers. There was
> a passage of which I cannot remember the exact words, but
> which seemed to conceal a veiled hint that an agreement of
> some kind must be reached   . .[11]

The Italian visit had given a welcome boost to Paul's self-
confidence, but he was aware that Berlin would be the real test.
His health and his nerves were better and, through the mediation of Šubašić he had persuaded Maček to resume negotiations
on the Sporazum. The breakdown of these talks had been one of
the reasons for his earlier bout of depression for, as long as

174

Yugoslavia remained politically divided, his position was undermined in negotiations with the Axis.

The state visit to Germany began on 1st June. It was the first royal state visit to Berlin since Hitler had come to power and he was determined that it should be an impressive one, not merely for the greater glory of his guests, but for his own prestige as well. For days beforehand the German magazines ran articles on Yugoslavia, its fairytale charm and its beloved royal family. The official press comment followed the line that the visit, coming immediately after the one to Rome, would once more demonstrate the determination of Germany's Yugoslav friend to continue to regard co-operation with the Axis as the foundation of Yugoslav foreign policy.

The programme for the eight-day visit was a formidable one: on 1st June, arrival and a banquet given by Hitler at the Reichs Chancellery. On 2nd June, a military parade and in the evening a five-hour performance of the *Meistersinger* with a massive reception and exquisite supper in the interval. On 3rd June, a trip to Potsdam for a lunch given by Ribbentrop at the New Palace, tea with Goebbels and dinner with Hitler at the Kaiserhof. On 4th June, a tour of Berlin and a reception held by Goering at the Charlottenburg with a candlelight dinner, a ballet on the lawn and a display of fireworks and parachutes of flags. On 5th June, a lunch à trois with Hitler, and for Paul an afternoon alone with the Führer in Dresden. Then, for the last two days, a private visit to Goering's country estate, Karinhall.[12]

If an enormous amount of thought, effort and money went into planning the magnificent entertainment, smaller details were not forgotten. Everything possible was done to please the royal couple. Before the visit Olga had been asked which of her many relations she would like to see and she had replied: her sister, her brother-in-law and her three first cousins.* On 1st June, after a drive through the crowded streets in an open car with Hitler and Goering, Paul and Olga reached Schloss Bellevue where they were to stay. Already there and waiting to welcome them were Elizabeth and Toto. Later, at the various banquets and receptions, Paul and Olga found a mass of relations and old friends. The only one who was not included any more than diplomatic protocol required was Sir Nevile

* All sisters of Prince Philip of Greece, later Duke of Edinburgh.

Henderson, though Goering had the grace to invite him to tea one day at Karinhall, at Paul's request.

Hitler was the perfect host. He spent a lot of time with his guests, particularly with Paul, leaving Olga in the company of her relations or of Frau Goering, who was acting as first lady. But although Hitler was attentive, his behaviour was at times strange. This was particularly apparent at the lunch that he took alone with Paul and Olga. The three sat round a circular table and behind each chair stood a black-uniformed waiter. At exactly the same moment, as if in perfect drill, the waiters placed a sturgeon of gigantic proportions in front of each person. Hitler, Paul later discovered, had refused to see his royal guests given precedence over himself. And since this could not have been avoided with only one waiter, the solution was, of course, to have three.

For Olga the trip was a fascinating experience. She felt safe enough in the company of so many of her family, and she was dazzled by the make-believe world of power and opulence. One of the displays in particular was fantastic. The military parade lasted for over three hours and consisted of an endless succession of gleaming brand new tanks, armoured cars and guns rolling slowly past as aeroplanes flew in perfect formation overhead. About half way through this show Olga became suspicious of the similarity of some of the tanks. She was sitting with Frau Goering while Paul stood alongside Hitler, and so she was able to send an A.D.C. round to the back of the parade ground to take a look. The man returned a little later to report that the hardware was indeed trundling round for a second viewing.

The exhibition of personal wealth was also quite astonishing. Karinhall had not been changed in any way to impress its royal visitors, yet it was an incredible display of luxury and indulgence. The house was beautiful and set in a huge forest filled with bison, stags and elks for Goering to shoot. Paul and Olga were lodged in a small guest cottage and entertained in the main house. On their first evening there Olga inquired of Philip of Hesse, who was also staying, what she and Paul should wear. She had thought he was joking when he promptly replied: 'For us black tie: our host will dress as William Tell.' But indeed, when the moment came, Goering appeared for dinner with powdered hair, white breeches, a full shirt, a jewelled belt and, hanging from it, a dagger. His wife was dressed in full Croatian national costume.[13]

In spite of the almost demented eccentricity of their host, the two days Paul and Olga spent at Karinhall were pleasant and relatively relaxing. Goering was fascinated by jewels and riches. Even his desk set was encrusted with precious stones and the centre of the long dining-room table was filled with a solid row of silver beasts, each one a model of one he had shot. However, best of all, Goering liked amassing treasures for the purposes of dressing up. His own appearance had become an obsession. So much so, that in the basement of Karinhall he had installed a complete Elizabeth Arden unit where he could have his hair washed and waved, and exercise on a roller to remove his rolls of flab. It had been a bitter disappointment to Goering when Ribbentrop had been chosen as Ambassador to Britain for he had longed to take part in the glittering pomp and ceremony of King George's coronation.

For Paul the state visit was less of a happy family gathering. Although he enjoyed some of the receptions he was always aware that behind the display there was a darker side. Hitler had invited him to Berlin for a specific purpose and both he and his Foreign Minister had been permanently on their guard. While Ribbentrop worked on Cincar-Marković, Hitler himself tackled Paul. Olga caught but glimpses of this, as on the occasion when she was forced to entertain her relations to tea in the garden at Schloss Bellevue, rather than in her rooms. Paul had ordered an A.D.C., who was trained as an electrician to check their rooms and the man had found microphones secreted behind the damask wallpaper.

The Germans were keener than ever that Yugoslavia should make a friendly gesture towards the Axis. In the nicest possible way, they pointed out the advantages that a declared policy of friendship with the Axis would bring. It would simplify the Serbo-Croat question, as the separatists could no longer look to Germany or to Italy for assistance, and it would end the threat of aggression from Italy. The Yugoslavs were naturally sensitive to these thinly veiled threats. They knew full well the extent to which Germany could infiltrate the Croat separatist movement and that Hitler's influence over Mussolini was extremely powerful. But neither Paul nor Cincar-Marković could be drawn. They rejected the suggestion that Yugoslavia should withdraw from the League of Nations: they refused to sign the anti-Comintern pact; and they avoided committing themselves in any way to the Axis.

Hitler was furious. All his planning and expense had been for nothing. The Prince Regent, he raged, was 'slippery as an eel: each time he thought he could extract a firm agreement from him, the Prince would claim sanctuary behind his Parliament'. As for Olga, she was a 'typical ice-cold Englishwoman [sic] only concerned with high living'.[14] It was probably no coincidence that Olga, who had been showered with Dresden clocks and china at the beginning of her stay, and who had been asked by Frau Goering what she would most like as a souvenir (to which she had suggested a cigarette lighter with her initials engraved on it) never received the present which she had thus been led to expect.

At the official level, Paul's apparent stubbornness and other signs that he basically sympathized with Britain and France prompted Hitler to suggest, in a moment of pique, that the Italians should immediately overrun and liquidate Yugoslavia. Fortunately for Yugoslavia, Mussolini was so unprepared for war in August, when this outburst took place, that he was obliged to resist the almost irresistible temptation.

While Olga was at once both delighted and disgusted with Nazi Germany, Paul was profoundly alarmed. The military parade, even at half of its apparent size, had given him some idea of German fighting strength and his conversations with Hitler had convinced him that there would be a war. Although Hitler still believed the British would back down over Danzig, Paul did not. Furthermore, he thought that Hitler was mad. He said as much to Alfonso of Spain who came to a family lunch at Schloss Bellevue on 2nd June. Writing to Paul in 1954, Alfonso told how he had been reading through his old diaries: 'and I now copy what I wrote on 2.6.39 Berlin: "Dentista: Voy almorzar (con Ataulfo) Palacio Bellevue con Paul & Olga y mucha familia (Friedel, Margarita, Chri, Tiny, Berthold, Dotta, Woolly, Toerring etc). Talk with Paul. He fears war sure. Says Hitler is mad. I tell him I fear Germans know nothing of R.A.F. and A.D. [Air Defence] G.B., [and] will get a nasty shock." So those people who tried to accuse you of trying to push your country into the war on Hitler's side can see how you talked in June 1939, to a Spanish airman who was certainly most friendly to Germany because the Germans had come to fight against the Reds on our side in 1936 when other nations were helping the Reds.'[15]

As a result of his visit, Paul had also become highly suspicious of Germany's relations with Soviet Russia. Both Hitler and Goering had been strangely vague and uncommunicative when he had asked them what they knew of Russia's policies, and from this and other signs he guessed that either they had started talks already or that the idea at least was beginning to gain ground. On his return to Yugoslavia, sensing that the outbreak of war in Europe was imminent, he immediately sent his chief of staff, General Pešić (the man whom King Alexander had chosen to lead the army in the event of war) for top level consultations with his opposite numbers in Britain and France.

Without delay, too, he decided to avail himself of a charming and most insistent telegram from King George asking him to visit London. As in November of the previous year, Paul and Olga stayed at Buckingham Palace. But this time the entertainment was more spectacular. It was as if London was somehow vying with Berlin. On 17th July, the day after their arrival, King George and Queen Elizabeth held a dinner party for them with sixty guests. On 19th, the King gave Paul the Garter and in the evening a glittering ball for 900 people was held at Buckingham Palace. Paul and Olga enjoyed it enormously. They saw all their old friends and danced till 3.30 a.m. But Paul had not only been invited to London to be fêted. The government was anxious to show him the strength and readiness of the allied forces, and to make sure that German hospitality had not made too deep an impression.

On the same day that he was made a Garter Knight, Paul lunched at Downing Street with the Prime Minister. His invitation listed his fellow guests: Viscount Runciman (Lord President of the Council); Viscount Halifax (Secretary of State for Foreign Affairs), Lord Chatfield (Minister for the Co-ordination of Defence); Sir Thomas Inskip (Secretary of State for Dominion Affairs); Sir Kingsley Wood (Secretary of State

179

for Air); Mr Oliver Stanley (President of the Board of Trade); General the Viscount Gort (Chief of the Imperial General Staff) and Admiral Sir Dudley Pound (First Sea Lord and Chief of Naval Staff). Underneath this formidable list it stated, somewhat unnecessarily, 'As you will see, there will be no ladies present.'[16] At this luncheon, Paul repeated to the assembled company Hitler's opinion of the British. He also warned Chamberlain of his own deeply-felt suspicion that Russo-German negotiations were in progress. Chamberlain did not take this seriously, as the U.S. Ambassador in London, Joseph Kennedy, reported back to Washington:

I have just seen the Prime Minister. On the whole, he is fairly optimistic about the outlook for the next 30 days. He is planning to go on vacation on 5th August and hopes to be away a reasonable length of time.

He told me he was sick and disgusted with the Russians and while he believes that the Russians are willing to continue talking without accomplishing anything, his patience is exhausted. He told me he had a conversation with Prince Paul of Yugoslavia and Prince Paul was definitely of the opinion that if England did not consummate a deal with the Russians, Germany would. The Prime Minister said he does not feel there is any danger of that. He thinks that the Russians have made up their minds probably not to make a deal with anybody but to watch them all tear themselves apart . . .

Chamberlain is now convinced that Hitler is definitely aware that England proposes to fight if need be; he is not one of those who believes that Hitler is not most intelligent. On the contrary Chamberlain believes that Hitler is highly intelligent and therefore would not be prepared to wage a world war . . .[17]

A day later, after meeting Paul at dinner at No. 3 Belgrave Square, Kennedy considered the Prince Regent's views sufficiently important to warrant a further telegram: 'He [Prince Paul] said on his visit to Hitler he was impressed with three things: first of all Hitler was convinced that the British Empire was decadent and therefore would not be able to fight very strenuously even though their dispositions were courageous; secondly he found the same condition that he has in London and Paris: when he asked Hitler and Goering what they knew about Russia they told him "nothing"; third, he found Goering a most decent fellow, very able, with a real desire to be constructive. Ribbentrop, however, at that time was definitely no longer top.'[18] Kennedy was not to know it, but Paul had already told Bliss Lane, the U.S. Ambassador in Belgrade, that Danzig would trigger general war in Europe.[19]

To his obvious delight, Paul's six-day visit to London had to be extended. An operation to remove his wisdom teeth turned out to be more complicated than he had expected and it was over a fortnight before he and Olga were able to return home.

They arrived back in Yugoslavia on 4th August, and as it was still high summer, went straight to Brdo. For the next few weeks the house was full of children and family. The Kents and the Toerrings came to stay, as did Albrecht of Bavaria. Albrecht had left Germany because he could no longer tolerate the Nazi regime, and Paul had given him employment running his estates and shoots at Petrovcić and Belje.

But the late summer of 1939 was not a relaxing time, and Paul was still convalescing from his operation. His recovery was not hastened by the dreadful news that came to him from all sides. The rumours reached a climax on 22nd August, when it was confirmed that Germany and Russia had signed a non-aggression pact. His suspicions, which Neville Chamberlain had chosen to disregard in London, were being proved right. Although Paul had anticipated the worst, he had hoped that something would happen to prevent it. But now there was no longer hope: Poland was at the mercy of Germany, and Britain and France would have to fight.

Both Georgie and Toto left Brdo as soon as the news arrived, one to England and the other to Germany. Paul and Olga debated what to do with the children and eventually decided that it would be wisest for the two boys to go back to England. On 26th August they left with Marina, furious to have their summer holidays broken up when they had only just begun. Olga's mother and Elizabeth remained, but the house seemed strangely empty and hanging over all their heads was the question of when or whether they would see each other again.

The mounting tensions and uncertainty in Europe, however, had one salutary effect in Yugoslavia. On 20th August Maček finally accepted the terms for an agreement between the Serbs and Croats, which Prime Minister Cvetković had proposed. These were taken to Prince Paul who immediately gave them his assent. On 23rd August the Sporazum was signed. On 26th a new government was formed with Cvetković as Premier and Maček as Vice-Premier.

Because the communist state of Yugoslavia which developed out of World War II was so fundamentally different from the kingdom that entered it, the significance of this political concordat is not easily appreciated. Yet it was an achievement of overriding importance and it brought, for the first time, a hope of real unity to the Yugoslav people. It was certainly the supreme achievement of Paul's regency and one for which he had worked untiringly since 1934.

During King Alexander's reign Paul had seen that suppression did not work; autocratic methods were, in any case, against his principles. From the very beginning he had set out personally to bring the Serbs and the Croats together in some form of contract. It had taken him nearly five years and it had caused the downfall of two of his administrations.

Paul's first step as Regent had been to order the release of Dr Maček. From then on, things had slowly improved. There was a period when Stojadinović did little to further the search for an agreement but, upon realizing this, Paul had re-established contact with the Croat leader himself. After Stojadinović's fall Paul chose, as the next Prime Minister, the man most likely to succeed with the Croats. He chose well, as Cvetković was both a likeable and convincing politician. And, most importantly, Paul had won the trust of Vladko Maček. The Croat had consistently remained loyal to the crown, if not to the constitution, and his loyalty to Prince Paul was both personal and lasting. It was a tribute to Paul's character and to his resolution. Maček's negotiating style had been uncompromising. For him, Croatia had come first and Yugoslavia second. On occasions his conversations with the Prince Regent had lasted for five or six hours and still ended in stalemate. But

Paul had remained willing to listen and to try to understand, and in 1939 his patience was rewarded. As he confessed in a letter to Bernard Berenson: 'it was indeed a satisfaction to have succeeded in settling one question at least after years of perseverance and many efforts.'[20]

By the terms of the Sporazum, the Croats were given a considerable degree of autonomy. Croatia, Dalmatia and seven other regions which were predominately Croat, were grouped together under a single governor (or Ban) in Zagreb. Foreign affairs, foreign trade, defence and other matters where policy had to be national rather than regional, remained under the control of central government in Belgrade, but the new Croatia was to have its own legislature and budget. The Governor of Zagreb was to be Dr Šubašić, the man who had so often played the part of intermediary in the negotiations.

For the first time since 1929, the Croats were to take their seats in Parliament. Moreover, the new government was to be formed out of all the parties, with four members of the Serb Radical Party, four members of the Croat Peasant Party, and one member each of the Serbian Agrarian and Independent Democratic parties, the Slovenian Populist Party and the Yugoslav Moslem Organization. The two leaders, Cvetković and Maček made a good combination, the former being involved in foreign affairs, the latter in implementing the new constitution.

The political situation in Europe had forced Maček into a decision. But though developments in northern Europe hastened the Sporazum, they also prevented its consolidation, for eight days after the Yugoslav agreement was signed the Germans marched into Poland and two days later Britain declared war on Germany. Ronald Campbell, who was by then Ambassador in Paris,* was not usually sentimental, but he bordered on it in a letter to Paul in January 1940: 'What a happy country you would make of Yugoslavia if only your neighbours would leave you alone.'[21]

Hitler's attack on Poland was preceded by a frantic burst of negotiations. Both Henderson and the self-appointed Scandinavian mediator, Dahlerus, flew in desperation between

* Sir Ronald Hugh Campbell had left Belgrade for Paris in October 1939.

London and Berlin with offers and counter-offers. But there was never any real hope for peace: Hitler had relied on the British backing down and this they were not prepared to do. On 4th September, Henderson left Berlin for good and from England he replied to a letter of sympathy from Paul:

> It was kind of you to write to me. I got back here broken in mind and body at the failure of my efforts, and the tragic consequences of that failure. It is a nightmare which just goes on and on, and merely saying that I did my best is no consolation.
>
> I pray that you will succeed in keeping your part of the world out of the conflict. That is vitally important not only for your own country, which suffered so much in 1914–18, but for Europe in general . . .[22]

In 1939 Paul had little difficulty in keeping Yugoslavia out of the war for, following his victories in Poland, Hitler was preoccupied with his ambitions in the West. Yugoslavia remained on the sidelines, welcoming Polish refugees and waiting.

It was a strange time for Paul and Olga. After the German victory in Poland there was a lull. Berenson came to stay for a few nights, and Elizabeth and Toto for a little longer. But gradually they had to get used to the idea that they were going to be separated from most of their family and friends, probably for a very long time. Olga became occupied with the Red Cross while Paul speculated on Hitler's next move. He took to spending periods alone at Brdo to rest and to think, for he was now thrown back very much on his own resources. He could not talk politics with Toto because their views were quite different and Ronald Campbell was in Paris. The new British Ambassador, Ronald Ian Campbell, arrived in December and it was clear from the start that he was not going to be such a close friend.

CHAPTER X

1940

Regency IV
Neutrality

In Yugoslavia the first major event of 1940 was the official visit of the Prince Regent and Princess Olga to Zagreb, the capital of Croatia-Slavenia. The visit had been planned at the signing of the Sporazum, but it had been postponed when difficulties arose in working out some of the details of the agreement.

The visit was to be a public demonstration that the conflict between Serb and Croat was finally at an end. As such it was of the greatest importance. Although Zagreb was the second largest city in the land with a population of over 185,000, a cathedral, a university and many government buildings, the split between Serbia and Croatia had kept the royal family away. Indeed, it was Olga's first visit to the city for sixteen years, and Paul's first as Regent. They had kept away for good reasons. The history of royal visits to the Croatian capital was not a happy one: in virtually every instance something unpleasant had taken place.

But this time Paul and Olga had little to fear. They were under the protection of Dr Maček, and he was an immensely powerful figure. His power stemmed from the solid backing of every peasant in Croatia for the Croat Peasant Party was far more than just a regional political party. When the Radić brothers had founded it at the beginning of the twentieth century they had aimed to combine the purity of peasant society (about 80 per cent of the population) with the humanist ideas then prevalent amongst the Croat intelligentsia. The brothers decided that the dignity of the individual required that society should be organized from below, not above. Whilst one developed the theories, the other set about putting them into practice. Hiking from village to village and sleeping rough, Stepjan Radić soon became well known and trusted by the peasant communities. He encouraged the peasants to combine their resources and to put their labours to profit. He set up systems, too, whereby those who knew how to read and write passed on their knowledge to others. By 1928, when the leadership fell to Maček, the peasants were organized into efficient economic co-operatives and wide ranging cultural societies, all of them members of the Croat Peasant Party. Maček, elected unanimously after Stepjan's murder, was by no means brilliant, but he had been one of the party's founders and he possessed in abundance the characteristics which appealed to the Croatian peasants—honesty, common sense and patience. Despite the fact that Maček spent much of the time between 1929 and 1934 in prison he continued to develop and exert his own authority over the party and his popularity grew steadily. By 1939 he had a sizeable Peasant Guard at his disposal and people had begun to refer to him as the uncrowned King of Croatia.

From the outset Maček had made his feelings towards the Prince Regent absolutely clear. When, at last, the Regent came to Zagreb in celebration of the Sporazum it was he, rather than the Governor or the Mayor, who delivered the welcoming oration. In it he described Prince Paul as having three qualities rarely found united in one man—a sense of justice, wisdom and courage. The first because he had recognized the justice of Croat claims; the second because he had seen that the satisfaction of these claims was for the good of Yugoslavia; and the third because he had been determined to cut the Gordian knot. 'Therefore,' Maček had concluded, 'the Croat people today welcome you with open arms and wish you a happy and agreeable stay in the capital of all the Croats.'[1] And this was not all. In a subsequent interview with the press Maček stressed the part the Prince Regent had played. After describing Paul as the 'first promoter of the Serbo-Croat agreement' he stated that, 'It is to Prince Paul that the credit for the happy result of the negotiations opened last spring with the Premier Cvetković is largely due.'[2]

The royal train arrived in Zagreb at three o'clock in the afternoon of 14th January. After the welcoming speeches, Paul and Olga drove through the town in state. Their open carriage was surrounded by a mounted detachment of the town guards with drawn swords, and was preceded by the mounted band of the King's bodyguard. It was bitterly cold, but it was beautifully sunny. Parts of Zagreb dated back to the twelfth century and the narrow winding streets and architecture in the old part of the town reflected both German and Magyar influence. In contrast, the modern areas were spacious, with wide streets and open squares and gardens.

The carriage halted at St Mark's Church, the mother Church of Croatia. Paul was greeted by the Archbishop and the traditional Te Deum was sung. The royal couple then moved on to watch a march-past of the town and peasant guard. In Serbian political circles Maček's Peasant Guard had been something of a joke but when he saw their numbers and discipline the Minister of War was overheard to say, 'They are not a negligible quantity. Give them rifles and they will be the best division in my army.'[3] In fact the force paraded before Prince Paul was only about a quarter of those drafted to Zagreb for the purposes of security during the state visit, and this in turn was but a fraction of the total strength.

In the evening of the first day Paul and Olga attended a huge banquet at the Governor's official residence. On the second day they received 800 townspeople and, in the evening, visited the theatre, about which Olga commented 'very good staging and costumes but too long and patriotic'.[4] On the third day, whilst Paul toured the museums, Olga visited the nursery schools. The visit finished with a ball for 1,800 people.

Throughout the celebrations the atmosphere was somewhat restrained. The visit was a serious occasion and the Peasant Party leaders had given orders that there was to be no wild cheering. They had made it clear that the royal visit was not an excuse for a Roman holiday. For them it symbolized the end of a struggle which had lasted since 1918, and most of the functions which Paul performed over the three-day visit had some significance in the context of this struggle. Probably the one which meant most to the people was the visit which he paid to Dr Maček at his home in Kupineć. Paul and Olga were formally received by Dr Maček and his wife, amidst his cows and peasant friends. Only once before in Croatian history had a monarch returned ceremoniously the visit paid him by a subject, so this was a great honour to Vladko Maček and to all his peasant following. It was also a particular pleasure for Paul for he had grown to like and respect the stolid Croat leader.

The official visit ended in a snowstorm on the morning of 17th January. Olga had not enjoyed it much. It was not so much that it had lacked the glamour of Berlin and London, for, if anything, Olga preferred simplicity to grandeur. It was rather that the endless displays of loyalty had bored her. Besides, she had had to hide a cold and a high temperature. Though Zagreb was not exactly Paul's spiritual home, for him the visit had meant a great deal. He could feel, with the peasant leaders, that it was the conclusion of a very long struggle. The public, too, were delighted. As the British Consul reported to Belgrade: 'Prince Paul and Princess Olga played their parts magnificently, their prestige and popularity increasing visibly as their stay proceeded with hardly a discordant note. There can be no doubt that at the outset the attitude of the population was reserved but they gradually melted to such an extent that more than one person has suggested that some resemblance could be found to the conquest of Paris by King Edward VII at the time of his visit in 1904.'[5]

During the months which followed, Maček and the other Croatian leaders made every effort to co-operate with the work of government. They were pleased with the terms of the Sporazum, and anxious to see it implemented in full as soon as possible. But at almost every point they met with resistance from the right wing Serbs. Cvetković did his best to counteract this resistance but he was in a weak position because he had no real following. He had picked up the remnants of Stojadinović's party, the J.R.Z., but in his last months of power Stojadinović had alienated many members of the party. Cvetković had tried to remedy the situation by forming a union with the largest of the other Serbian parties, the Radical party, but through no fault of his the negotiations had broken down. The fact was that since the Serbian parties had splintered during King Alexander's dictatorship, they had bickered and quarrelled over everything except the Croat question. This last had become their only point of real agreement. After the Sporazum they had had to reassess their positions, but only slightly. Their new bond became criticism of the terms of the Sporazum which, they complained, had conceded far too much to the Croats both in territory and in administrative and political rights.

Of their grievances, the two most problematic were the reorganization of finance and the restructuring of the army. By threatening to resign, Maček eventually succeeded in getting the financial settlement through. But the army was a far more complicated problem. The Croats resented the fact that there were very few high ranking Croat officers in the army, and the Croat soldiers found it strange and difficult being commanded almost exclusively by Serbs. The army, of course, harboured some of the most reactionary Serb elements. They held stubbornly to their opinion that the Croats were untrustworthy and that they were poor fighters, and there was nobody who could persuade them otherwise. The army was the one area where Paul himself had practically no influence. He had never really been accepted by them for he was not a soldier, like King Alexander, nor was he traditionally Serbian in his outlook. Consequently the army refused to make the suggested changes and the Croats became deeply resentful.

Cvetković's attempts to deal with the stubborn contingent of old Serbs were in no way helped by the subversive influence of Stojadinović. The former Prime Minister was indulging in all kinds of intrigues in order to regain power. He claimed to have started a new political party and he began to circulate scurrilous pamphlets about his successor. More dangerous than this, he was in contact with both German and Italian secret agents. By May, Paul felt obliged to order his internment in Bosnia, far away from the German and Italian borders and at a safe distance from any of the contacts that he had in Belgrade.

Largely as a result of the lack of cohesion amongst the Serbs, the unity which the Sporazum should have brought about was slow developing. Yet, as Campbell wrote to Halifax: 'If given time and peace, Yugoslavia should be able to find equilibrium between her component parts.' And he continued: 'In any review of the internal situation in Yugoslavia full account must be taken of the personality and character of the Prince Regent, who works tirelessly for the country's welfare and unity and whose political skill and judgement have enabled Yugoslavia to survive more than one serious crisis.'[6]

Whilst Cvetković was occupied with the aftermath of the Sporazum and with trying to form some sort of coalition out of the Serb parties, Paul concentrated on foreign affairs.

In the late summer of 1939 the British and French had discussed the possibility of landing a military force at Salonika. Paul and his ministers had been involved in the plans and had shown themselves to be fully prepared to co-operate. Paul, in fact, had been in favour of immediate action and had passed on his views to Brugère, the French Ambassador: 'He [Prince Paul] concluded from all, that we are faced with a shameless plot, of which Europe and his country in particular will be the victims if we do not impose guarantees of neutrality on Italy allowing us to overtake the German-Italian bloc on the only vulnerable point that offers itself to us at the present time . . . *he wants us to come to Salonika as soon as possible with or without Italy's consent.*'[7]

The French had had to refuse Prince Paul's request, because, as General Weygand explained, it would have taken at least three months to get the French expeditionary force to Greece. But Weygand was no less keen on the idea of a Salonika front than Paul, and through October and November 1939 he continued to work on plans for an allied landing in the Balkans.

Salonika was of vital importance to Yugoslavia. Since the creation of Albania, after the Balkan wars, this port had been her only outlet to the Mediterranean. Paul wanted the allies to come to Salonika in order to preserve the link between Yugoslavia and the West, so that Yugoslavia could remain neutral until the opportunity arose for her to join the war on the allied side. He also wanted them to come because he feared that if they did not, the Italians might. He had no faith at all in the Italian declaration of neutrality. As he told the French Ambassador, on the very day that the Italian Ambassador in Paris informed the French government that Italy had decided to observe a strict neutrality throughout the entire war, Count Ciano had received the Yugoslav minister in Rome. To the Yugoslav the story had been slightly different. 'Italian neutrality would be "watchful" and would last only as long as the interests of the Axis, not engaged in the affair of Danzig, were not at stake.'[8]

But Paul did not need evidence to bolster his mistrust of Mussolini. He had negotiated with the Duce for ten years and was sure he knew exactly how his mind worked. Mussolini would wait until it looked as if he could, with little cost or hurt, share in the glory. Then he would join in as a belligerent. As for the Axis, Paul was convinced that it was unbreakable. He had already reached this grim conclusion during his visit to Rome in May 1939 when, as he later told Terence Shone 'Mussolini had talked of Hitler in terms of affection ("tenderness")'.[9] Every day reports reached Belgrade of the build up of Italian troops in Albania and Paul was terrified that the Italians would march on Salonika, protected in the north by German troops released from Poland. With the Axis in control of Salonika, Yugoslavia would be forced to come to terms with Germany.

The French interest in Salonika arose out of an impatience and a desire for military action of some kind, as well as out of the memory of her victorious campaign in the 1914–18 war. Before the outbreak of war the British had also shown some interest in a Salonika front but this was when they had been expecting Mussolini to take sides with Hitler. When he did not, the preservation of Italian neutrality became an all important factor in British policy.

The British alternative to a Salonika front was the idea of a neutral Balkan bloc strong enough to withstand German pressure. As a political, rather than a military strategy, they reasoned that this would be less likely to anger Mussolini and force him into hostilities. The Balkan Entente was to form the basis for the bloc, but somehow Bulgaria had to be persuaded to join in. The policy was not new to Yugoslavia: it was the one that Stojadinović had started to pursue in 1936. Since then relations with Bulgaria had improved, albeit slowly. In 1937 Yugoslavia and Bulgaria had signed a Treaty of Friendship. In 1938 the States of the Balkan Entente and Bulgaria had signed an agreement by which all parties renounced force in their mutual relations, permitted Bulgaria to increase the size of her army, and accepted a proposal for discussions on revision of the Thracian frontier. But Bulgaria wanted more than this. The Balkan Entente had been created, in part at least, to protect Yugoslavia, Greece, Rumania and Turkey from Bulgaria's revisionist claims. In the words of the British Minister in Sofia 'it represented to the Bulgarians the prison warder far more than the friendly policeman'.[10] Before Bulgaria would consider joining a Balkan bloc she demanded specific frontier revisions, and in particular the southern Dobruja from Rumania.

191

British ministers in the Balkan countries set to work. An agreement was imperative and the British government looked forward optimistically to the forthcoming Council of the Balkan Entente. Meanwhile they worked on the French in an effort to dissuade them from pursuing the Salonika front strategy. At staff talks in October, the French appeared to accept the British view that their project was unsound, but at the end of November news reached Britain that General Weygand had returned to Paris from Syria and the Balkans with extensive plans for further staff talks with the Balkan countries. Weygand had achieved considerable fame in the 1914–18 war and was a powerful figure in France.

For the first months of the war in 1939, Paul continued to support the idea of a Salonika front. In November he asked the French military attaché in Belgrade to arrange closer collaboration and permission for a Yugoslav military mission to visit France. In return, Weygand wanted to send an air force officer to Belgrade to establish contact with the Yugoslav, Rumanian and Greek high commands, without involving the British. But gradually Paul's enthusiasm waned. He did not like the fact that the British disapproved of the plan and he reckoned that the available French forces would not have a chance against the Germans. But, most important of all, he objected to the way the French were 'trumpeting the project in the press, giving Germany full warning for preparing counter-measures'.[11]

By the beginning of 1940 Paul had turned his attention to the scheme for a Balkan bloc. Since the early days of the war the Yugoslav foreign minister, Cincar-Marković, had been discussing the Bulgarian problem with his Rumanian counterpart. The two had concluded that on all accounts it was vital that Bulgaria should join the Balkan Entente and in order to persuade her to do so each member state would have to be prepared to give up territory. The details of the concessions were left for discussion at the Council of the Balkan Entente which took place in February 1940. But though Bulgaria knew of the plans to grant her territory she refused to join the Entente. In mid-February the moderate Bulgarian government had fallen and the new administration was much more sensitive to the influence of Russia and Germany. For both these countries it was convenient to kindle the flame of Bulgarian revisionism.

Through the winter and early spring of 1940 the British government remained hopeful about the formation of a Balkan bloc, but at the same time they were forced to consider seriously a Salonika front. General Weygand had not been deterred by the lack of enthusiasm and was planning a drive through the Balkans to defeat the Germans on their own soil. The British were furious when they discovered that the General had taken to signing himself 'Commander in Chief of the East Mediterranean Theatre of Operations', for they considered the Balkans to be primarily a sphere of British influence.

After the unsatisfactory conclusion to the Council of the Balkan Entente, Paul had picked up the threads of the French negotiations. He and his ministers and the Yugoslav General Staff together kept the French constantly up-to-date about German troop movements, German deliveries of materials to Bulgaria and the internal situation in Germany. Paul also welcomed the suggestion of a French inspection of the Yugoslav airports, as the French Ambassador reported in his telegram home: 'As was agreed with the Prince Regent, I continued this afternoon the exchange of thoughts with General Neditsch about the best way of renewing the general staff discussions. Since, according to the view of General Weygand, the question of airports and their usage is the most urgent one, General Neditsch would agree that an appropriate co-worker of General Weygand's come here in civilian clothes under the greatest secrecy, who could travel around the country and to whom a Yugoslavian officer, also in civilian clothes, would show all existing installations.'[12]

But, with the British and French on the defensive, nothing came of the Salonika front plan and in the spring of 1940 Hitler began, once more, to control the course of European history.

After the occupation of Poland Hitler had wanted to begin the Western campaign immediately. He had scheduled the invasion of the Low Countries for 12th November 1939. But he met with opposition from the army. His general staff did not share his confidence in the superiority of German forces and they could see no sense in extending the war gratuitously. And

then, on 8th November, an attempt was made on Hitler's life.*
Although the bomb exploded after Hitler had safely left the
building, the incident, together with the deteriorating weather
conditions, persuaded him to postpone his attack on the West.
Successive postponements followed and finally he decided to
wait until the weather improved in the spring.

Meanwhile Hitler sat back and watched the Russians take
over Finland. It was an unusual experience for him but he could
not interfere. The importance of Russian raw materials to
Germany was paramount. Then, in January 1940, he became
absorbed in a plan for the occupation of Denmark and Norway.
Admiral Raeder had first suggested the idea in October 1939 as
a means of attacking British sea routes. In December, when the
threat of an allied landing in Norway was being rumoured,
Hitler began to take a greater interest in Raeder's plans. The
result was 'Exercise Weser', a surprise invasion of Denmark
and Norway on 9th April 1940. It was a brilliant success and, as
Winston Churchill admitted, the British were 'completely
outwitted'.

Up to that point the British had been talking of 'the phoney
war'. Hitler had remained remarkably quiet and, after the Finns
had signed an armistice with Russia, there was little action
anywhere in Europe. Morale in England was low: people were
suffering from the strain of uncertainty and from a lack of
inspiration and direction in the country's leadership. This mood
filtered through to Yugoslavia, particularly in the Duke of
Kent's frequent letters to Paul. In December 1939 he was
writing: 'Everything goes on here the same—and it seems years
since war started—and the boredom is immense—three months
without anything really happening,' and again, in March 1940:
'The war drags on—everyone seems to be talking—but I
cannot see any result from it'; and then in April, at the peak of
his frustration: 'I have been at the Admiralty (awful waste of
time) and so I went to see Chamberlain weeks ago and asked
him if he could find me something which I could do which, being

* The bomb was planted in a Munich beer hall by Georg Elser, a
Swabian watchmaker. It exploded eight minutes after Hitler had left
the building early to catch a train. Had Hitler spoken for his
customary ninety minutes he would, almost certainly, have been
killed.

what I am, would be really useful to the country—you see—we are used for anything and everything in peace but when war comes no one wants us as we don't know enough of any particular subject which seems unfair.'[13]

Nevertheless, life in England was relatively normal. In fact things were so quiet that Marina invited Olga to stay for Easter, so that she could be with her two boys during the school holidays. Olga had already spent part of January and much of February in Athens with her mother and as the day of her departure drew near she began to regret having to desert her husband once again. Her feelings were heightened the day before she left when news arrived of the invasion of Denmark and Norway.

However, when she arrived in London she had little time for misgivings. Alexander had to be amused and Nicky, who had caught mumps, had to be nursed. In addition, social life seemed hardly to have suffered. True, there were no more enormous parties, but reviews and plays and films continued and Olga had a gay time escorted by Georgie and Chips, and entertained by the Buccleuchs, the Mountbattens, the King and Queen and a host of other friends.

At the beginning of May the atmosphere in London changed. Olga was brought sharply back to reality when she heard from Paul that he had despatched Elizabeth and her nurse to Lausanne because of the danger of an Italian attack on Yugoslavia:

My own love,
    It was a relief to hear that you crossed the Channel safely and I only hope that you weren't frightened and didn't find it unpleasant. The news has been consistently bad and every few hours we get alarming reports about Italy's intentions towards us. I had a talk with Nursie* and came to the conclusion that it was better to get Pixie† out of the way while there was time. She didn't at all relish the idea of Greece as she doesn't consider Mummy's house safe and this is what we decided. Nursie is leaving tomorrow night with Pixie for Geneva where she will stay in the neighbourhood and see

* Miss Ede, Elizabeth's nurse.
† Elizabeth, aged four.

how things turn out. If all is normal, on your way back, you can pick them up and bring them back here. If not, baby will be taken to Paris and from there you can arrange about her joining you. We also thought that if she went to Greece and Italy declared war, you'd be cut off from your daughter completely.

Like this, at least, you'll have all three children under your wing . . .[14]

In the event, Elizabeth was sent off the very next day with her nurse to Lausanne. From there they made their way to Paris and eventually to London. Paul wrote again to Olga on 21st April summarizing the general feeling of frustration at England's apparent inability to take up the initiative and displaying his own sense of disappointment at the missed opportunity over Salonika: 'I am still very mistrustful of Muti's* intentions and nothing would surprise me on that side. If England delivers a striking blow in the north everything will improve but they are always so slow and one nation perishes after another before they even begin to move. Then they are always surprised by something as they go on trusting everybody till the last minute.'[15]

On 10th May, Hitler put his Western Campaign into operation. In the early hours of the morning German troops marched into Holland, Belgium and Luxembourg, once again taking the Allies completely by surprise. In the afternoon of the same day the Chamberlain government fell: discontent in Britain had been growing for some time. It had been brought to a head at the beginning of the month when the Allies had been routed in Norway and stormy debates had taken place in the House of Commons on 7th and 8th May. By 10th May Chamberlain's fate had already been decided. Strangely, Olga was one of the last to see the Prime Minister before he resigned: 'Subbotić phoned at 9.30 to announce the news that Germany marched into Holland, Belgium and Luxembourg at 4 a.m. this morning! Help is being rushed from here to stop or check the advance but it is feared there may be air raids on the coast and docks here. I had lunch upstairs (at the Dorchester) with the Halifaxes, Chamberlain and General Dill—most interesting.

* Mussolini.

'At 5.30 the government here fell and Churchill is now Prime Minister.

'What will it mean? . . .'[16]

Not surprisingly, Olga found it almost impossible to get home. Hitler's invasion proceeded relentlessly and on 13th May Queen Wilhelmina of the Netherlands was forced to leave her country on a British destroyer. She arrived at Buckingham Palace with her jewels but no clothes, determined to return to Holland at the first possible opportunity. Meanwhile Olga was, for her part, becoming increasingly anxious to get back to Yugoslavia. On 15th May the Yugoslav Ambassador received a reply to his coded wire asking for Prince Paul's opinion on whether or not she should travel. Paul advised that she should leave at once or not at all, so Olga packed her belongings and booked the first available seat. But on 17th May, the day of her departure, all flights were stopped. The Germans were in Belgium threatening Brussels and it was no longer considered safe to fly the Channel. Olga thought she was completely stranded. In despair she telephoned Georgie, who promised to see what he could do. That afternoon she flew from Heston to Le Bourget in the King's new private bomber. She arrived in time for high tea at the Yugoslav legation in Paris, from whence she boarded the train to Yugoslavia.

Paul met Olga at the station in Belgrade. He was looking thin and worried. He had spent some anxious weeks alone and life at Beli Dvor had been especially gloomy without Elizabeth and her nannie. Elizabeth had provided Paul with an escape from serious matters and the nannie had contributed, in the way that British nannies do, a touch of strictness and stability to the household. Paul had been in the habit of taking her the daily Reuter's news summary, in case she felt homesick or cut off, and he had missed his evening trips to the nursery.

Politically, Paul's chief worry had been Italy. The threat to Salonika had temporarily disappeared, but in the early spring of 1940 Mussolini was looking about for easy victory. He had always coveted Croatia, Dalmatia and the islands of the Adriatic. In March Yugoslavia had been spared only because Hitler had warned him off the Balkans. But in April Mussolini again became acquisitive. He was jealous of Germany's advances and anxious to assert what he deemed to be his right over the Balkans and their minerals. Furthermore he had remembered Pavelić, the Croat terrorist. Mussolini was eager to employ Pavelić before the Germans did and he and Ciano set about preparing plans to put Pavelić at the head of a Croat army.

The Yugoslavs were well informed about the state of affairs in Rome. They had an efficient team of spies in the city and in the Vatican, and in addition all they had to do to assess the Italian mood was to monitor the movement of Italian troops near the Yugoslav frontier. In mid-April the signs had been particularly bad, and indeed rumours had reached France and Britain that an Italian invasion was imminent. Paul knew that Yugoslavia was virtually defenceless and suspected that the Allies were in no position to come to her immediate rescue. He was right. In Britain at least, preservation of Italian neutrality was considered of paramount importance. Lord Halifax had told Olga as much when he had seen her in May. She had asked him what Britain would do in the event of an Italian attack on Yugoslavia and had been told: 'we should naturally wish to do anything in our power to help but . . . we must recognize that if the Italians, as . . . was likely, mined the entrance of the Adriatic, the navy would presumably not be able to do much.'[17]

When Olga arrived back in Yugoslavia on 19th May there had been a change in the focus of attention. Italy had moved into the background in the light of Hitler's spectacular offensive in the West. The German army was achieving victory after victory. By 20th May the Germans had overrun Denmark, Norway, Holland and Luxembourg and were fighting fiercely in Belgium and France. Then, on 27th May King Leopold of the Belgians capitulated and the First French Army and the British Expeditionary Force were very nearly encircled by German troops converging from the north and south. They were saved by the Dunkirk evacuation, but this was a miraculous escape not a victory, and it left the defence of France to the depleted forces of General Weygand. The old general put up a brave resistance but could do little to halt the German onslaught. By 14th June the Germans had occupied Paris, and on the 16th the Prime Minister, M. Reynaud, resigned in favour of the collaborationist, Marshal Pétain.

On 10th June, at a moment when a German victory was

already within sight, Mussolini declared his intention of coming into the war on the side of the Germans. Despite the fact that the Italians could play but an insignificant part in the campaign, Mussolini hoped to pick up some spoils, especially in French North Africa. Paul had consistently predicted this turn of events, as Sir Ronald Campbell, writing from the British Embassy in Paris, acknowledged: 'How right you were in so many, many things. I often think of that.'[18]

Mussolini's entry into the war brought with it a slight reduction in the risk that he would launch an independent attack on Yugoslavia. He was now, at least temporarily, occupied elsewhere. But Paul and his ministers had been badly frightened in March and April, and as a consequence had begun to look around for some protection and for a supply of arms. The Allies had refused to commit themselves and Paul had had no desire to make his country still more dependent on Germany. This left Russia, the only other power with enough influence to check an Italian move in the Balkans.

But for Yugoslavia to approach the U.S.S.R. for help there had to be a major reversal of policy. For twenty-two years the Yugoslav government had refused to recognize the Soviet Union. This was not altogether surprising. After the October Revolution and throughout the 1920s Yugoslavia had received many thousands of émigrés from Russia. These refugees had been welcomed for there were ties between the houses of Karageorgević and Romanov, and the two peoples shared a common Orthodox religion. Besides, the immigrant Russians soon became influential members of society for many of them were professional people—doctors, musicians, military experts and the like.

The existence of a strong Russian minority in Yugoslavia, coupled with the geographical proximity of the two countries, meant that news of the atrocities and murders filtered through with a regularity which fuelled the dread of Bolshevism. Paul himself subscribed to it wholeheartedly: he detested the regime and feared Soviet ambitions. But despite his personal views, Paul had realized back in 1939 that the time would come when he would have to seek a rapprochement. In preparation, he had approached his old friend Mr Strandtman who had once been the counsellor at the Imperial Russian Embassy and, since the Revolution, had continued to represent Tsarist Russia in Belgrade. Mr Strandtman had complied with Paul's request. He had removed the double eagle from over the door of his embassy and had announced that he was no longer acting as the representative of a government which no longer existed.

Shortly after these preparatory moves had been made, Russia invaded Finland. Unwilling to annoy the Allies, the Yugoslavs put off their formal rapprochement.

It was not until the Italian threat seemed imminent, in March 1940, that they began to reconsider it and this time seriously. Once the first move had been made progress was fast, for the Russians had their own reasons for favouring an agreement. On 15th April economic talks began between the two governments, and on 11th May a treaty, covering trade agreements, was signed. On 10th June the Russians agreed to open negotiations about the possibility of official recognition and on the 24th diplomatic relations were established between the two countries. The Yugoslav government chose as their Ambassador Milan Gavrilović, a leader of the Serbian Agrarian Party. His instructions were concise: to make the U.S.S.R. aware of the dangerous position of Yugoslavia and the Balkans; to obtain armaments, and, in case of Axis aggression against Yugoslavia, to secure the help of the Soviet army. Mr Gavrilović left for Moscow in July and in the same month the first ambassador from the U.S.S.R. arrived in Belgrade. If Paul did not exactly enjoy receiving him, Olga found it positively diabolical: 'I had the ordeal of receiving the Soviet Minister and wife at 11! I wore a cross round my neck which I held all the time.'[19]

Throughout the whole of July Paul and Olga waited for news that the Germans had invaded England. After the defeat of France, Hitler had assumed that Britain would sue for peace, leaving him free to pursue his aims in the East. He made what he considered to be a generous offer: he was prepared to recognize the British Empire provided Britain returned the German colonies and recognized German supremacy in Europe. Hitler waited for an answer. But he had misjudged the mood of the British people and he waited in vain.

On 19th July Hitler made a speech giving Britain a last chance. By this time he cannot really have expected to receive a response for he had already given orders for the invasion of Britain ('Operation Sea-Lion') three days earlier. Throughout the summer months the British expected an invasion any day, but it never came. Gradually Hitler realized that he was quite unprepared for the immense difficulties such a plan involved. Operation Sea-Lion was postponed in October and finally cancelled in January 1942. As a substitute Hitler put all his energy into a massive bombing campaign ('Operation Eagle') which had initially been planned to eliminate the R.A.F. as a prerequisite of invasion.

Far away, as it seemed, in Yugoslavia, Paul found it almost impossible to get accurate information. He was worried about the extent of the damage in England and had no means of knowing whether or not the German boasts were true. He longed for news, and was thrilled when, on 3rd July, a letter arrived from King George. But it was a disappointment, for it was not written in his friend's own casual style. It was stiff, long-winded and full of propaganda:

In the anxious times through which we are all passing my thoughts have often been with you and with the extremely difficult position in which you have found yourself. Although, happily, your country is still at peace, the entry of Italy into the war must have intensified many times over the special problems which you, as guardian of your people's security, have been called upon to face. Italy's attack is now directed against my Empire, but I realize that her belligerency has already involved momentous decisions for Yugoslavia, and I am deeply conscious of the anxieties which these must have caused you.

Here in England we have all admired the skill and foresight you have shown in guarding the policy of your country, and we are confident that you will succeed in maintaining this policy on the firm and independent lines you have chosen. I feel sure that you are right in holding that in this direction alone lies the best hope of maintaining Yugoslavia's honour and integrity. It is not an easy line to follow but, as I say, we understand the difficulties of the position and we are not under any illusions that such a policy carries with it any implication that in your country the cause of Germany and

Italy is regarded in the same light as that of my own peoples . . .

I think you may be interested to hear a little of our own efforts and prospects. The cruel fate which has overtaken France has in no way altered our determination to continue to the end of the struggle in which we are engaged, and never for one moment have we thought of laying down the burden that we now have to carry almost alone. There is today concentrated in Great Britain an army stronger than any this country has seen before. Another powerful army waits ready in the Middle East.

At sea, now that Italy has entered the war, the control by my Navy of the imports and exports of the enemy can not only be continued, but even accentuated. Good proof has already been furnished of our ability to keep open the line of supply to the forces which are stationed in the Middle East. East of Suez the Italian submarines have already been reduced, during the first twelve days that Italy has been at war, to one half the number that they were before . . .[20]

The letter had in fact been drafted at the Foreign Office, probably in a clumsy attempt to counteract the shock of the fall of France. It was precisely the sort of communication calculated to irritate the Prince Regent. He had looked forward to a letter from a friend. He had instead received a Foreign Office circular. What Paul missed most was the presence of people whose opinions he respected and from whom he could seek advice. In previous years, the British Legation had provided him with exactly this element of support. But now it was to all intents and purposes empty. Terence Shone had gone and Ronald Ian Campbell was unsuited to fill the personality gap left by his namesake and predecessor. Paul liked him well enough but he soon gave up hope of getting on confidential terms with him, or of enjoying his company as a friend.

It was difficult for Campbell, for he was used to sticking by the rules more rigidly than had Sir Ronald. Thus, when Paul asked him if he might see some confidential information, in return for all that he showed Campbell, the Minister referred the matter home. The reply was that Prince Paul could be shown certain papers but not those marked 'secret'. Since anything of the slightest importance or interest was marked 'secret', this was of little use. The outcome was that Paul learned to regard the new Minister as a man of negligible influence. This opinion was continually reinforced by the letters Paul received from Sir Ronald in Paris. These served to accentuate the differences between the two men. Sir Ronald's letters were affectionate, perceptive and full of the kind of harmless political gossip that brought Paul nearer to Europe and the centre of the war:

Thank you very much for your interesting and amusing letter. I should have answered it before, but I have been more than usually overwhelmed. Among other things we have just had one of our periodical visits from 'Winston'. He drops on us from the skies at one hour's notice—turns the house upside down, puts a stop to all work not directly connected with him, makes a vast hole in my cellar and departs in the same sort of whirlwind as that in which he arrived. At night he walks up and down my room like a caged lion till 2 a.m. expounding all his schemes for killing Germans and then goes off to bed leaving me to cope till 3 or 4 a.m. with the more pressing work on hand. But although exhausting, his visits are very stimulating.[21]

But Sir Ronald's letters ceased after he left France and Paul also lost Brugère, the French Ambassador, who left Belgrade broken and sad, and intent on giving up his career.

In August Paul and Olga were cheered by the arrival of their two sons. At the beginning of July, amidst talk of German invasion, the Foreign Minister had advised that it was no longer safe for them to be left in England, so their journey back to Yugoslavia had been arranged. They came via Lisbon and Vichy, and for three weeks their parents waited nervously for news of their safety. On 3rd August they reached Yugoslavia. It was the first time Paul had seen them for almost a year.

Immediately the atmosphere at Brdo lightened. Alexander was sixteen and Nicky twelve and they were both high spirited. To begin with tennis, swimming and shooting kept them occupied but soon reckless driving, tutor baiting and 'unsuitable' girls joined the list of amusements. Nicky was too young but

Alexander and Peter quickly became the greatest of friends in these exploits.

Even before the boys' arrival, Peter had spent much of his time with Paul and Olga. His mother, Queen Marie, had finally decided some time late in 1939 to stay in England for the duration of the war. She was living with another woman in Bedfordshire and suffering from an indeterminate 'nervous break-down' associated with a gallstone operation and the menopause. She wrote frequently to Paul, both for money and to describe her symptoms in the greatest detail. She had her two younger sons with her but seemed in no hurry to return to see Peter. Only occasionally did she refer to him in her letters and then usually in such a way as to put the responsibility firmly on Paul's shoulders. Fortunately, Paul's relations with his nephew had improved considerably. They had begun to discuss the future together and Paul had arranged for Peter to attend the Minister of Court's daily report, as a gradual introduction to the business of government. But even so, neither Paul nor Olga could feel very close to him—he seemed to be quite unlike their children.

Having the house full of young people and attempting to keep control over them was certainly a diversion from politics, but it was not the same as the Brdo house-parties of previous years. Most of all Paul missed the Kents. Georgie and Marina wrote almost every week and each time there was a bad air raid over London they sent a message of reassurance to Brdo.

As the end of July approached, so too the Kents began to realize that for the first time since their engagement they would be unable to come out to Slovenia: 'This is just one line for the boys to take with them. It's sad they are leaving—but I can imagine how you must feel about leaving them here and it is an added worry for you in a very difficult time with wild beasts all round you—and liable to fight each other over the morsels— what a hell of a world we live in—with evil pushing its way everywhere. . . . It's horrible to think that in only a week's time in ordinary years we should be leaving to see you all, and here we are stuck for ever.'[22]

Albrecht was still around and usually accompanied Paul and the boys on shooting expeditions. Olga's mother and Elizabeth and Toto came to stay. But Princess Nicholas was anxious about Italian intentions in Greece and with Elizabeth and Toto there was now a certain coolness. Relations were all right until the subject of politics came up and then the differences of opinions made things awkward. As Olga wrote in her diary: 'Talked a lot to Fael—discussed the situation quietly—alas, so much we see with different eyes.'[23] It was difficult for Olga, with one sister in England and the other in Germany, and a strain for Paul who found Toto's views unappetizing.

The Germans did not at all approve of Yugoslavia's new relations with the U.S.S.R., and Paul was under constant pressure from the German consul in Belgrade. Neuhausen was a close friend of Goering and his appointment had been chosen with care. The disapproval stemmed from the rivalry which had been growing throughout the summer between Germany and Russia. Each country suspected the other of trying to gain an unfair influence in the Balkans. Whilst Hitler was involved in the West, the Russians had occupied the territory which had come into their sphere of influence under the 1939 agreement. After the defeat of France Hitler determined to put a stop to Russian expansion. But before he could deal directly with the Russian threat, he had to settle matters in Europe. In July he quashed yet another of Mussolini's plans for attacking Yugoslavia and on 30th August he brought to an end the simmering dispute between Rumania and Hungary over the region of Transylvania. Having summoned the Foreign Ministers of the two countries to Vienna he dictated a settlement agreeable to the Axis powers. By the terms of this accord Rumania was forced to give up part of Transylvania to her northern neighbour.

When the Rumanian Foreign Minister first caught sight of the partition line on the map he fainted. When he returned home the Rumanian people were outraged. An attempt was made on King Carol's life and a military dictatorship took power. By 6th September the King had been forced to abdicate. Paul's reactions were mixed. King Carol had not been a popular king: he had abdicated once before, in 1925, after eloping with his mistress, and although he had returned in 1930, his treatment of his young, long-suffering and courageous wife, Helen, had given great offence. But although Paul disapproved of Carol's behaviour, he liked him as a man, and he was saddened by reports of his hasty and undignified departure.

Weeks later, Paul received a series of pathetic letters from Carol, who was being held in Spain regardless of the fact that the Portuguese had agreed to his establishing himself in their country. There was nothing Paul could do to exert pressure on the Spanish or Rumanian governments, but he was able to help in a small way by ensuring that King Carol's letters reached his son. Michael was nineteen when he was proclaimed King for the second time, and to help him rule the new government invited his mother, Princess Helen, back to Rumania. Sitta had lived an unsettled life since her marriage had been dissolved in 1928. At first she was thrilled to be going back in her capacity as Queen Mother. She telephoned Olga on her arrival in Bucharest to describe the fantastic reception she had received from the people as she drove through the town with Michael, in an open carriage. But before long the new military dictator, General Antonescu, began to show his true colours and by mid-September Sitta and Michael were living the lives of political prisoners with no court and no freedom of movement.

The fact that Antonescu was pro-Nazi, and from the start collaborated with the Axis, brought the German threat even closer to Yugoslavia's frontiers. For a year, Belgrade had been able to maintain its distance, for the attention of the main protagonists in the war had been elsewhere. But now, as autumn approached, the focus of their attention began to shift towards the Balkans and Greece.

In September 1940, relations between Hitler and Mussolini were at their best. Italy and Japan had just reaffirmed their mutual commitments by signing the 'Tripartite Pact' with Germany. But Hitler, at the signing, had kept the fact of his settlement of the Transylvania question from Mussolini. When, exactly one week after the signing ceremony was over, the Italian leader found out about it, he was furious. Accusing Hitler of acting behind his back, he determined to make an independent move to remind the Führer that, if nothing else, he was not conducting the war alone. On 15th October Mussolini issued orders for an attack on Greece and on 28th October Italian troops stationed in Albania marched into Greece.

For Yugoslavia, the Italian invasion of Greece was another step in the gradual encirclement by the Axis powers. It constituted, besides, an unprovoked attack by a common enemy on a friend and ally. But, short of declaring war on Italy, and risking retaliation from Germany and Hungary in the north, Yugoslavia could do nothing officially to help the Greeks. Unofficially, however, there was a lot of activity. A number of Yugoslav citizens were sympathetic to the Greek cause, including the owner of one of Yugoslavia's largest armament works. The government also was involved and so was the Prince Regent. Being married to a Greek princess he was more intimately involved with the Greek cause than most, and he had the best connections. He could communicate directly with King George or Prime Minister Metaxas, or pass messages to them indirectly through Olga's mother and other friends and relations.

In November and December 1940 the Greek army received armaments, food and all the horses that they required from the Yugoslavs. Through Paul, they also obtained permission to set up a secret supply depot on Yugoslav territory, and during the Albanian campaign hundreds of tons of materials left Yugoslavia for the Greek lines. But this was not all. Paul was able to use his country's official position to prevent the Germans sending supplies through Yugoslavia to the Italians in Albania. The Yugoslav Foreign Minister, Cincar-Marković, played his rôle of naïve neutral to such perfection that it was some time before an angry and frustrated German foreign ministry eventually decided that it was time for punishment. At Count Ciano's request, Ribbentrop cut off the supply of aviation materials to Yugoslavia.

The British government heartily approved of the Yugoslavs' declaration of neutrality. The last thing that the British wanted was for the Germans to be directly drawn in and they knew that this would happen if the Yugoslavs were to fall upon the Italians. To encourage Paul the Foreign Office drafted yet another letter from King George VI.

We have been thinking so much of you and Olga since I last wrote to you in July. So much has happened everywhere and the situation in your part of the world has become so much more critical in the last month. Italy's attack on Greece has brought the war nearer to you than ever before.

I know and realize how difficult your position is, and that

you may have to make concessions to the Axis on non-essential matters. At the same time I am sure you will never give way where the sovereignty of your country is concerned, and I do so admire the skill and patience with which you are conducting this very difficult policy.

I wonder whether you may think that now is a good moment, from your somewhat lonely geographical position, to talk to your courageous neighbour Greece, and also to Turkey, on the subject of closer co-operation with these two countries.

I know that you are badly in need of armaments of different kinds, and I only wish that it was possible for us to supply you with them at once. I am sure you realize that it is only a matter of time before we are in a position to do so. Owing to the tragic collapse of France, we lost much of our material, but I am glad to say we are now making up fast our losses, and will soon be able to supply the needs of others besides our own.

I am sending you with this letter some notes I have had collected from the various Departments, as I know it will please you to see why we are so sure of ultimate victory . . .

The notes on the 'British War Effort' were nothing but propaganda but the letter was more personal than the previous one and it ended with an endearing post-script which was genuinely from the King: 'P.S. I wear your wrist-watch every evening. I have changed the strap as you suggested, and it is a very good timekeeper.'[24]

The policy of neutrality had not been easily arrived at in Belgrade. On receiving the news that the Italians had crossed the Greek frontier Paul had summoned an emergency Crown Council.* Present at the meeting had been the Prince Regent, Prime Minister Cvetković, Foreign Minister Cincar-Marković, Minister of War General Nedić, Chief of Staff General Kosić and Minister of Court M. Antić. The subject of the discussion had been Salonika, and the general reaction one of alarm. They had all agreed that the Italians should not be allowed to capture the port, but they could not agree on what measures to take to prevent them doing so. Paul had favoured immediate mobilization

* The Crown Council acted as an executive committee of the cabinet.

on the southern border; Cvetković had supported him but had suggested that they should not react too hastily; General Nedić had advocated waiting until the Germans had made their position clear.

Although no decision had been reached on 28th October, the Crown Council generated a series of events which were to have important consequences. Two members of the Council, Milan Antić and General Nedić engaged in a little private enterprise. After the meeting, the General sent instructions to the Yugoslav military attaché in Berlin to test out the German reaction to a Yugoslav march on Salonika. Although the military attaché was surprised by the nature of the telegram, which violated all coding rules and appeared to be from General Nedić rather than from Kosić, the Chief of General Staff, with whom he normally communicated, he carried out the necessary investigations. His reply was clear enough: Italy would not negotiate but Germany might be willing to mediate in Yugoslavia's favour, in return for the right to make certain demands on her.

A few days later Nedić was dismissed. Though his scheme was short-lived, the Germans had been accurately alerted to the fact that Salonika might be a useful lever in any future negotiations with Yugoslavia and they were soon in a position to make use of this.

It was not General Nedić's involvement in the Salonika plan that brought about his summary dismissal, for at the time Paul was unaware of the secret communications. Rather, it was the result of a conversation which the General had with Paul over the Italian bombing, 'by mistake', of a town within Yugoslav territory. Paul had been disturbed by Nedić's slow reaction to this act of aggression and had asked to see him to obtain an explanation. During the conversation Nedić propounded the view that Yugoslavia had reached a point in the war at which she should state her position. He thought that if she ceded a small part of her territory to Germany the Axis would spare the rest. Paul was almost as angry as he had been with Stojadinović over the scheme to divide Albania with Italy, and when General Nedić continued with the opinion that Yugoslavia would have no need for an army if she had a clever diplomatic policy, Paul asked for his resignation. In 1941 General Nedić was to become the Marshal Pétain of Yugoslavia.

To replace Nedić Paul chose General Pešić, the man he had sent for talks with military leaders in London and Paris in July 1939. Pešić was considered anti-German and his appointment pleased the British as much as it displeased the Germans.*[25] Pešić was a man of action and an optimist, but he had taken over at a bad time. As November progressed so Yugoslavia's position worsened. By 23rd November, both Rumania and Hungary had agreed to sign the Tripartite Pact. Out of Yugoslavia's neighbours this left only two, Bulgaria and Greece, outside the Axis camp. At the best of times Bulgaria was an unreliable friend, and Greece was already under attack.

On the day that Rumania signed the Tripartite Pact, Mr Campbell telegraphed to the Foreign Office that Yugoslavia was exposed to 'the immediate possibility of most severe Axis pressure'. He asked the Foreign Office to do something to 'strengthen the hands of the Prince Regent and other staunch elements'.[26] On the request, Winston Churchill minuted: 'The moment is appropriate and the action needful. . . . Is there any aid and assistance we can give them, except by carrying on the war by ourselves as we are doing? If we cannot promise any effective material aid, we can at any rate assure them that, just as we did last time, we will see their wrongs are righted in the eventual victory.'

The British could not promise any effective material aid. Land forces were out of the question, air assistance could only be given over southern Yugoslavia and the Navy were uncertain whether or not it would be possible to keep open the supply line through the port of Salonika. The reply to Mr Campbell's request was inevitably vague: 'If the Yugoslav government and people should be called upon to defend again their freedom and independence, they may rest assured that H.M.G. will make a common cause with them. Yugoslavia will be fighting side by side with us and our allies and we could look forward once again to achieving a victory by our joint effort that would secure to Yugoslavia all her rights and interests.'[27]

By this time too, the first of many 'invitations' had arrived

* In the Epilogue of her book *Black Lamb and Grey Falcon* (page 1134) Rebecca West mistakenly says Nedić 'was replaced by a pro-Axis General'. (See pages 290 to 292 below.)

from Hitler. The Prince Regent had been asked to Berlin. Paul refused to go, but sent his Foreign Minister instead. On 28th November Cincar-Marković left for Fuschl, with instructions to avoid committing his country to anything at all. Hitler did his utmost to persuade Cincar-Marković that Yugoslavia should sign a non-aggression pact with Germany and Italy. In return he promised to give Salonika to the Yugoslavs and to demand no transit rights through Yugoslavia. But Cincar-Marković did not give way: he left Hitler with a vague assurance that his country would consider the offers and send a reply through the German Minister in Belgrade. For once, Yugoslavia was in quite a strong position. Just before Cincar-Marković left for Germany the Russians had announced that they were willing to supply all the war material that the Yugoslavs could want and, in addition, the Italians had suffered such a series of defeats in Albania that the chance of their actually reaching Salonika was remote.

Hitler was unsure of the outcome of the interview as his note to Mussolini indicates: 'Yugoslavia: I've had a talk with Yugoslav Foreign Minister Marković. I sought to render obvious to him that his only chance is in joining the Axis—which will win this war in one way or another—in a relationship of close friendship. . . . I've by-passed talking of a German-Italian guarantee but have indicated a possibility of a non-aggression pact. . . . Whether now we will be successful in winning Yugoslavia, whose benevolent neutrality is very important, I wouldn't know. As soon as I receive an answer from Belgrade, or another conversation comes about, I will inform you, Duce, at once by a communication to this effect.'[28]

The position was not much clearer when the answer from Belgrade finally arrived on 7th December: 'Yugoslavia is willing to discuss with the Reich government and the Italian government the possibilities of signing a non-aggression pact.'[29] In making this announcement the Yugoslav government clearly hoped to be able to play for time a little longer.

To understand why Hitler, who had been so impatient to get an answer, took no notice of the Yugoslav reply until late December it is necessary to trace the development of German policy throughout the autumn of 1940.

At the end of the summer Hitler had decided not to carry out the invasion of England, but to transfer the war to the Mediterranean and to defeat the British in Egypt. This was his Peripheral Strategy. When he first heard that Mussolini planned to invade Greece Hitler had had no objections. In fact he had considered the move quite useful as it fitted in well with his Peripheral Strategy—the Italian occupation of Greece would have shifted the balance of power in the Eastern Mediterranean significantly in favour of the Axis. But, from the very outset, news of the Italian invasion was disappointing. Not only was it slow but it was also in the wrong direction: south towards the strategically useless region of Epirus instead of north to Salonika. Angered by the complete incompetence of the Italians, Hitler began to look for a means to carry out his Peripheral Strategy despite them. When, on 12th November, plans for the peripheral operation were finally drawn up in Directive 18, orders for the invasion of Greece were included. These orders were specifically directed against the British. The German plan was to invade Greece in order to obtain air bases for use against the British in the Mediterranean. The route was to be from the north, through Bulgaria.

The Bulgarian operation was not a simple one. First, the Germans had to persuade King Boris to allow the passage of German troops through Bulgaria, something which Boris was under heavy pressure from the U.S.S.R. and Britain not to do. And secondly, supposing Boris did agree, they had to get the troops to Bulgaria and ensure their safe passage through the country. In both these last matters Yugoslavia was a factor.

In conveying troops to Bulgaria the Germans had two potential routes. One was through Hungary and Rumania, the other through Austria and Yugoslavia. The latter was infinitely shorter and easier. It meant that troops could travel by rail from Austria, via Belgrade, directly into Sofia, cutting by half the distance they would have to cover by road once in Bulgaria. The Germans reckoned that if the Yugoslavs could be coerced to grant them rights of transit, the build-up of troops on the Greek border would take four weeks less than if the Hungary–Rumania route had to be utilized. Furthermore, even if Yugoslavia did not actively co-operate, it was vital to the Germans that she should, at the very least, remain neutral. The German route through Bulgaria lay parallel to the border with

Yugoslavia for hundreds of miles, and the Bulgarian railway which the Germans planned to use came, for much of its length, within thirteen miles of the Yugoslav border and, at its closest point, within six miles.

It was in an attempt to settle these questions that Hitler had invited the Yugoslavs to Berlin on 28th November. Sensing the level of resistance, he had not pressed for rights of transit but instead had gone all out for a non-aggression pact. This would at least have ensured the safety of his troops within Bulgaria and, at the time, speed was not of overriding importance.

But when the Yugoslavs replied nine days later that they would be willing to consider a non-aggression pact Hitler, surprisingly, took no notice. Though the Yugoslavs were not to know it, there had been, in the short interval, a major shift in German policy. Hitler had shelved his Peripheral Strategy and had decided to give absolute priority to an attack on Russia, in the spring of 1941. He had always planned one day to turn on Russia, but his decision at the end of November, to attack as soon as possible, was reached after his attempts to draw the Russians into a grand coalition against the British had failed. The Russians had agreed in principle but had not accepted Hitler's terms. At the end of November they had produced their own, and these Hitler was not prepared to countenance.

This fundamental change in German policy put the conflict in Greece into a new perspective. Hitler had lost all interest in the Eastern Mediterranean, but at the same time needed, more than ever before, a stable situation in the Balkans. Above all, he did not want the British in Greece with the threat of a Salonika front developing in the future. Suddenly, Mussolini's blunders had become a major obstacle.

Hitler's first reaction was to try to settle the Greek question by diplomatic means. But his offers of peace were refused. The Greeks were flushed with success by their victories over the Italians and they were encouraged to stand firm by the British who had their own reasons for not wanting German mediation in the Italo-Greek conflict. For one thing the commitment in Greece diverted the Italians from Egypt, for another it gave the British an opportunity to establish air bases in the Eastern Mediterranean. Because of the rejection of his peace offer, Hitler was forced to fall back on military means. He had been prepared for such an eventuality: On 13th December he had signed Directive 20 for 'Operation Marita' and on 18th December he had signed Directive 21 for 'Operation Barbarossa'. The former was for an attack on Greece, the latter for an attack on Russia and the two were interdependent. The strategy for Greece contained in Directive 20 had a very different purpose from the earlier one set forth in Directive 18. It was a preliminary to the Russian campaign rather than part of the war against Britain, and it was primarily defensive rather than offensive. Its aim was to secure the southern flank in readiness for Operation Barbarossa.

The difference in emphasis between Directive 18 and Directive 20 was to affect Yugoslavia. Whilst Hitler was pursuing his Peripheral Strategy he had been prepared to accept a non-aggression pact with Yugoslavia. But with the prospect of Operation Barbarossa in the spring, it became essential for him to complete Marita as swiftly as possible. This being the case, a non-aggression pact with Yugoslavia was no longer enough for it meant that Yugoslavia would be able to close her frontiers to the passage of German troops and war materials. On the other hand, an agreement which gave Germany the right of transit and thus the use of the Yugoslav railways would mean a time schedule for Marita of six weeks instead of ten. This was an advantage which the Germans could not afford to ignore and it was what lay behind the telegram which Ribbentrop sent to his minister in Belgrade on 21st December 1940: 'The Führer and I . . . gave consideration to the proposal that a non-aggression pact be concluded between Germany, Italy and Yugoslavia . . . the conclusion of such a pact would of course not meet the specifications for the strengthening of Yugoslavia's relations with the Axis powers that we had envisaged in the conversations with Cincar-Marković at the Berghof and Fuschl.'[30]

From December 1940, it became imperative for Germany to secure the right of transit for their troops and war materials through Yugoslavia. For Yugoslavia and for the Prince Regent such a concession was—and would always remain—completely out of the question.

CHAPTER XI

JANUARY–MARCH 1941
Regency V
The Tripartite Pact

1941 was the year that Paul had looked forward to as the last of his regency, for Peter's eighteenth birthday was in September. However, he had little time to contemplate his plans for the future.

He and his ministers had ignored the menacing note from Ribbentrop which had arrived in Belgrade in late December, but they could not so easily ignore the German troops which were moving into Rumania. If the Germans joined forces with the Italians in Greece, their country would be surrounded and virtually defenceless. Britain had failed to provide Yugoslavia with arms; the magnanimous offer from the U.S.S.R. had never materialized; and the German supply had ceased in November 1940, at about the same time that the war minister General Nedić had been dismissed and that Cincar-Marković had refused the Italians the right to transport war materials across Yugoslav territory.

To make things worse, the internal political divisions were growing instead of diminishing in the face of external threat. Cvetković and Maček were working in closer harmony, but, in spite of all his efforts, Cvetković had been unable to gain any real support among the Serbs. His party, the J.R.Z., was weak in comparison with some of the older Serb opposition parties. Their leaders were, in many cases, ambitious men who hoped to utilize the reactionary Serb element to their own advantage. The Serb Democratic party was a case in point. The two leaders had hoped for the posts of premier and foreign minister, respectively. When Cvetković refused to give in to their claims, the Democratic Party reversed its policy of twenty years and attacked the agreement with the Croats.

Paul had reached one of his lowest points and, in desperation, had drafted a letter of resignation at the end of 1940. In faultless Serbian, it read as follows:

More than six years have passed since the tragic events of October 1934 put me at the head of this state and placed on my shoulders a heavy burden. I doubt that more fateful events have ever happened in the history of the world than in this short period. From all these difficult and dangerous situations Yugoslavia has emerged unharmed. My main aim has always been to reconcile the domestic disagreements and passions and to keep peace on the borders. In connection with this I have made every effort to preserve the dignity of Yugoslavia. Today I have the peace of mind of having done what I considered to be in the best interest of our country. I think that throughout the world all countries, without exception, look upon Yugoslavia as one solid, sound and independent state. However, I have always intended to remain in this position only so long as I am able to serve my country. Unfortunately, I have come to the conclusion that my further presence at the head of the state is no longer in the best interest. I do not wish to go into the polemics because I do not consider this an appropriate moment. I can only say that I have failed—perhaps through my own mistakes—to inspire confidence in those who should have been my closest collaborators and from whom it would have been natural to expect support. I believe the future of this country lies in the fraternity and the understanding of the three peoples (Serbs, Croats, and Slovenes) gathered in concord round their King.[1]

Paul had always been especially sensitive to gossip and intrigue. He felt increasingly isolated at home, his health and confidence were near breaking point and the bloody turmoil of war seemed to swirl ever closer to Yugoslavia's frontiers. In a sense the resignation note was Paul's Gethsemane. He knew that appalling decisions lay ahead and he longed for the cup to be taken from him. But it was not to be. The moment his counsellors heard what he proposed to do they gathered round to dissuade him. They spent hours urging him to remain and in the end he grudgingly gave in. He knew, as well as they, that he could scarcely abandon Peter at such a time.

Until January 1941, Paul had at least been able to count on one important factor: the interests of Yugoslavia had never crossed those of Britain. Throughout his regency Paul had been anxious for one thing above all else: to discharge his duties in a manner consistent with his British training, friends and emotional allegiance. His evenings with successive British Ministers, his diligence in keeping them at all times well informed, had been prompted not only by his need for kindred companionship but by a deeper reverence for British standards and values.

But at 6.00 p.m. on 12th January, this state of affairs came to an end. On instructions from the Foreign Office, Campbell called on Paul to inform him that Churchill had decided that mere neutrality was not enough. The British were going to send a mechanized force to Greece and proposed to form a united Balkan front.

Paul was horrified. He considered the plan impetuous, irresponsible and doomed to failure. The landing of British troops in Greece would provoke Hitler into a Balkan offensive. Britain would call for a Yugoslav act of suicide and in the end the whole of the Balkans would be overrun.

It was the arrogance which infuriated him. As neighbours of Greece, both Yugoslavia and Turkey would have no choice but to become involved. Yet neither country had been consulted. For once Paul could not contain himself. He completely lost his temper and dismissed Campbell with the words 'this stinks of Anthony'.[2]

In fact, the plan did not originate with H.M. Secretary of State for War. It was Winston Churchill's decision rather than Anthony Eden's and it was based on political rather than military considerations. Churchill had already decided to support the Greeks and, as he minuted on Campbell's report from Belgrade, Prince Paul's views left him quite 'unchanged'. 'Prince Paul's attitude,' he wrote, 'looks like that of an unfortunate man in a cage with a tiger, hoping not to provoke him while steadily dinner time approaches.'[3]

Churchill's attitude towards the Balkans had changed considerably since 1938. When, in that year, Hitler had marched into Vienna, Churchill had spoken in the Commons, warning of the threat posed to the countries of the Little Entente: 'Rumania has the oil, Yugoslavia has the minerals and raw materials. Both have large armies and both are mainly supplied with munitions from Czechoslovakia. . . . A wedge has been driven into the heart of what is called the Little Entente, *this group of countries which have as much right to live in Europe unmolested as any of us have the right to live unmolested in our native land.'*[4]

When in April 1939, Albania had been overrun, Churchill had foreseen the dangers which lay ahead for Greece and Yugoslavia. On that day he had written to Neville Chamberlain, the Prime Minister: 'What is now at stake is nothing less than the whole of the Balkan peninsula. *If these States remain exposed to German and Italian pressure while we appear, as they may deem it, incapable of action, they will be forced to make the best terms possible with Berlin and Rome.* How forlorn then will our position become! We shall be committed to Poland and thus involved in the East of Europe, while at the same time cutting off from ourselves all hope of that large alliance which once effected might spell salvation.'[5]

Until the beginning of 1941, Yugoslavia had been allowed to live 'unmolested'. Unable to obtain any assistance from Britain, France or the United States, her ministers had indeed been forced, within certain limits, to make the best terms possible with Berlin. Now, for reasons not explained to Paul, the British were bent on a foolish and tragic undertaking. An undertaking which London, with brilliant understatement, referred to as 'a sideshow' in the Mediterranean theatre of war.

The reasons for British intervention in Greece were prompted by the need to raise morale in London and, pressing the advantage gained by Wavell's successful military operations in North Africa, to engage as many German troops in northern Greece as possible.

Early in 1941, British victories against the Italians in North East Africa had swept Wavell through Bardia, Tobruk, Benghazi and El Agheila, covering 500 miles in two months

* Authors' italics.

and taking him to the borders of Tripolitania. With the loss of 438 British troops Wavell had effectively wiped out ten Italian divisions. The Sudan had been cleared of Italian troops, Italian Somaliland had been overrun and British Somaliland regained. Eritrea had been invaded by British armies and in Abyssinia a patriotic uprising had been stimulated and fed by British officers and arms.

In the Balkans, the picture was very different. Rumania was already a German satellite and Hitler, having amassed an army on the Rumanian/Bulgarian border, expected Bulgaria to succumb with equal ease. When on 1st March King Boris signed the Tripartite Pact the German troops were, at last, within striking distance of Salonika.

It was precisely at this time that it suddenly became an unchangeable feature of British military and diplomatic policy to use the breathing space provided by Wavell's successes in North East Africa to send troops to Greece, to form a Yugoslav/Greek/Turkish alliance, and to engage German troops in the southern part of the Balkan peninsula. The northern provinces and the greater part of the land mass of Yugoslavia would of course have to be sacrificed; the Yugoslav army could, however, be expected to advance south to Albania to trap the Italian army facing Greece. As Eden wrote from Athens on 24th February, to the Prime Minister: 'The President of Council, after reaffirming the determination of Greece to defend herself against Germany, reiterated the misgivings of the Greek government lest insufficient British help should merely precipitate German attack and stated that it was essential to determine whether available Greek forces, and forces which we could provide, would suffice to constitute efficacious resistance to the Germans.'[6]

With Yugoslav help, it was thought possible to hold a line from the mouth of the Nestos to Veles in the extreme south of Serbia, just covering Salonika. If Yugoslavia was unable to help, the only line that could be held that could give time for withdrawal of troops from Albania would be a line west of the Vardar, through Olympus—Edessa—Kajmačalan.

On 12th February, Anthony Eden, Secretary of State for War, and General Dill, Chief of Imperial General Staff, set off for Cairo with sealed orders from Churchill first to 'send speedy succour to Greece' and second 'to make Yugoslavia and Turkey fight or do the best they could'.[7] These instructions, as Eden knew full well, marked a change in attitude. Where before, Yugoslav neutrality had sufficed, now she was to be asked to fight. It was this new demand that Paul found unacceptable.

In stark contrast to his views in April 1939, and as a consequence of the appalling responsibilities and exigencies of war, Churchill had been driven to the conclusion that it was the right of a great power to sacrifice a smaller neutral state for the sake of ultimate victory. The British accordingly required Prince Paul to adopt 'the right strategic plan, i.e. abandonment of Croatia and withdrawal to old Serbia'.[8] Churchill, thinking in terms of pre-World War I Serbia, saw a golden opportunity for the gallant Serbs to attack the Italian rear flank in Albania—crushing the Italians and releasing arms for use in Yugoslavia. But Paul, after what must have seemed to him a lifetime's effort to bring Serbs, Croats and Slovenes together, viewed things very differently. He was Regent of the Kingdom of Yugoslavia, not Serbia, and considered it his duty to do what was in the best interests of all his people. He could not abandon the Croats and Slovenes in order to further a British cause, however much he believed it to be right.

Over the next few weeks a totally demoralized and lonely Prince Regent was to try in vain to explain his position to the British. But he did not only have the British to think about. Whether he liked it or not, Paul had also to negotiate with Hitler.

On 14th February, the Yugoslav Prime Minister and Foreign Minister travelled to Salzburg. The initiative for the meeting had come from the Yugoslavs and was prompted by the number of German troops that were streaming into Rumania. Hitler had taken it up after receiving a message from his generals about the very slow rate at which the build-up for Operation Marita was proceeding. The generals were pressing for the use of the Yugoslav railways. However, in the meetings of 14th February, neither Ribbentrop nor Hitler were able to extract any promises from the Yugoslavs. Instead, they were forced to listen to Cvetković's own schemes for keeping the peace in the Balkans. Ribbentrop, particularly, found himself in an embarrassing position. He had maintained that all the Germans wanted to do was prevent an extension of the war and that they were being hindered in this noble aim by British aggression in Greece. If, Cvetković replied, throwing the British out of Greece was Germany's objective, Yugoslavia would be willing to assist: she could try to mediate for a diplomatic solution to the Italian-Greek war and then construct a neutral Balkan bloc, also including Turkey, with the aim of keeping the British out. The pre-requisite, of course, was that Germany should also stay out. What did the Reich's Foreign Minister think of such a plan?[9]

The Reich's Foreign Minister did not think much of it—and nor did Hitler. But Cvetković refused to be bullied and the question of right of transit through Yugoslavia never arose. However, Cvetković knew that he had merely stalled. This became all the more apparent when Hitler turned to him as he left and asked if perhaps the Prince Regent might come to Berchtesgaden.

For Hitler, the meeting of 14th February was most unsatisfactory. He had gained nothing from Cvetković and shortly afterwards had had to face further questions from his generals about the possibility of troop transportation through Yugoslavia. For the Yugoslavs it was also unsatisfactory. Although they had successfully evaded the issue of joining the Tripartite Pact, German troops were getting nearer and stronger every day. Paul had ordered the mobilization of 700,000 troops on the eastern border with Bulgaria, but he knew that they could not hold out for long on their own. In a last attempt to discover whether the British would give Yugoslavia any aid in the event of a German attack, Paul turned to Campbell. He asked if British troops, then on their way to Greece, would be able to stay in Greece as long as they were needed. He got no reply. Mr Campbell was only prepared to give the standard Foreign Office line that Britain believed that the Balkan States could successfully resist the Germans if Greece, Yugoslavia and Turkey would only stand together. In other words he could promise no immediate military support or supply of arms. It was clear to Paul that if he refused to sign the Tripartite Pact, after an ultimatum date which would no doubt soon be delivered, he would be sacrificing his people. His only hope was to play for time and hope that things might somehow change.

Eden made his first direct approach to Paul on 22nd February. It was an appeal to Paul to make a statement about his government's position. Paul replied that he would not allow Axis troops to pass through Yugoslavia but he remained non-committal about what Yugoslavia would do in the event of a German move through Bulgaria against Greece. This was not enough for the British. They wanted the Yugoslavs to fight even if their country was not invaded. From 27th February, when he received Paul's reply, to 24th March, when he left for London, Eden made repeated attempts to speak with Paul in person. He approached the Prince Regent by letter and through Mr Campbell and the sense of urgency in his messages suggests that he placed great importance on a meeting. 'Mr Eden states that he would greatly value a meeting which would enable him to give you information which he cannot communicate in any other way . . .'[10] 'I have received further telegrams from Mr Eden dispatched at 6 p.m. on 28th February, and at 11.50 on 1st March, instructing me to make a further pressing appeal in favour of a meeting between your Royal Highness and him.'[11]

Eden declared himself ready to fall in with any suggestion that Paul should make as regards a place and time for the meeting but Paul steadfastly refused all invitations. At the time, and afterwards, Paul claimed that it would have been too risky, that it would have given the Germans an excuse for an ontright invasion of Yugoslavia. Although this may have been part of the reason, it was not the whole one. Paul knew only too well what the British wanted him to do, and that he almost certainly would not be able to do it. He also knew Eden, and that Eden would neither try to understand his argument nor realize how painful it was for him to have to defend it. This being the case, there was no point in their meeting. It was this decision to keep Eden at arm's length that gave grounds for the view, subsequently put about, that the Prince Regent had cooled towards Britain.

Having failed to make any headway by approaching Paul directly, Eden turned his attention more and more to the Turkish-Yugoslav negotiations. Some time towards the end of January the Turkish government, prompted by the British, had approached the Yugoslav government about plans for a common policy in the event of German aggression in the

Balkans. The initial instructions which the Turkish Minister of Foreign Affairs had sent to the Turkish Ambassador in Belgrade for communication to the Yugoslav Minister of Foreign Affairs read as follows:

According to information reaching him, arrival of German troops in Rumania increases daily. The object of these concentrations is not clearly known and various possibilities suggest themselves, namely (a) that although Germany entertains no idea of aggression, the concentration is designed to afford support for pressure and imposition on one or more Balkan States (b) it is designed for an attack on one or more Balkan States (c) it is a preparation for an attack on the Soviet (d) it has a defensive purpose and is designed as a precaution against all eventualities (e) its object is to establish Germany more firmly in Rumania for the purpose of exploitation of that country. (a) and (b) are of immediate concern both to Turkey and Yugoslavia and the Turkish government considers Turkish and Yugoslav governments should get into touch in regard to protection against these two possibilities, and work together to arrive at a [plan] of operation and action. The Turkish government enquire whether the Yugoslav government share this view and if this is the case whether the latter will [name] time, place and procedure for the conversations . . .[12]

The Yugoslav reply was described as being 'neither negative nor positive but rather negative'.[13] Understandably, this was regarded as unhelpful by both the Turks and the British. After about a week it was discovered that the original message had been muddled by the Turkish Ambassador in Belgrade and that the part about aiming at a 'community of decision and action' had been left out entirely. This went a long way to explaining the Yugoslav attitude, but by then it was too late. The Foreign Office and Sir Hughe Knatchbull-Hugessen, the British Ambassador in Ankara, had become impatient.

Over the next few weeks little progress was made, although telegrams passed in all directions between Yugoslavia, Turkey and the British Foreign Office. The main difficulty lay in the fact that each country accused the other of having failed to define its position clearly enough. In addition to this, the Yugoslavs had a number of specific objections about the degree of 'formalism' appropriate for the talks. As Cincar-Marković explained to Mr Campbell, 'formal negotiations or an agreement would be equivalent to making Yugoslavia an ally of Great Britain and Greece who were belligerents and it was inconsiderate of Turkey to have made the suggestion'.[14] The quibbles about what the Turks meant by a 'specially authorized person' to conduct the negotiations and other such matters of procedure so annoyed Knatchbull-Hugessen that on the 15th February 1941, he sent a strongly worded telegram to the Foreign Office and to Belgrade, which concluded:

> It is utterly unreasonable to expect the Turkish government to listen to such arguments:
> (a) 'Formalism' of Turks is imaginary, Minister of Foreign Affairs having assured me that he will entertain any proposals put to him by Yugoslav government on less 'formal' issues.
> (b) Idea that Turkish government wish Yugoslav government to send a 'special negotiator' has no justification. Yugoslav Ambassador here or anyone else should have authority to discuss matter on hand.
> (c) Nor does it appear from this end that Yugoslav Ambassador has as yet received necessary instructions.
> (d) Turkish position should be as clear as daylight. See Ankara telegram No . . .

The conclusion of this telegram was that '. . . if shilly shallying on part of Yugoslav government continues it will have worst possible effect here'.[15]

The Foreign Office joined with Knatchbull-Hugessen in putting all the blame on the Yugoslavs. Their attitude to Prince Paul had hardened a lot over the last two months. His code name remained 'F' for 'Friend', but he was no longer referred to as a 'staunch element' as he had been in November. On the contrary, the idea that he was a 'very weak character' had begun to creep into Foreign Office minutes. Paul and his government were accused of deliberately misunderstanding the Turkish approach and of picking on minor points in order to avoid conversations.

14. Foreign Secretaries meet. Dr Stojadinović with Anthony Eden at Victoria railway station, 1937.

15. Prince Paul, Regent of Yugoslavia, leaving the Elysée Palace after being received by President Lebrun, 1939, accompanied by French officials.

16. An uncomfortable drive: state visit to Germany, June 1939.

17. Prince Paul's eldest son, Alexander, getting his RAF wings.

18. Prime Minister Cvetković, c. 1940.

Although Campbell endeavoured to point out that the Turks were not entirely without blame, his reports carried little weight compared with the tirades from Knatchbull-Hugessen.

The Yugoslav reluctance to rush headlong into negotiations with the Turks was not unreasonable. In spite of Knatchbull-Hugessen's protestations to the contrary, the Turks had not made their position clear. The British certainly believed that because the Turkish government had asked for conversations to take place to devise common action in the event of a German attack, it had thereby given indisputable evidence of its readiness to take such action. The Yugoslavs thought otherwise. They had had considerable experience in negotiating with the Turks and they were not so trusting. Furthermore, Paul had heard a report of the Turkish Ambassador's views on the subject. In a talk with Mr Subbotić the latter had expressed the opinion that Turkey could not be counted on, and that the U.S.S.R. might become a threat in Asia if Turkey were to intervene as a result of German entry into Bulgaria.[16] In addition, on 17th February, the Turkish government had renewed a non-aggression pact with Bulgaria. This was not a move likely to inspire Yugoslav confidence for it effectively cleared the way for the Germans to invade Thrace. The threat of a Turkish attack had been even more of an obstacle to the Germans than that of a Yugoslav attack, and Hitler had been prepared to wage war on Turkey as well as on Greece. In the event, he did not have to. When the German troops crossed into Bulgaria on 2nd March the Turkish Foreign Minister, Mr Sarajoglu, received the Führer's reassurances 'in a very friendly way'.[17]

From the moment that King Boris signed the Tripartite Pact, Yugoslav opposition was all that lay between Hitler and Greece. Paul had received an invitation to visit Berchtesgaden and he knew what Hitler would demand. A few days before, Cvetković had sent him a document drafted by himself and the Minister of Justice, Konstantinović, summarizing the various possibilities. The two men had hoped that a thorough analysis of Yugoslavia's position from the German point of view would reveal a solution, but they had worked in vain. One after another they had listed hypothetical German proposals as 'unacceptable', 'totally unacceptable', and at the end they had been forced to conclude: 'It is better for us to be directly attacked than to be slowly tormented. Although our end would be the same in both cases, the means of attaining this end would not be the same. If we are attacked and we resist, our honour will be served, and this will mean something at the time the war is over.'[18]

Paul had agreed wholeheartedly with the document, little knowing that it would devolve on him to act it out in front of Hitler. Reluctant as he was to go to Berchtesgaden, there was no alternative. Cvetković, Cincar-Marković and Maček all begged him to go. After a long cabinet meeting at which the Cvetković-Konstantinović document was used as a basis for discussion, Paul left for Brdo.

On 4th March 1941, he journeyed secretly to Berchtesgaden. There he spent five hours with Adolf Hitler. Ribbentrop was also present but only as an interpreter on the odd occasion when Paul needed help with his German. The conversation was entirely between Paul and Hitler and the subject was the Tripartite Pact. Hitler did his utmost to persuade Paul to sign, while Paul produced countless reasons why it would be impossible for him to do so. For a start, he said (with reference to Italy) that he would not remain Regent for a week if his government were to sign a military alliance with the country whose leader had murdered King Alexander. But Hitler waived these objections aside. Throughout the interview he remained calm, self-possessed and sure of victory. Only twice did emotion break through, once in anger and once in a rambling, partly incoherent monologue denouncing the tragedy of war between Britain and Germany. His eyes became misty as he described how it disturbed him to think of a 'pretty' English boy lying dead on the battlefield beside a 'beautiful' young German.

This curious aside of the Führer's, which Paul interpreted as a manifestation of the man's inherent homosexuality, was probably designed either to appeal to Paul or to relieve the pressure. But Hitler did not relieve the pressure again. Even the objection that it would be quite impossible for Yugoslavia to sign the Tripartite Pact because of its military clauses, was sidestepped, for Hitler immediately offered to omit them.

Hitler had given way on virtually every point but Paul still refused to sign the Pact. He explained to his host that the decision was too serious for him to make on the spot, that he would have to consult his cabinet and that for this he would need more time.

Although for years afterwards it was to be put about that at this meeting Paul had capitulated and that, having capitulated, he had returned to Belgrade to urge his cabinet to do likewise, the records paint a different picture. Paul's own explanation for the start of this rumour was as follows:

On leaving Berchtesgaden to gain my own train which I left at a small station (I forget the name) I was accompanied by a tall red-haired man called Von Doornberg, a kind of master of ceremonies and not a political person. When we departed he immediately started bombarding me with questions, 'Were you pleased with your visit, what did you think of the Führer?' etc., etc. The whole thing was so obvious and I had no intention of discussing politics with him—I naturally said I was very pleased with my visit and that the Führer had been quite charming, etc! What I felt in my heart was different but I wasn't to let him know it, especially as I left convinced that war was inevitable but that we had to gain time to be able to mobilize.[19]

Faced with the realization that neutrality was no longer an option, Paul resolved to fight rather than to sign the Tripartite Pact. Yet two days later, at a hastily summoned Crown Council, he changed his opinion.

Present at this meeting on 6th March 1941, were Paul and his co-regents Stanković and Perović; Prime Minister Cvetković; Foreign Minister Cincar-Marković; Minister of War Pešić; Minister of Court Antić; Vice Premier Maček the Croat; and Kuloveć, the Slovene. Paul opened the session with an account of his conversation with Hitler. Cincar-Marković followed with an analysis of Yugoslavia's position with respect to Germany and then the meeting was thrown open. Two or three of the Council members expressed their opinions immediately: Kuloveć, the Slovene, in favour of signing; Cvetković and Stanković against. Then Maček brought the arguments into focus. He turned to Cincar-Marković and asked him to tell the Council frankly whether refusal to sign would really mean war with the Axis. The Foreign Minister said it would. Maček then turned to General Pešić and asked for a breakdown of Yugoslavia's prospects in the event of war. The old General spoke calmly and with authority: in the event of war the Germans would very soon be in possession of the entire northern part of Yugoslavia including the three main cities, Belgrade, Zagreb and Ljubljana. The army would have to withdraw to the mountains of Bosnia and Hercegovina where it could exist for about six weeks. After that there would be no food or ammunition, and there was little chance of any aid, for the British were not in a position to give substantial military help and had admitted as much. At this point, said Pešić, the army would be forced to capitulate.

Pešić's speech provoked an immediate response from the Croat and the Slovene. Maček declared that he could not allow Croatia to be overrun whilst the Serbs retreated to the mountains in the south, and Kuloveć followed by saying that he felt the same about Slovenia.[20] All of a sudden, Yugoslavia's position was painfully clear. Paul remained silent but, among the rest, an argument broke out and tempers ran high. At length, Cvetković called the meeting to order. He summarized the arguments and called for a vote. As was customary, all the members of the Council, except for Paul, voted. All voted in favour of signing the Pact provided that Germany agreed to the concessions of which Cincar-Marković had spoken. The Council then adjourned, after the members had sworn to keep both their meeting and the results of their discussions secret.*

* According to one account (Jukić, *The Fall of Yugoslavia*, p. 52) the Crown Council was also strongly influenced by reports, from Gavrilović, the Yugoslav minister in Moscow, that Germany was planning to attack the U.S.S.R. by 22nd June, at the latest. Whether or not this is so, it is certainly true that relatively detailed information about an attack in late May had reached the Yugoslav government by the end of the second week in March, from Vauhnik, the Yugoslav military attaché and intelligence officer in Berlin. (J. B. Hoptner, *Yugoslavia in Crisis, 1934–1941*, pp. 231–233, Vauhnik to J. B. Hoptner.) If the Yugoslavs had indeed been aware of this information before the Crown Council of 6th March, it would explain the importance they attached to their stalling tactics, such as the imposition of terms which they were convinced Hitler would refuse. Intelligence from Vauhnik, which was received later in the month, undoubtedly added strength to the view that their only solution lay in postponing signing for as long as possible.

Secrecy was all important for the government had still to wring the necessary concessions from the Germans. Cvetković and Paul were convinced that their demands would prove too much for Hitler. At worst, if their terms were accepted and they were obliged to sign the Pact, they would have rendered it ineffectual. They could probably gain further delay by quibbling over terms. Furthermore, if Hitler did agree and then broke his promises, the Croats and Slovenes might be provoked into fighting. It had been obvious at the Crown Council that they would not do so of their own accord.

When Cvetković called on the German Minister on 7th March, he explained that the Council required the Axis partners to guarantee a number of points before a final decision could be reached. The list he presented to Von Heeren read as follows:

—The sovereignty and territorial integrity of Yugoslavia will be respected.

—No military assistance will be requested of Yugoslavia and also no passage or transportation of troops through the country during the war.

—Yugoslavia's interest in a free outlet to the Aegean Sea through Salonika will be taken into account in the reorganization of Europe.[21]

These points were the ones that Prince Paul had mentioned at Berchtesgaden a few days earlier. Exactly how it came about that the Yugoslav designs on Salonika were included in the list remains unclear. It is possible that at a moment of personal and national humiliation, an element of self-interest crept into their deliberations; it is possible, too, that they felt they should counter Italy's claims on the port; and according to Dr Maček's account of the meeting Cincar-Marković argued that refusal of Germany's offer of Salonika would cause the Germans to doubt Yugoslavia's sincerity.[22]

Paul was both physically and mentally exhausted. The emotional strain of having to stand firm against pressure from abroad had taken its toll. Almost every evening King George of Greece or one of Olga's other relations would telephone. Obvious messages like 'are you going to play bridge with me soon?'[23] were passed on and Paul seemed unable to make them understand why he could not immediately throw in his lot with the Allies.

The British were similarly deaf to his explanations and they too piled on the pressure. And so did the Americans. Roosevelt had approved Churchill's plan for a Balkan front and the U.S. Minister in Belgrade, Mr Lane, worked hard to promote it. In January 1941, he had been assisted by a special envoy from Roosevelt, Colonel William Donovan, who had spent some weeks in the Balkans talking with the various political leaders. At the end of the mission, a report of Colonel Donovan's views had reached the British Foreign Office. Of the Prince Regent he had said: 'While his [Prince Paul's] early training had unfitted him for dealing with people like the Yugoslavs, it had left him with a strong sense of doing the "right thing". He would not like his English friends to think that he had played a mean rôle'.[24]

This information was certainly no revelation to the British, but both they and Colonel Donovan failed to understand its real significance. The very fact that Paul had a strong sense of duty and of doing the 'right thing' prevented him from falling in with the British, Greek and American designs. Paul was horrified that his duty to Yugoslavia was inevitably gaining him the reputation of a poor friend to Britain. Yet, presiding over the Crown Council he had heard his Minister of War describe the prospects for his country in the event of a German attack and he had watched all his senior ministers vote in favour of joining the Pact.

Might Paul, even then, have swayed the decision the other way? It is possible that another man in the same position, prepared to risk the immediate dismemberment of the nation and the almost certain destruction of a large part of its population, might have intervened decisively to turn the vote the other way. Paul's love of Great Britain, his natural inclination and basic instincts all cried out for solidarity with her. But heroism, if it came at all, would come only from Serbia in the south. The Croats and Slovenes, if given time, might leave the government and strike an independent deal with Hitler. Serbia would once again have to show its military integrity and courage. Paul could claim to have acted in the interests of the

Allied cause, of Greece, and even of Serbia as an independent state. Yugoslavia was itself, after all, only the product of war and he had done his best to preserve its unity.

It was a tempting prospect and, at the end of it all, a triumphant welcome in Athens and in London. His wife's family in Greece and his brother-in-law's in Britain could be expected to receive him with open arms. Olga, Peter and the children could easily be sent across the frontier to Greece. He might have to move south more slowly with the remnants of his government. He would have to head up a government in exile—probably out of London—at least until Peter's majority in the autumn. He could then retire to the English countryside to pursue his lifelong and peaceful interests, in relative comfort and obscurity.

Against all these arguments in favour of Serb heroics stood the inexorable fact that, as long as he remained Regent, Paul saw himself pledged to the thankless task of preserving a unified Yugoslavia; and, as trustee for King Peter, in honour bound to hand the country over intact to its lawful heir. It was thus in a mood of absolute despair that Paul met his moment of truth. He remained silent and, with a sense of deep foreboding, stood by the Crown Council's unanimous decision. Perhaps it was easier to let others decide for him; perhaps he feared the nature and extent of German military retaliation too much. But even if he had felt that he had the constitutional authority to influence and reverse the decision in Council (which he did not), he would not have used it. He thought then and he continued to think for the remaining thirty-five years of his life, that at that particular moment he had not the right, and that Britain had not the right, to call for a unilateral act of Serbian heroism. The price this would exact in terms of Serbian, Croat and Slovene life, was far too high. It was as simple as that. His ministers had agreed in Council and, though unconvinced, he was in agreement with them. Unquestionably, the decision was in the interests of Yugoslavia; it was probably also in the longer term interests of the Allies and of Greece.

It would be said of Paul that he acted out of fear. He would be called a traitor to Yugoslavia and to the Allied cause. He would be jeered at as a quisling. He would even be accused of wanting to usurp the crown, of being a fascist, pro-Nazi,* jealous of Peter and ambitious for himself.

As they left the Crown Council meeting, however, neither Paul nor Cvetković considered that they had given way to the Axis. Cvetković sincerely believed that the Yugoslav demands went beyond what Hitler would be prepared to accept and Paul may have believed this too, although he was less optimistic on this point than his Prime Minister. More probably, he reckoned that the demands would cause delay and while there was time there was still hope—though not much. However, he was prepared to clutch at anything, and when Campbell returned from Athens, where he had been having talks with Eden, Paul agreed to the suggestion that a Yugoslav staff officer should travel there for talks with British officers.

Major Perišić's journey was a dismal failure. It was probably doomed from the start for he travelled, inadequately disguised, on a British passport made out in the name of Mr L. R. Hope. L was for 'last' and R for 'ray'. But it was not the fact that the Germans knew about the mission within hours which made it so unsatisfactory. It failed because both the British and the Yugoslavs expected to have their questions answered, but to answer none themselves. General Wavell's chief of staff, Major-General Arthur Smith, represented the British government. Almost immediately Smith decided that as the Yugoslav attitude appeared so uncertain he and General Papagos should only give general replies. This was of little use to Major Perišić who was under strict orders to find out, in the most specific terms, what help could be given to the Yugoslav army

* For a good example of this general attitude, see page 1142 *Black Lamb and Grey Falcon* by Rebecca West (Macmillan, 1943):
'It turned out that peasants and the provincial intellectuals, who had no means of knowing what was going on in Prince Paul's head, had been right about his attitude and the experts who had intimate knowledge of him were wrong. *He had for some time been pro-Axis.* His lack of resistance to Nazi claims was not only due to the feeling, which any scrupulous person in his position must have shared, that a Regent had not the same right as a reigning monarch to pledge his country to an expensive policy; nor was it due to the lack of respect he had naturally enough felt for Chamberlain's England and distrust of it as an ally. *It was the result of a genuine admiration for Hitler's personality* and a desire that Yugoslavia should throw in its lot with the winning side.' [Authors' italics.]

should it be forced to withdraw either south to the Aegean or west to the Adriatic. However, even if the British had been prepared to be frank, their reply would not have given the Yugoslavs much encouragement, for as long as British forces were being moved to Greece they had no ships to spare for other manoeuvres.

After Perišić had left, Major-General Arthur Smith telegraphed the results of the discussion to Eden, who was by then in Cairo. Not surprisingly, the British were put out. Prince Paul did not seem able to make up his mind whether or not to join them. They therefore showed little interest in what he had to say and wrote him off as weak and indecisive. This was a pity, for during the next ten days, Paul tried to alert Campbell and Lane to what might happen. Both he and Cvetković made it absolutely clear that joining the Pact was a strong possibility, and they both spelled out the conditions under which Yugoslavia might be forced to sign. Campbell sent Eden, who was still in Cairo, constant bulletins of the latest developments. One of these Eden misunderstood. It was a message about the circumstances under which Yugoslavia might consider signing the Pact: she would resist attack, refuse passage of troops and use of the railways, and 'would not sign Tripartite Pact with military clauses'. Eden noted 'with satisfaction' that Yugoslavia 'will not sign the Tripartite Pact'.[25] This was only a slip, but it helps to explain Eden's reaction when he heard that Paul's government had signed the Pact, albeit without its military clauses. He showed little mercy.

Before leaving the Middle East, Eden made a final effort to bring pressure to bear on Paul. On 17th March 1941, he sent him a long letter by the hand of Mr Terence Shone, and on the following day he himself flew to Cyprus for top secret talks with the Turkish Foreign Minister, Mr Sarajoglu. The Yugoslav-Turkish negotiations had broken down at the end of February 1941, because of mistrust on both sides and because neither, when it came down to it, were willing to commit themselves. Eden now hoped to persuade the Turks to make a firm declaration that they would regard an attack on Salonika as a *casus belli* if the Yugoslavs would do likewise. This he felt sure would encourage Paul.

The Cyprus talks were not as successful as Eden had hoped.

For a start Sarajoglu would not agree to the proposal that an attack on Salonika should be taken as a *casus belli*. However, he was prepared to send a message to the Yugoslavs suggesting an exchange of views about the Pact. Eden accepted this as better than nothing. But a series of events followed which meant that even this message, for what it was worth, did not reach the Yugoslavs. First there was a straightforward delay: the message was not transmitted from the Turkish government to their Minister in Belgrade. Then the resignation of three ministers in the Yugoslav government was used as an excuse to withhold the message until the government crisis was over. The British reaction to this behaviour was one of bewilderment, followed by impatience and anger. Rather belatedly, the Foreign Office came round to the view that perhaps the Turks were more to blame for the failure of the Turkish-Yugoslav negotiations than they had thought: 'Doubt sincerity of Turkish government. Deduce (a) Turkish minister of foreign affairs ahead of his colleagues and was told that he had gone too far when he returned from Cyprus. (b) Turks will not fight unless attacked. (c) Turks do not want to make Greece too difficult for Hitler in case he turns instead on Turkey. (d) Turks' one and overriding determination is not to fight . . .'[26]

Whilst all this was going on, Terence Shone was with Paul in Belgrade. He had arrived quite unexpectedly, to the delight of Princess Olga. '. . . we kept him to dinner—so nice to talk to, he brings England so near . . .'[27] Paul was probably less enthusiastic. He liked and trusted Shone but he could not accept what the British wanted him to do. The all too familiar plan was repeated again in a long letter from Eden, which Shone brought with him. The letter was comprehensive and formal. It dealt briefly with the prospect of reinforcements and with the rapid progress of the African campaign, and then moved specifically to the Balkans:

> Now, Sir, let me turn to the Balkan situation. As it seems to me, you and your government have, if I may say so, skilfully built up a strong and defensive political position during the last few weeks. By your refusal to sign the Tripartite Pact and by making clear to the German government that the future of Salonika is a vital Yugoslav interest,

you have placed the German government in a difficult position. I have no doubt that their original purpose was to subject all the Balkan countries in turn to their rule without having to fight any one of them to secure this result. They have succeeded with Rumania and Bulgaria. On the other hand, the Greeks have made plain that they will fight rather than submit, and the Turks have done the same. The attitude that you and your government have taken up means that the German military authorities must take into account that a further aggression in the Balkans may bring them into conflict with Yugoslavia, Greece and Turkey, backed by all the resources that we can bring to bear. It seems to me of the first importance to hold this position, for as long as you, Sir, and your government can do this, there is always a chance of checking the German threat to the independence of Yugo-slavia, Greece and Turkey before ever that threat develops into military action. I feel sure that there can be no vestige of doubt in your mind that to come to an arrangement with Germany now would be to sacrifice the strong position you have built up and would lead step by step to Yugoslavia suffering the fate that has already overcome Rumania and Bulgaria.

I am distressed to learn from Campbell that your military authorities take so pessimistic a view of Yugoslavia's military position. Our military authorities here by no means share that view, and you will agree that they have recently proved on the field of battle that they are not men of light-hearted optimism. In particular, they point out to me how strong is Yugoslavia's position in relation to Albania. The Italians there are still ill placed. Their recent attempts to break the Greek line have once again failed, with heavy loss. Their communications with Italy are difficult, their units are confused and their morale is low. Campbell will have told you that traffic with Italy is not unimpeded. Attacks upon it are frequent and only two nights ago the Fleet Air Arm sank a ship in Valona Harbour. If Yugoslavia were to attack Albania from the north, Italian resistance would soon collapse and Italy's participation in the Balkan conflict would be at an end, except in so far as she could continue to play a secondary rôle with her Metropolitan air force. The elimination of Italian armies in Albania would give your army most valuable munitions of war and supplies of all kinds, while it would free the Greek army and our air force for operations elsewhere. It is difficult to estimate what the effect of such a defeat would be on Italian morale, more especially if it came at the same time as the final collapse of Italy's east African empire, but we can be sure that it would be most serious. It is indeed certain that with the passage of time Italy will become an increasingly heavy burden upon Germany. Moreover, surely such an early victory by the Yugoslav army in Albania would greatly hearten all sections of your people in the first stages of the campaign, and sustain them to face German attacks with us on other fronts.

I was very sorry not to be able to see Your Royal Highness and to discuss all these matters with you. Apart from all political considerations, it would have been like old times to have had a full talk together . . .[28]

Eden's argument, though plausible, was one-sided. He did not spare a thought for what the Germans might do in the northern provinces of Yugoslavia if the Yugoslavs followed the British plan and fell upon the Italians in Albania. It would have been more honest, though equally unproductive, to have asked Paul, outright, to sacrifice half his country for the Allied cause. As it was, Paul was unimpressed. Beside a vague promise of arms at some future date the letter contained nothing for him, and the appeal to 'old times' left him cold.

However, Terence Shone had also brought with him the news of Eden's approach to Turkey. This at least was something on which Paul was able to pin a little hope, but he waited in vain for the results of the talks to come through. Campbell and Knatchbull-Hugessen worked frantically to persuade the Turks, first of all to communicate the message, on which Eden and Sarajoglu had agreed, to their minister in Belgrade, and then to permit him to deliver it to the Yugoslav government. But the Turks obstinately refused, on the grounds that the 'attitude of the Cabinet in Belgrade was not susceptible of inspiring indispensable confidence'.[29]

As Paul waited for the Turks to approach him, as he had been assured that they would, he had to face up to the fact that, on 19th March, Hitler had agreed to accept all the Yugoslav conditions and had imposed a deadline for the signature of the Pact. On the following day, Paul attended a meeting of the Crown Council and one of the full cabinet. At the latter, only three ministers stood out against signing the Pact. They resigned in an unsuccessful effort to bring down the cabinet. Paul persuaded one to return to his post and the following day Cvetković filled the two vacant ministries.

On 23rd March 1941 Terence Shone decided that there was nothing more he could do. Before leaving Belgrade he telegraphed a report to the Secretary of State in Cairo:

F,* whom I had asked to see me once again to say goodbye, sent for me yesterday evening. We had an hour's conversation. He began by saying that his position was now most difficult. Whether the government did or did not sign the agreement with Germany, [the] country was likely to be split. I told him by all our accounts feeling against the agreement was running high especially in Serbia and the junior ranks of the army. How could anything else have been expected of a proud and brave people? Could not he use [the] internal crisis, including [the] resignation of three ministers, as argument with the Germans for not signing the agreement in the present form or at least for delaying the signature? He reverted to the desire of [the] Croats and Slovenes, as represented by their party leaders, to sign but said he was doing what he could to delay matters. We had [a] long discussion of [the] internal situation in which as an old friend anxious to help him in his difficulties I sought with many arguments which I need not enumerate, to lead him back to what I felt sure was the right path for his people. So far from taking exception, as he might have done to such advice from a foreigner, he said he welcomed my frank speaking. But how far I moved him I cannot say. He made the point that if he did not sign the agreement and his country were involved in the horrors of war, many of his people and not only Croats would blame him for having failed to take the chance which the agreement offered of peace.

* F for Friend. FO code name for Prince Paul.

I repeated all [the] arguments I could think of against signing the agreement, and enlarged on the deplorable effect which that must have on public opinion in Allied countries. I gave him, to read, a page in the *Daily Sketch* for 22nd March which contains quotations from the Bible strikingly appropriate to the situation, especially second Corinthians Chapter 6, verses 14 and 17. I said that this was just what Allied opinion would feel if he joined the powers of Darkness. He was visibly moved and said 'I know'.

I asked him for information as to [the] general line of [the] agreement. These have been embodied in Mr Campbell's telegram. I enquired what he would do in [the] event of Germany demanding passage of troops through South Serbia. He said emphatically 'then we shall fight'. I questioned whether the morale of the people and army would not by then have been too far undermined for resistance. He doubted this and said that the army would remain mobilized but he feared [the] Bulgarian army would fight with [the] Germans.

When on the subject of Turkey he asked why [the] Turkish ambassador had not made the communication referred to in your telegram no. 101. On [the] strength of Ankara 150 I said that [the] ambassador had his instructions and urged him to tell [the] President of the Council to send for His Excellency. If the latter is now unable to make [the] communication [the] effect will be deplorable.

F expressed renewed regret at not having been able to see you, bade me thank you for sending me and sent you cordial messages.

I regret having been unable to accomplish more. Events, he considers, worked strongly against us before my arrival (Turco-Bulgarian Agreement, German occupation of Bulgaria, persistent doubts about Turkey's solidarity with us, weakening of Croat and Slovene leaders' will to resist). Acceptance by Germans of Yugoslav conditions (which happened I believe [the] day after my arrival) still further reduced any chance of success. Strain under which F himself has been labouring for so long has told on him. One feels that he has now lost that reserve of courage which sufficed to meet less critical decisions in the past; he has, I believe, been so reluctant to let personal feeling weigh that he has not let beliefs on which they are founded count enough; and in his dilemma he has fallen back on advice, and failed to control the actions of men who lack wide vision, courage and decision, and amongst whom are evil counsellors.[30]

Shone's observation that Paul was reluctant to let personal feelings weigh, was shrewd. Like Campbell and Lane, Shone had taken full advantage and played mercilessly upon this reluctance. After a long harangue over dinner on 20th March Paul's sense of misery and isolation was at its peak. Looking sad and exhausted and with a note of resignation in his voice, he turned to the U.S. Minister and said, 'You big nations are hard, you talk of our honour but you are far away.'[31]

Germany on the other hand was drawing nearer than ever. German troops were in Bulgaria and the German deadline hung over Yugoslavia. Hitler had been annoyed by the delay caused by the resignation of the Yugoslav ministers and had made it clear that he would wait no longer than 24th March for the Yugoslav answer. Marita had to begin, and anyway he wanted to have everything settled by the time the Japanese Foreign Minister arrived in Germany for a visit. Yugoslav accession to the pact had become, for Hitler, a matter of prestige.

It was obvious to the Yugoslavs that they could delay no longer. Hitler had accepted their conditions and had agreed to incorporate them into the protocol in the form of appended notes. He had even consented to publish two of them—about sovereignty and exemption from any obligation to provide military assistance. Had he agreed to publish the other one as well (that he would make no demands on Yugoslavia to permit the march or transportation of troops across her territory), the fate of Paul might have been different. But, although keen to gain Yugoslavia's signature, Hitler was not prepared to publish this clause. It would have been tantamount to a public admission that the Yugoslavs had signed a pact that meant next to nothing.

At the hour of the deadline, midnight 23rd March 1941, Cincar-Marković informed the German ambassador that the Yugoslavs would sign. The following day, Cvetković and Cincar-Marković left for Vienna. Prince Paul remained in Belgrade with a telegram from King George: 'I am absolutely convinced that both the true interests of your country and of your trusteeship demand that no agreement of any kind should be signed with the Germans whose word is never, and least of all now, to be trusted. We count on you.'[32]

These were the words that brought home to Paul the fact that he had finally forsaken his link with Britain. But it was too late, even if he had had the power to do it, to turn back. As to the future, he had no idea what would be in store for him, or for his teenage sons and five-year-old daughter. Olga, he knew, was probably a thousand times stronger than he, yet he could never hope to explain to her how these events had come about. Olga, as it happened, was about the only person at that time who remained both strong and absolutely trusting.

On the same day that the ministers left to sign the Pact, Eden telegraphed to Campbell: 'Prince Regent's attitude shows such a hopeless sense of unreality that there is nothing to be expected of him . . .' This was in response to Shone's report and went on to give Campbell 'full authority for any measures that you may think it right to take to further a change of government or regime even by coup d'état'.[33] But Campbell was not optimistic about the chances of a coup d'état. As he explained to Eden in a long telegram on 24th March, a successful coup would have to be a military one and he thought it unlikely that any military uprising would succeed, certainly not without the backing of British arms supplies.

As the British could not supply arms, the atmosphere in the Foreign Office was one of despair. They knew that signature of the Pact was imminent and there was nothing that they could now do to prevent it. Official policy was therefore to maintain relations with the Cvetković government, even after signature of the Pact, while continuing to explore alternatives. Thus on 26th March, Churchill telegraphed to Campbell not to 'let any gap grow up between you and Prince Paul or the ministers. Continue to pester, nag and bite. Demand audiences. Don't take no for an answer . . . at the same time, do not neglect any alternative to which we may have to resort if we find present government have gone beyond recall . . .'[34]

Meanwhile, Anthony Eden was on his way back from Cairo to London, believing there to be little chance of further action in Yugoslavia.

PART III

CHAPTER XII

MARCH 1941
The Coup d'État

I wonder if Walter Lippmann isn't right about 'Neutral
European States' after all. He alone seems to realise
how easy it is to recommend heroism to a small defenceless country whose neighbour is a big strong bully and
how little one gains by it in the end.

Prince Paul to Bernard Berenson, 1949.

On 26th March 1941 the Yugoslav morning papers published
the news that the country had signed the Tripartite Pact.
Because only the first and the third of the Axis guarantees*
could be made public the people assumed that their government
had signed a military alliance with the Germans. In Belgrade
rioting broke out in the streets and schools, and foreign radio
stations broadcast the likelihood of German intervention.

It was against this background that Paul received his Prime
Minister back from Vienna. Cvetković was far from happy after
his ordeal at the Belvedere Palace and the two men spent a
dismal afternoon together. At 9 o'clock in the evening Paul left
by train for Brdo. Cvetković accompanied him for the first few
miles of the journey and then travelled back to Belgrade by car
as the train sped northwards. Exhausted, Paul retired to the
sleeping compartment. But he was to have little rest. In the
early hours of the morning his train was held up at the small
railway station of Viskovci and his A.D.C. was summoned to
the telephone. 'There is trouble in the capital' a voice said and
then the line went dead.

In Belgrade the citizens slept peacefully in their beds, but
down below in the dark streets soldiers moved swiftly and
silently towards the government buildings. In an office,
borrowed from his Commander-in-Chief, Brigadier-General

* See Appendix III, pages 313 to 315.

Bora Mirković of the Yugoslav Air Force, sat alone, issuing orders with icy efficiency. He had planned the coup d'état with the precision of a military exercise and he was entirely confident that it would succeed.

For Mirković the night of 26th March had begun at 5 o'clock in the afternoon—the hour that he had moved into his headquarters and assumed command. His first task had been to summon his fellow conspirators and inform them that he had decided to act. After that he had to alert all his lieutenants in the field and check that each one knew his duties. Mirković kept the overall strategy entirely to himself: he was obsessed with secrecy and proud of the fact that (so he claimed) 'no one in the whole world' knew of the plans but him. By 11 o'clock Mirković was satisfied that everything was ready. At 11.30 he gave the first order. At Zemun, Belgrade's main airport, one of his men quietly took over command; at the royal palaces, troops gathered outside the walls; and in the city, tank forces began to roll up the wide tree-lined avenues. Half way up, the tanks stopped, forming a massive steel barricade across the exit routes from the city. Mirković had allowed a bare three hours for the coup d'état and one event followed quickly upon another. After the tanks came the troops. The first squad made for the radio station of the Chief of the General Staff, in order to prevent communications between the government and the Commander of the Army. At the door, a policeman who tried to bar the soldiers from entering lost his life in a spray of gunfire. But he was the only casualty of the evening. At the Administration Buildings, and finally at the Belgrade Command, the soldiers met with little resistance. By 2.15 in the morning they were in complete control of the city and it was time for the specially selected officers of the Air Force to rouse the sleeping cabinet ministers and take them into custody.

Back at headquarters, General Mirković's tasks were almost over. He instructed one of his colonels to go out into the streets of Belgrade to calm the people and make speeches, and he put through a telephone call to wake General Simović, the man he had chosen to take over as Prime Minister. Then he prepared to leave, satisfied in the knowledge that he had done his duty.

For over three years, Bora Mirković had lived with a single ambition: to rid his country of the Regency government.

Strangely enough, Mirković was not particularly anti-German (in fact he kept a signed photograph of fellow airman, Marshal Goering, in a place of honour in his own quarters). For him, signature of the Tripartite Pact was just another in a long line of weak and unworthy acts perpetrated by Prince Paul and his ministers. He had no time for appeasement. He was a Serb, obsessed with a romantic dream of his country's glorious past—a past when the army had ruled and the country had been strong and independent.

Mirković had probably begun to formulate his plans about the time of the Concordat dispute and of the Italo-Yugoslav pact. Certainly by 1938 he had begun to look round for someone to take over in the event of a coup d'état; a man who would provide a strong military leadership. Thus, in secrecy, he had in turn approached Generals Nedić, when he was Minister for War, Stanković, when he was Commander of the Royal Guard, and Ilić. But one after the other these had turned him down. It was not until 1941 that he found a willing candidate in General Dušan Simović, Commander of the Yugoslav Air Force. Simović was a Serb and extremely ambitious.

Mirković did not bother Simović with the details, he merely exacted a promise that the general would take over when the time was ripe. For the organization of the coup Mirković looked to one or two trusted friends in the Belgrade Officers Club, and to the Knežević brothers. Major Živan Knežević was a young and popular commander of a Guards Infantry battalion and a useful contact in the army. His brother, Professor Radoje Knežević was equally useful. Radoje was an intellectual, a politician and a leading light among the dissidents in the Serbian Cultural Club. As such he was well placed to extend Mirković's range of acquaintances into areas which would otherwise have remained closed to him. Radoje Knežević's motives were not entirely unselfish: he had, at one time, been French tutor to King Peter but had been dismissed on account of his radical tendencies.

For Simović, the reality of the coup d'état was a shock. When he had given Mirković his word at the beginning of the year, the coup had seemed a vague idea and he had not thought much about the responsibilities which he would have to accept. On 26th March, Mirković's cool announcement caught him unprepared and he reacted nervously, doing his utmost to persuade Mirković to postpone the operation. Mirković was firm. He told Simović that his decision was final and that he neither wanted to wait a moment longer nor did he have reason to do so. At nine in the evening General Simović left his own office a worried man. He did not return home immediately but visited his relations in the city, bidding them goodbye. When he finally got to bed it was one o'clock in the morning of 27th March. At four o'clock his telephone rang and he was ordered out of bed to take command.

The problems which faced General Simović that morning were numerous. He had to form a cabinet, persuade the Croat leaders to join it, face the German threat and deal with the Regents. But before anything else he had to establish the legitimacy of his own position. This meant obtaining the King's written approval. So Simović and his fellow conspirators drew up a document declaring King Peter's accession to the throne and the appointment of Simović as Prime Minister. This they entrusted to Major Živan Knežević with orders to go as fast as possible to the royal palace and to obtain the King's signature.

When Knežević arrived at Dedinje at 6 a.m., he found that his route to the King was blocked; for within the walls of the palace the King's governor, General Petar Kosić, was still loyal to the Regency. He was ignorant of developments that morning, but he had with him all the adjutants and orderly officers of the palace guard. Between the two sides stood Captain Božidar Delibašić who, as commander of the external palace guard, was in charge of the main gate. Delibašić was not party to Mirković's plans but he had seen enough to have some idea of what was afoot and, like many other soldiers, he was not unsympathetic to the idea of replacing Prince Paul's civilian government with a more militarist and Serbian one. Recognizing Knežević immediately, Delibašić explained the dangers and offered to take to the King the envelope that Knežević was waving about in the air so excitedly. Knežević agreed, but within minutes Delibašić was back with the news that the King was no longer in the palace: he had gone to the headquarters of the guard with General Kosić. It was Delibašić who then suggested that they should proceed as if the document had actually been signed.

The troops which had been sent to surround the royal palaces had moved quickly and stealthily and had carried specific instructions not to harm the King, as he was essential to the new government. Thus it was that Peter had slept on at Dedinje, while at Beli Dvor neither Olga nor any of the children had stirred. It was not until morning that Alexander noted the unusual strengthening of the guard inside the palace grounds and the presence of soldiers outside the gates. Immediately he rang Peter and shortly afterwards drove across the park to Dedinje. Peter had already been taken, at about 6.30 a.m., by an utterly distraught General Kosić, to inspect the headquarters of the guard. Now, puzzled by the soldiers and the silence, the two boys drove round the palace grounds together. The time was 8.30 and, had they switched on their radio, they would have heard the voice of a young man, supposedly the King, declaring that he had dismissed the Regency and assumed full powers himself.

Peter and Alexander were confused by all the commotion but they put it down to some elaborate military exercises and, together, made their way back to Beli Dvor. Here, gradually, news of the previous night's events began to filter through. Olga tried again and again to contact Paul by telephone but with no success. Without Paul they were helpless—particularly Peter, who was already being harassed by General Simović who was anxious for him to come out and associate himself with the new leaders. Eventually, Peter agreed to a short drive round the regiments but immediately afterwards returned to Beli Dvor—he would do nothing until the return of his uncle.

Meanwhile Paul was in Zagreb. His train had been detained there early in the morning and in order to find out what was going on, he had sent for Maček. When Maček arrived, he found Paul half-dressed in crumpled clothes, still in the sleeping compartment. One of Mirković's officers stood outside the royal train but otherwise there was no show of force and Paul had only a vague idea of what had happened. Having just received a telephone call from one of the Croat ministers being held by General Simović, Maček was able to give a clearer picture of the state of affairs in Belgrade. At the end, Paul sighed deeply and asked: 'What's to be done?'[1]

Maček's answer was to take Paul and the three officials of

the Croat Peasant Party who had accompanied him, to the governor's palace in Zagreb. There, while Mirković's officer waited outside the door, he put forward a plan of resistance. He urged Paul not to accept the coup as an accomplished fact and offered him the services of the fourth army which was composed almost entirely of Croats and was therefore loyal. With this army he reckoned that Paul would be in a position to negotiate with the rebels and to influence the large number of army officers who had not been actively involved in the conspiracy.

But Maček was wasting his time since, for Paul, civil war was inconceivable. Besides, as he reminded the Croat, his wife and children were in the hands of the rebels. To this kind of argument Maček had no reply.

Paul opened the door to the officer and quietly accepted the order, 'in the name of the King and the new government' to return to Belgrade. He asked that his train should be ready at noon and, before leaving, made contact with the British Consul. The following telegram thus preceded the Prince to Belgrade: 'Prince Paul wishes message to be conveyed to H.M. Minister to the effect that he is returning to Belgrade and wishes to leave the country as soon as possible for Greece, with the eventual intention of proceeding to England. He requests H.M. Minister to intervene with present government and facilitate departure.'[2]

At the end of the telegram the British Consul noted that the Prince was 'taking the situation calmly and philosophically'. In a moment of weakness and sensing the inevitable, Paul had told Maček that morning that he was sick and tired of the problems of government and that he wanted nothing so much as to leave the country. Naïvely and pathetically, he assumed that, now that his duties and commitments in Yugoslavia seemed at an end, the British would help him and his family to get to London. But he knew his responsibilities were not quite over. He went out of his way, even after he had agreed to resign, to persuade Maček and the other Croat ministers to join the new Simović government. They were reluctant to have anything to do with it but Paul knew that a split in the country would only make easier the German attack which he knew would now be unleashed.

Paul travelled back to Belgrade with Dr Šubašić, governor of Croatia and an old and trusted friend. The journey took the whole afternoon and it was after seven o'clock when the royal train arrived at Zemun railway station. General Simović was waiting on the platform accompanied by a few officers and a detachment of infantry. There were no signs of the over-excited crowds that had been celebrating in the streets all day and there was no suggestion that Simović was a national hero. As one of the escorting officers reported, the reception was a restrained and pathetic occasion:

When the train drew into the station and stopped, an orderly officer got out of one carriage and I* at once went up to him and asked him in which carriage was the Prince. He replied that the Prince was in the same carriage and opened the door of the carriage for me. We went into the carriage: myself, Rupcić and the orderly officer. In the corridor the orderly officer asked me whether he should announce me. I said 'yes'. He then opened the door of a small drawing-room, went in and announced me: 'Colonel Dragutin Savić.' I heard the Prince ask him: 'Is that Colonel Savić who was formerly our adjutant?' The orderly officer answered in the affirmative and the Prince then said that I could come in. When I went in, and saluted him, the Prince said: 'Good evening' and shook my hand and presented me to the Ban [Governor] of the Croatian Banovia, Dr Šubašić, who was with him. Dr Šubašić shook hands with me warmly, and greeted me cheerfully, as if he wished to express his joy that we had carried out the coup d'état, and that he wished to congratulate me. Standing at attention, I informed Prince Paul: 'Your Highness, the Prime Minister is awaiting you on the station platform.' The Prince was in civilian dress, his face a little pale, and he asked me: 'May I take my coat?' When I heard this request I felt very uncomfortable, because I had the impression that the Prince saw us not only as revolutionaries, but as his executioners, and probably

* Colonel Dragutin P. Savić who had been chief of staff of the Air Force Command since 28th January 1941, and whom Mirković had entrusted to hold Zemun aerodrome for the rebels on the night of 26th March.

believed that I was taking him to the gallows . . . so that I might make a favourable impression psychologically on him, I not only answered that he could take his coat, but added also: 'Yes, Your Highness, you should certainly take your coat because it is quite fresh outside.' After I had personally held his coat for him, we all went out on to the platform, where the detachment of infantry was lined up. Then came the command: 'Attention' and 'Salute'. The Prince did not inspect the guard because that was not expected. He greeted General Simović and the officers of his escort. Immediately after that we left in army cars for Belgrade. I was in the first car with Col. Rupcić; in the second car were the Prince and Simović; and behind them were two more cars with the officers.[3]

The fleet of cars drove first to General Staff headquarters in the War Ministry, where Paul, with his co-regents Stanković and Perović, signed the document of abdication. Immediately afterwards, they set off in the same army cars for the royal palace and Beli Dvor. Upon arrival, Paul and Simović went straight to Paul's office, where Peter was waiting for them. The officers of the escort and the members of the palace guard who had accompanied the cars were left waiting in the hall, uncertain as to what was going to happen, as Božidar Delibašić recalls:

> After approximately fifteen minutes, Prince Paul came out of the office and set off upstairs to his apartments. Simović stayed longer with the King. After 45 minutes, the Prince came down again and went into the office to the King and Simović. (As I later learned, the Prince went to his apartments to give the orders for packing.) Soon afterwards Simović came out from the office, but the King remained alone with the Prince for almost a whole hour. During that time we were all waiting in the foyer, where we were served with food and drink. During that time servants in a great hurry carried out from the Prince's apartments the packed trunks and loaded them on to the palace cars which stood in front of the White Palace.
>
> Perhaps it was like that till about 11 p.m., when the King

and the Prince came out of the office. The Prince set off for his apartments, but the King approached us and shook hands with all the officers present.

Soon after that Prince Paul appeared on the stairs with his whole family. As soon as the King noticed them he at once went up to them. We then all knew what this meant. We knew that the Prince and his family were going into exile, that this would now be the King's last farewell to his uncle, who had been to him a counsellor in the place of a parent, and who now, by a strange game of fate, was leaving him and going into exile in the moment when the young King was assuming power and a throne, and alone was taking for himself the greatest responsibility . . . in the moment when he needed his uncle most. . . . Tears were running down all our faces. The King was also weeping and the Prince and Princess Olga and their whole family. The King first kissed Princess Olga, the Princes Alexander and Nikola, then Princess Jelisavetta. Lastly he embraced and kissed his uncle, Prince Paul. This was the most touching moment. They stood a long time embracing, crying and kissing each other.

After the farewell with the King, the Prince and his family set off towards the exit. We stood to attention and the Prince, while passing through, gave the military salute. He did not shake hands with anybody. When they were seated in the car, the driver moved off and they soon disappeared.[4]

The cars headed straight for the railway station for Paul had been advised that he should leave immediately for Greece. Besides himself, the party consisted of Olga, the three children, the English nurse, two maids and two escorting officers. Their pictures and possessions had been left behind for there had been no time to pack.

For Olga no less than for Paul the prospects ahead were unfathomable. The day had been a nightmare and her heart went out to Peter: 'Poor little Peter tried to be brave and sensible, it was heartrending to leave him alone. As we parted he cried and begged to go with us—the British radio broadcast several times we had fled to Germany.'[5]

If the British radio had got it so wrong, she could well

imagine that others would get it wrong too. She longed to see her family in Athens, yet she dreaded the reaction that her husband might find there. Worse still, she knew that the effects on Paul would be catastrophic and that now, more than ever in her life, she would be called upon to draw on her reserves of courage and endurance.

At the station both Ronald Campbell and Terence Shone were waiting to see them off. Paul took this as a demonstration of friendship on the part of the British and was particularly touched and grateful. If he had seen the celebration at the British Legation that morning he would have known better. On the morning of the coup d'état the *New York Times* correspondent had telephoned the British Legation. To his 'Who's there?' he had received the reply 'Bloody well everybody, we're having champagne. Come on.'[6] The entire staff had been assembled, as well as a number of outsiders, and champagne corks had popped. Congratulations had flowed almost as freely as the drink, for everybody assumed that the coup d'état was British-inspired. Nobody seemed to know quite who had engineered it but one and all agreed that it was a very good thing.

In fact, only a small group of people at the party had known that a coup d'état was planned. The majority of these belonged to Special Operations Executive, or S.O.E., which had its Balkan headquarters in Belgrade. S.O.E. had been formed in July 1940 from the cream of Section D of the Secret Intelligence Service and Section M.I. (R) of the War Office, specifically to organize sabotage and subversion. Its overall director was Hugh Dalton, the Minister for Economic Warfare. Dalton was an ambitious man and he had been pleased by his S.O.E. appointment but from the start he had found it frustrating. Permanent government departments kept their distance and professional diplomats and soldiers treated S.O.E. with mistrust. They dubbed it the Department of Ungentlemanly Warfare.

The lack of respect shown to S.O.E. in its first few months was not unwarranted, for the early British attempts at irregular warfare had been at best amateurish and at worst extremely embarrassing for the governments concerned. Dalton was anxious to change this state of affairs and in December 1940 he was given his chance. As the German army advanced through one Balkan country after another Churchill 'sent for him and told him it was the acid test for S.O.E.—he must do everything possible to hamper the German effort in the Balkans'.[7] This was both a challenge and a threat to S.O.E. for in subsequent remarks Churchill let it be known that he was not impressed with their record. Dalton acted quickly. He had already placed a responsible man, Tom Masterson, in charge of Belgrade. Now he sent out a second, George Taylor, then chief of staff to the executive head of S.O.E., with instructions to investigate and co-ordinate S.O.E.'s Balkan operations.

When Taylor arrived in Belgrade he found that S.O.E. already had a wide network of contacts, particularly in the field of public relations. They had helped to establish a supposedly independent news agency, Britanova, from which they distributed British propaganda and they had also infiltrated the National Associations. Organizations like the Chetniks, the Veteran Associations, the Order of the White Eagle with Swords and Narodna Odbrana were hangovers from Serb resistance movements in the First World War. S.O.E. had chosen to subsidize Narodna Odbrana. It was the most active of the organizations and its leader, Ilija Trifunović Birčanin was president of all the National Associations and a man of considerable influence.

Nor had S.O.E. neglected politics. At the time of the Cvetković-Maček alliance many hard-line Serb politicians had been forced out of government. Amongst these men S.O.E. found a number who were disillusioned and willing to co-operate with the British. In addition, Serbian political parties were not above bribery—both the Independent Democratic Party and the powerful Serb Peasant Party were subsidized by S.O.E. The leader of the Serb Peasant Party, Milan Gavrilović, had had extremely close links both with Section D and with the British Legation but in June 1940 he had been posted as Minister to Moscow. His deputy, Miloš Tupanjanin, maintained the contact and he was one of the most useful men that the British had in government circles.

Through February and the early part of March 1941, Masterson and Taylor made full use of this network of contacts in the hope that Paul would respond to the pressure of public opinion. Encouraged by S.O.E., the National Associations flooded Belgrade with pro-British and anti-German leaflets and, as a telegram on 15th March from Campbell reported, neither Paul nor the government were spared: '48 patriotic societies have presented a petition to the Prince Regent urging resistance to German demands. . . . Letters and telegrams urging a firm attitude are reaching the Yugoslav government in some numbers'.[8]

But the propaganda only infuriated Paul. He realized that the British cared little for the unity of his country and he had no time for the very right-wing Serbs. As it was, the atmosphere in Belgrade was highly volatile, with crowds gathering in the streets and a virtual stoppage of work. Even without outside interference, the country was in danger of disintegrating.

By 18th March it had become clear to Masterson and Taylor that if they did not embark on a more active policy, the Tripartite Pact would be signed. Consequently they determined to encourage as many members as possible of the existing government to resign in protest. Such a crisis, they hoped, would bring down the government. Over the next twenty-four hours S.O.E. exerted pressure through all possible channels and, on 20th March, the day that Cvetković announced the terms of the pact to the full cabinet, three ministers duly resigned. Of these three, two, Cubrilović and Budisavljević, belonged to parties subsidized by S.O.E. The third, Konstantinović, was an independent. He had come heavily under the influence of Tupanjanin but was later persuaded to withdraw his resignation by the Prince Regent. Ironically, the resignations not only failed to bring down the government, for replacements were immediately found, but caused the fatal delay in the transmission of Eden's Cyprus message.

On 24th March 1941 the Yugoslav government delegation left for Vienna, and S.O.E. concluded that a coup d'état was the only course of action left. Fortunately, that very day, S.O.E. had had word, via Trifunović-Birčanin, that preparations for a coup d'état were already well advanced. On 25th March the news was even better: Trifunović-Birčanin reported that the conspiracy was ninety-nine per cent certain of success and that action could be expected in forty-eight hours. How much more S.O.E. learned of Bora Mirković's plans is uncertain, though one factor, at least, indicated a fair degree of confidence. On 25th March S.O.E. turned down a suggestion from London, in response to the news of the signing of the Pact, that the train bringing the Yugoslav ministers back from Vienna should be blown up.* S.O.E. feared that such action would lead to the introduction of martial law and the disruption of plans for the coup d'état.

From 24th March onwards S.O.E. worked hard, mostly through Trifunović-Birčanin and Radoje Knežević, to encourage the conspirators and to prepare public opinion. But whereas S.O.E. involvement was peripheral, that of two members of the British Legation (neither of whom belonged to S.O.E.) was not.

Group Captain Macdonald and T. G. Mapplebeck were employed, respectively, as Air Attaché and Assistant Air Attaché at the British Legation. Mapplebeck had lived in Belgrade since 1923 and had had various jobs in the aircraft business before being appointed honorary attaché at the British Legation in 1940. In his work he had come across Mirković, and over the years he had developed quite a close relationship with the Yugoslav. According to some accounts, Mirković later claimed that T. G. Mapplebeck had played a crucial part in persuading him, on 26th March, to carry out the coup d'état within forty-eight hours. Whether or not this was so, there is certainly evidence that Macdonald knew something of the plans—from Simović, if not from Mirković. On 26th March, Macdonald sent a long telegram to the Director of Intelligence at the Air Ministry reporting an interview he had had that morning with General Simović, 'head of an organization intending to carry out a coup d'état'. In the telegram he quoted Simović's view that they 'should not have to wait more than a few days before coup d'état'.[9]

With S.O.E. and two members of the official legation expecting a coup, the fact that the British Minister sent no advance warning to London is odd. At the time, Campbell was

* Dilks ed. Cadogan Diaries, p. 365 entry for 24th March 1941: 'Cabinet at 5. After we met I got Transocean message that 7 Jugs are off tonight to sign Pact. Told Cabinet. A. [Eden] is doing all that is possible, and that is unavailing. Can only ask G.J. [Gladwyn Jebb, chief executive officer to Dalton] to blow up Jug train. But he probably can't do that.'

receiving information from a number of sources and it may be that he chose to rely more heavily on what Lieutenant-Colonel Clarke, his military attaché, told him, than on Masterson and Taylor from S.O.E. Certainly his telegram to the Foreign Office of 24th March, in which he stated that a coup d'état was unlikely if not impossible without supplies of British arms, was based on the assumption that a coup d'état would have to come from the army.

Campbell knew that S.O.E. had little influence in the armed forces and this may have been his only reason for discounting their talk of a coup d'état. However, there may have been another reason. A year later, when he was Ambassador in Washington, Campbell put down his opinion of S.O.E. in a letter to Orme Sargent at the Foreign Office: 'They did a great deal of [political dabbling] in Yugoslavia and usually did it pretty ignorantly.' They were 'always toying with the idea of staging a coup d'état in favour of the very political leaders who are now [1942] in the Yugoslav government. I always resisted this on the ground that the political leaders in question were well past their prime, and that it was not at all certain that they any longer represented Yugoslav opinion and I was certainly sorry that after the coup d'état these men were called into the government by Simović.'[10]

When details of the coup d'état finally arrived at the Foreign Office, enthusiasm was unbounded. For weeks there had been nothing but 'bad news from Juggery' and the atmosphere had been one of gloom and despondency. Then, literally overnight, the tables had turned. And they had every reason to be pleased for, following close upon the news of the coup, came the telegram from Macdonald the Air Attaché. The telegram had been dispatched without the knowledge of the British Minister, at 7.40 p.m. on the 26th, but somewhere along the line it had been delayed. As well as reporting Simović's prediction of the coup d'état the telegram made the following points:

1. Simović expected that war with Germany would result and hoped that Britain would defend Salonika.
2. Simović predicted that the Yugoslavs would also attack Albania.

19. Portrait of Princess Olga painted by her youngest sister, Princess
Marina, Duchess of Kent.

20. Prince Paul of Yugoslavia.

3. Simović had asked what help the British could offer and had seemed satisfied with the very vague assurances that Macdonald had been able to give him.

4. Simović considered it probable that the Prince Regent would not be permitted to remain in power after the coup but would be handed over to the British.[11]

The Foreign Office could hardly have asked for more. Simović had refrained from tiresome requests for British military support and seemed prepared to fight the Italians in Albania and join the war against Germany.

For propaganda purposes the British government made out that it was a strictly Yugoslav rebellion, but in private there was no restraint. Praise was lavished on the men in Belgrade and the Defence Committee noted that 'an expression of appreciation should be conveyed to Dr Dalton for the part played by his organization in bringing about the coup d'état in Yugoslavia.'[12] This was the kind of recognition of which S.O.E. had been so desperately in need and Dalton was only too pleased to accept it although, in the privacy of his diary, he noted that 'it was the air attaché who went to Simović and finally persuaded him to act'.*[13]

Dalton was not alone in his attitude and, in the mass of post-war memoirs and accounts, the part played by S.O.E. in the coup d'état of 27th March became grossly exaggerated. Correspondingly, the part played by the Yugoslavs was reduced. Now that the balance has been restored there is a tendency to forget that S.O.E. was not the only British Intelligence Agency operating in Yugoslavia. S.I.S. (Secret Intelligence Service or MI6) had been in the Balkans far longer than S.O.E. and was generally considered better informed and more trustworthy. S.I.S. reports went only to the highest levels in government, and in the utmost secrecy, and to this day their contents are shrouded in mystery.† The rôle of S.I.S. in Yugoslavia in 1941 has still to be explained but there is evidence

* S.I.S. records are not open for inspection and those individuals who were involved at the time are bound, under oath, not to reveal the facts.

† Dalton was probably wrong to attach so much importance to Macdonald, the Air Attaché.

to suggest that, at the very least, some members of the British cabinet had prior knowledge of the coup d'état. How otherwise could Leo Amery have timed his speech on B.B.C. radio so perfectly—the speech, on 26th March, in which he exhorted the Yugoslavs, and particularly the Serbs, to acts of heroism in keeping with their ancient traditions?

Towards the end of his life, Prince Paul was asked whether he or his government had had any idea at all at the time of the nature and extent of British involvement in the coup d'état and whether his own intelligence services had been aware of the contacts and movements of the various British departments and agents. His reply displayed the almost incredible naïvety with which his regency government had believed and trusted in Britain: for he replied that he had given strict orders that neither the British Legation in Yugoslavia nor any of its officials or official communications were at any time to be monitored or in any way interfered with.[14]

Yet, whether or not the coup could have succeeded without British encouragement and involvement, its effects on morale in Britain were immediate, though wholly disproportionate to its military or political significance.* Churchill was quick to maximize its morale-boosting impact. In his speech to the nation that day he told the people of Britain: 'Yugoslavia has found its soul.' In his subsequent book, *The Grand Alliance*, he developed the romantic theme further, drawing more from his imagination than from the facts: 'The streets of Belgrade were soon thronged with Serbs, chanting, "Rather war than the Pact; rather death than slavery." There was dancing in the squares; English and French flags appeared everywhere; the Serb national anthem was sung with wild defiance by valiant, helpless multitudes. On 28th March, the young King, who by climbing down a rain-pipe had made his own escape from

* Harold Nicolson, writing to his wife on 27th March from the Ministry of Information, had this to say:
'I truly believe that if this Yugoslav thing is as real as we imagine, we have won the war. Of course the Germans may now invade Yugoslavia and Greece. It will take them a great effort and it means that during these vital months of 1941 (when all their efforts should be concentrated on defeating us) they will be diverted to side-shows. What a triumph! Truly it is all over. I think you should hoist the flag on Sunday.'

regency tutelage, attended divine service in Belgrade Cathedral, amid fervent acclamation. The German Minister was publicly insulted, and the crowd spat on his car. The military exploit had roused a surge of national vitality. A people paralysed in action, hitherto ill-governed and ill-led, long haunted by the sense of being ensnared, flung their reckless heroic defiance at the tyrant and conqueror in the moment of his greatest power.'[15]

Churchill did not pause to question the suitability of the new leaders. When the War Cabinet met on 27th March he informed them that he had authorized Campbell to tell the new Yugoslav government that 'on the basis that they were determined to denounce the pact with Germany, and to help in the defence of Greece'[16] Britain recognized them as the new government of Yugoslavia. What Churchill did not know, and what nobody in Britain discovered for many months, was that, at almost exactly the same time that this recognition was received in Belgrade, General Simović's chosen foreign minister, Momcilo Ninčić, was assuring the German Minister in Belgrade that the new government intended to carry on Prince Paul's policy with virtually no change. This was no bluff. Faced with the reality of the political and military situation the new minister had panicked. Very soon they were following exactly the same policies that they had condemned under the Regency.

For a few days, at least, the British would hear nothing against the new government in Yugoslavia. Simović was the saviour and Paul a traitor. The only problem left was what to do with Paul. He had been delivered into British hands: but his own idea, that he might proceed via Greece to England, was out of the question. As Eden simply notified Campbell: 'Endeavour to facilitate Prince Paul's departure via Greece to Cairo. Not, repeat not, proposed that they should come to England.'[17]

But after Cairo, where? The Foreign Office applied themselves with zeal to the task of finding a suitable colony for their erstwhile 'Friend'. Not Cyprus (for Stojadinović was there) but perhaps Mauritius, or Ceylon, or the Seychelles. . . . 'There will be strong feeling here if the wretched and treacherous creature (the public will never believe any other version of him) is treated with anything but rigour. It need not and should not be harshness; but better men have gone to such places as the Seychelles. If he is relegated to somewhere too "cushy" it will of course at once be said that this is due to his connections—royal, aristocratic, ministerial, snobbish as the case may be—in spite of his having done his damnedest to stab the Greeks and us in the back. Any reasonable island should be good enough.'[18]

When a telegram arrived from Sir Michael Palairet, H.M. Ambassador at Athens, with the news that King George of Greece had requested that Prince Paul might be allowed to remain in Greece, the Foreign Office was at once embarrassed and annoyed. King George's offer was a generous one. Yugoslavia's accession to the Tripartite Pact had spelt disaster for Greece, yet King George was not vindictive. After hearing the full story, he accepted Paul's account of it. For Yugoslavia, he agreed, there had been no other course of action. In fact, of all the family, only one member maintained that Paul had behaved dishonourably. As Olga recorded in her diary on 29th March: 'Mummy the only one to greet Paul very stiffly. . . . Mummy, Paul & I retired to her salon to talk quietly and for him to explain his point. She listened, then turned on him terribly, implying our country could be sacrificed to save Greece! Freddie* came, then Zin† talked to Paul and Mummy, as he [Paul] was decided to leave at once if he is disliked here! Thank God, for my sake, all is patched up.'

It was a hard time for Olga but, although her feelings were torn in two, her loyalty to Paul never wavered. The more he was attacked the stronger she became in his defence. And the battle to justify his actions was a frustrating and hopeless one. The family were prepared to listen, but the British were not. Paul was 'advised' not to go into Athens, the British Minister was under orders not to receive him and when Eden himself visited the capital Paul's suggestion that they should meet was summarily turned down. Paul's voice was heard only through intermediaries: King George, who was very much in British hands, and Elim Demidoff. The latter might as well not have bothered for the British Minister was far from sympathetic:

* Frederika, Princess, and later Queen, of Greece.
† Mme Lilia Ralli, an intimate friend of Princess Olga and her sisters.

Prince Demidoff, who is the uncle of Prince Paul of Yugoslavia, came to see me today to explain how distressed the latter was that he should be regarded by us with disfavour, whereas he was now and always had been strongly pro-British and anxious for British victory. He had been hurt by your not seeing him when you were here. Prince Demidoff suggested (he said without having consulted Prince Paul) that I should see him and listen to his convincing explanation of how he had only acted in what he believed to be the best interests of his country, which would have been attacked at once if he had refused the pact. Acting on your instructions (but without mentioning them) I said that I was afraid that I could not go to see Prince Paul, nor would he be able to convince me that a friend of England would have concluded a pact with her enemies, the enemies of freedom, which placed his country in the hands of Germany and exposed Greece to immediate attack. Such friendship seemed to me merely sentimental and not real.[19]

Two copies of this telegram were made, one for the Secretary of State and one for the Prime Minister. 'Sounds to me as if Prince Demidoff was not up to much good himself—who is he?' Eden scrawled on the bottom of his copy. Churchill was more direct: after commenting 'good' alongside the sentence 'he had been hurt by your not seeing him when you were here' he wrote briefly at the bottom: 'The sooner Palsy is interned and out of the way the better.' With an example like this from their leaders, the Foreign Office needed no further encouragement: attacking Paul became quite a game.

The British had no wish to leave Prince Paul in Greece in comfort and among his wife's relations, so when the Yugoslav government presented them with an excuse to move him on they jumped at it. Prince Paul, the Yugoslav government complained, had been trying to intrigue. Their evidence was twofold: first, Princess Olga had made attempts to speak with their young King on the telephone and secondly, Prince Paul had actually sent a telegram to Maček, asking that Šubašić might come to see him in Athens. The Minister of Foreign Affairs was particularly disturbed: he was sure that the Prince's continued influence on the Croats would be highly undesirable and he begged Mr Campbell to arrange for Paul to be sent further afield.

Certainly Olga had telephoned Peter, for she was worried about him, and wished to reassure him. And Paul's telegram to Maček, far from being an attempt to alienate the Croats, had been intended to encourage them to bear with their new and aggressively Serbian government. But whatever the motives, the pretext for removal was there. A series of telegrams travelled from London to Athens and from Athens to Cairo, and before H.M. minister had had time to inform the authorities in Egypt, Prince Paul and family had landed at Heliopolis— to stay until such time as they could be moved on to Kenya.

Sir Miles Lampson had but one day to look for suitable accommodation for them 'not, of course, at H.M. Embassy'.[20] It had not been easy and the house to which Olga and Paul were taken was filthy dirty and ridiculously small. Yet Cairo had its compensations. Terence Shone was the First Secretary at the British Embassy, and Peter Coats, an intimate friend of Chips', was A.D.C. to General Wavell. Both the Shones and Peter Coats were welcoming and kind and so too, in so far as they were allowed to be, were the Lampsons. Sir Miles displayed a more independent approach than his colleague in Athens, and after visiting Paul and Olga for tea at their house he sent a personal telegram to Eden. 'H.M. Ambassador expresses perturbation at humiliating conditions in which Prince Paul and Princess Olga are held, and suggests it would be wise to entertain them and generally help in purely unofficial and informal way.'[21]

The reply, initialled in red ink by Eden himself, was short and to the point: 'Royal Highnesses do not have anything of which they can justifiably complain. Bad idea to entertain them or exceed original instructions.'[22] Paul and Olga did not see the Lampsons again, but other British friends continued to look after them. It was thus with sinking hearts that they were forced to leave for Kenya.

But Paul's despair, prior to his departure for Kenya, was not confined to his own or his family's pitiable circumstances. While he had been in Cairo, his country had been torn to pieces by the Germans.

On 30th March the new Foreign Minister of Yugoslavia had

delivered the following statement to the German Minister in Belgrade: 'The present Royal Yugoslav Government remains true to the principle of respect for international treaties which have been signed, among which the protocol signed on 25th of this month at Vienna belongs.'[23]

But by 30th March it was too late. On hearing the news of the coup d'état on the morning of 27th March, Hitler had at once determined to destroy Yugoslavia 'militarily and as a national unit' without waiting for any of the declarations of loyalty that he knew would be forthcoming. His arrangements had been upset and he was all the more enraged by the fact that he saw the British behind it all. Although word of Macdonald's interview with General Simović did not reach London until 27th March, a report from von Heeren arrived in Berlin on 26th: 'A lengthy conversation took place this morning between the British Air Attaché and General Simovitch, during which precise details were discussed regarding British aid in the event of war with the Axis powers, which Simovitch regards as unavoidable should the coup d'état proceed'.[24]

On the afternoon of 27th March, the Führer summoned a conference and to the assembled company (Keitel, Jodl, Goering, Halder, Brauchitsch, Heusinger, Rintelen, and Ribbentrop) declared his intention to attack Yugoslavia. Speaking in curt, tough sentences he outlined a plan which later that evening was drawn up as Directive 25:

The Führer and Supreme Commander of the Armed Forces	Führer Headquarters 27th March, 1941 13 copies

Directive No. 25

1. The military revolt in Yugoslavia has changed the political position in the Balkans. Yugoslavia, even if it makes initial professions of loyalty, must be regarded as an enemy and beaten down as quickly as possible.

2. It is my intention to break into Yugoslavia in the general direction of Belgrade and to the south by a concentric operation from the Fiume-Graz area on one side, and the Sofia area on the other, and to deal an annihilating blow to the Yugoslav forces. Further, the extreme southern region of Yugoslavia will be cut off from the rest of the country and

will be occupied as a base from which the German-Italian offensive against Greece can be continued. The opening of traffic on the Danube as soon as possible and the seizure of the Bov copper-mines are important for economic reasons. Efforts will be made to induce Hungary and Bulgaria to take part in operations by offering them the prospect of regaining the Banat and Macedonia. Internal tensions in Yugoslavia will be encouraged by giving political assurances to the Croats.

3. I issue the following detailed orders . . .[25]

Fortunately for Hitler his army was not taken unawares. Halder and Heusinger had thought for some time that action in Yugoslavia might become necessary and already in October 1940 they had done some work on the idea. Hitler's scheme of invasion on four different sides came as no surprise: his plans were similar to their own. Virtually all the army had to do was complete the plans for movement of materials and this did not take long. At 5.15 a.m. on the morning of Sunday, 6th April, German bombers flew over Belgrade, flattening the city and leaving 17,000 Yugoslavs dead. 'Operation Punishment' had begun.

The war in Yugoslavia lasted precisely twelve days. The German forces were vastly superior in numbers and equipment but it was not so much this as the behaviour of the Yugoslav troops that made the defence such a pathetic and half-hearted affair. Some Serbs and Slovene units fought bravely on their native soil, but where the troops were of mixed nationality the Germans met with no resistance. On 8th April alone some 40,000 Yugoslav soldiers surrendered without fighting, allowing the Germans to take Skopje and Monastir—important landmarks on the route to Salonika. In Croatia the story was even sorrier: the Sporazum had hardly had time to take effect and any feelings of unity that had developed did not survive the coup d'état. The moderate Croats criticized it as a Serb affair that put not only Serbia but the whole country at risk: the extreme Croats welcomed it because they saw in a German invasion the possibility at last of an independent Croatia. Neither group was interested in fighting. There were some cases of outright treason—for instance, the air force officer who, on 3rd April, flew from Belgrade to Austria to hand over to the

Nazis a list of all Yugoslav air bases—but in the main it was just mutiny. Unit after unit of Croats abandoned their positions, threw away their weapons and went home. On 11th April Zagreb fell to the Germans. It was exactly as Paul had feared, except for one final touch: Anté Pavelić, the murderer of King Alexander, was proclaimed leader of the independent state of Croatia.

Meanwhile the Yugoslav government ministers moved hastily through Serbia, Bosnia and Montenegro in advance of the German forces. They held council meetings on the way but, as they gradually lost contact with the fighting, business became trivial and unrealistic: a salary advance and two months' leave for evacuated civil servants; an amnesty for all prisoners except those convicted of espionage and treason; a decree that all 10,000 dinar notes were worthless and that all other notes were to be released for circulation.[26] The farce ended on 13th April when General Simović informed them that he had authorized his senior general to arrange a truce with the invading forces. One after another the ministers fled the country. By 15th April, when von Weichs arrived in Belgrade to draw up a document of unconditional surrender, there was not a single member of the Simović cabinet left to sign it. They were all on their way to England.

In the devastated cities and villages of Yugoslavia even the most patriotic Serbs must have wondered if the coup d'état had been worthwhile. For the Germans it came at just the right moment, since its overall effect on their Balkan campaign was to increase the speed of their military operations, in particular the transportation of their troops northwards from Greece to the Russian front.*

---

* As a result of subsequent propaganda put out by the British and Yugoslav governments it became accepted that the Belgrade coup had caused a fatal delay in the opening of Operation Barbarossa (Germany's attack on the U.S.S.R.) and had therefore significantly altered the course of World War II in favour of the Allies. Churchill, amongst others, supported this claim and it was widely held for many years. Within the last decade research into German as well as British documents has suggested that this view may be wrong. Modern scholarship indicates that, overall, the coup d'état was more of a help than a hindrance to Hitler's planned invasion of Russia. For a detailed account see Van Creveld M.L., *Hitler's Strategy 1940–41 The Balkan Clue*, C.U.P. (1973).

For Paul and his family all this was far away. They were on a flying boat destined for Khartoum and the Sudan from where they were to travel by train to Nairobi.

In all, their journey took three days, and it was 28th April when they finally arrived at their destination, Osserian, a house near Lake Naivasha that had belonged to the ill-fated Lord Erroll. 'So they send me to the house of a murdered man on my birthday' was Paul's wry comment on arrival.[27] In the chaos of packing and travelling, the family had forgotten that it was his birthday and, confronted with their new home, they did not feel much like celebrating: 'We got to this place after half an hour's dusty drive from the station—house not lived in for months, dark and dirty, water filthy, no light—no wireless—garden a wilderness near the jungle, lake full of hippos, pythons seen quite near. A complete nightmare. Impossible to live here. We must not lose faith and courage.'[28]

CHAPTER XIII

1941–1943
Exile

Sir Henry Moore, the Governor of Kenya, had received hardly more warning of the Yugoslavs' arrival than had Sir Miles Lampson in Cairo. And he was given the briefest instructions: the status of the Prince was to be that of 'a political prisoner allowed the liberty of a normal visitor to the colony'. The Prince was 'not (repeat not) to be received at Government House'.[1]

In order not to draw attention to the new arrivals Sir Henry Moore chose Osserian because it was deep in the country, seventy miles from Nairobi. On paper Osserian may have looked suitable but in practice it was, in Olga's words, 'a complete nightmare'.[2] Probably it had once been a nice house, Moorish in design and covered with bougainvillea, but since the death of Lord Erroll it had been left to decay. Outside, the garden had reverted to a wilderness barely distinguishable from the surrounding bush. Inside, the rooms were gloomy and oppressive with black wood panelling and a lighting system that seldom gave more than half power. Nothing in the house worked; brown water oozed from the taps because the filter had long since ceased to function; the ice-box was worse than useless and the sunken bath was so cracked that it could not be filled. There was little china or linen and what blankets there were were pitted with cigarette burns.

The house was not the only depressing feature of life at Naivasha. Two British Secret Service men were on permanent duty outside the gate and a retired administrative officer had been appointed by the Governor to keep the Prince under surveillance. Fortunately Major Sharpe was not an objectionable man. Although he had to open letters, accompany Paul on journeys and generally be around, his behaviour was more that of an estate manager than a jailer. During the first few months it had to be, for, stuck in the middle of nowhere with three children, an English nannie and two Greek maids, Paul and Olga were very lost. Sharpie did his best: he helped them to buy necessities for the house; he taught Olga how to deal with the native boys and the cook who spoke only Swahili; he took Alexander off for jaunts in the bush and he entertained them all at his own farm which was eighty miles away. Though he could have been much more of a trial, his presence was a constant reminder of their status. It affected Paul the most for he, after all, was the prisoner. He was also the one who found it hardest to adjust: days that had once been occupied with politics seemed empty and pointless at Osserian, and he could summon no energy. As time passed he turned increasingly in on himself.

Olga suffered too, but in a different way. She worried about her mother and her sisters and she abhorred the isolation and discomfort, but she was not wounded like Paul. As he withdrew from life she threw herself into it. Somebody had to make the house habitable and so, with Nursie, Olga cleaned and scrubbed and knitted dishcloths out of twine. She even began to cook:

'I made scrambled eggs for lunch to eat with sausages . . .'[3]

And, of course, Olga had the children to think about. At five, Elizabeth was still safe in the hands of her nannie but Alexander, aged sixteen, and Nicky aged twelve, were problems. Nicky was a sensitive and intelligent child and at first without school or any children of his own age to play with, he was very much at a loose end. There had been no time for him to bring his games and hobbies from Beli Dvor and at Osserian the only books to read were murder stories. 'Nicky and I made ice cream today' became a frequent entry in Olga's diary. On the surface Alexander was less of a worry; he was a tough outdoor boy and the life in Kenya suited him well. Most of the time he was content, helping Sharpie, driving the car, and riding, shooting or boating with other boys. But, just occasionally, he stopped to think about the future. He was almost seventeen and his one ambition had been to join the R.A.F. With his father a prisoner of Great Britain, what chance had he now of that?

For Olga, the one redeeming aspect of life in Kenya was the kindness shown to her by the few people she met. Around Naivasha there were four families who lived within easy reach: the Perignys, who owned a large farm, the Marshalls, the Rawsons and the Traffords. Despite the rumours and the gossip and the secret service guards these people welcomed Paul and Olga into their little group, and before long Olga's days had settled down to a regular pattern broken only by the occasional trip to Nairobi. First, a French lesson for the boys, then household chores, shopping in Naivasha or ice-cream making; then lunch and a walk or gardening; then tennis at the Perignys or the Rawsons and perhaps a drink; then dinner at home or with one of the other families. It was not exciting, but it was bearable:

'Now we've got to know a few people and the boys have a friend it's not as awful as at first, if only the house was less depressing—still one must be grateful for a roof and food compared to the misery of others.'[4]

Paul could not feel the same way. He joined in with the tennis and the drinks and the bridge parties and sometimes played Chopin on the Marshalls' piano, but he rarely showed any sign of animation. He could not get over the fact that he had been rejected by England, the country he had adopted as his own. On 18th August 1941, Paul wrote to his brother-in-law, the Duke of Kent:

Your letter of 1st July was the first ray of sunshine since March. No words can express what we both felt when we got it or our deep gratitude for your unfailing friendship and understanding. I'll not even try to describe what we have been through these last months and our moral suffering at being misjudged and treated, overnight, as enemies! You, who know me, will understand what it means to me to be considered as an enemy of England. The whole of my life and the whole of my political activities are there to testify to the contrary. But to hear from you that people are beginning to realize the truth came as a balm to my wounded soul. Thanks again from all my heart. You will forgive my frankness, when I say that we have been treated with severity—no doubt at the demand and instigation of Simović—especially a woman and three children, but let me add that nothing can ever diminish our love for your dear country or change our feelings. We only live for the day when we can see the white cliffs and you all again. I know that that moment is far off and that it would be madness to suggest such a thing at present. To understand the situation one must know the inside motives of the so called Belgrade revolution. Now this is only for *your private ear*. One of the chief objects in view was the wish of a few ambitious (very few) military people to get hold of Peter and thro' him to rule the country. In consequence I must at all cost be kept away from the child so that he shouldn't fall 'under my influence'. This is an absurd conception I agree but that small minority of people (the three quarters of the Yugoslav government I am sure know nothing about this and the way we are treated) do not understand how much I hated my job (you knew it) and that the last thing I wish is to have anything to do again with Yugoslav politics! I was longing for Peter's majority to release me from a dog's existence and I was at the end of my physical strength when the March events took place. I did my best for my country, according to my lights, during nearly seven years among the most eventful and difficult in the history of the world. During all that time I walked hand in hand with your country till the last minute when I was unable to act differently owing to internal complications when my efforts tended to prevent the splitting up of my country as Croats and Slovenes insisted on the Pact being signed as well as the Minister and Chief of General Staff. The short, disastrous campaign that followed proved that the country was unable to resist and that a large part of it did not desire to fight. I am touched by what you say about Peter. He was like one of our own children: bless him. Alas! since you wrote O. received M.'s letter of 16th July. I can well imagine the intrigues going on against me to try and discredit me still more. General Simović's only successful and relentless offensive seems to be directed against me, although he has periodically sent me sugary messages of devotion and friendship. If he could only understand that he can sleep in peace—that I'll never try to play a political or any other part in Yugoslavia again. It is hard to see O.'s suffering and the children sitting and doing nothing for 4 months. We found, for Sept., some sort of agricultural school for A, miles away in another wilderness and another one for N. who according to one of the masters is already beyond it. But then it is so bad for them to sit and do nothing. N. hasn't *seen* even a boy of his age since we are here. O. gives them French lessons and that's all. Why in the whole of the British Empire and the Americas there isn't a single place near a civilized centre where we can live without being objectionable, is difficult to grasp. Why must we be exiled to this desert where there is no church, chemist, dentist, hairdresser, etc? Olga is wonderful: so brave and so efficient, doing things you wouldn't expect servants to do. She looks so tired and is suffering from a bad cough caught from Nicky who has just recovered from bronchitis. What we went through without a proper doctor and only a village practitioner who hasn't even got a telephone! There isn't even a postman in the whole district and we have to motor 16 miles both ways to get a letter. All this can be borne if necessary but the moral suffering is the worst. To read in one of your papers that we tried to run away to Germany and in another to Hungary really upset us beyond words. Why must such false statements be published? If you see Campbell, an honest man, I'm sure he'll tell you the truth as he came to the station to see us off.[5]

It was characteristically naïve of Paul to attribute all the adverse publicity to the Yugoslavs rather than to the British, but in one sense at least he was right. Through April, May and June 1941, the British had been occupied with the invasion of Greece and Hitler's declaration of war against Russia and they had had little time for Paul. There had been the odd joke, as in the Foreign Office memorandum which, mis-typing 'intern', called for Paul to be 'interred',[6] and the occasional reminder when the question of Paul's request to move to South Africa came up; but on the whole the Foreign Office simply wanted to forget. 'He has to stay where he is for the present at least. I feel sure that General Smuts would not wish to have him'[7] was Eden's comment on 2nd May and later, when King George had tried to intervene, the following note was added on a letter to

Sir Henry Moore: 'S. of S. tells me that the King thought that there were educational difficulties in Kenya. S. of S. would like us to consult Union government *hypothetically*.'[8]

This state of affairs ended abruptly when General Simović and his government arrived in London towards the end of June. General Simović was in an embarrassing position for he had to explain both the swift and complete collapse of Yugoslavia and the reasons why he and his ministers had attempted to negotiate with the Germans and Italians. Paul's observation that 'General Simović's only successful and relentless offensive seems to be directed against me' was not idle self pity. However, Paul was wrong in putting so much of the blame on Simović, for Foreign Minister Ninčić was a far worse enemy. Whilst General Simović concentrated mainly on the state of the army under the regency and on the lack of preparation for war, Ninčić worked behind the scenes to blacken Paul's character. 'Prince Paul doubts integrity of Ninčić, new Minister of Foreign Affairs',[9] the British consul in Zagreb had wired on 27th March 1941. But such wires had long been forgotten by the time a member of the Foreign Office paid the first official visit to the Yugoslav minister in June.

Dr Nintchitch stated that the Prince Regent was personally responsible for the signature of the Tripartite Pact. The coup d'état government had found a document signed by Mr Tsvetkovitch, the former President of the Council, putting forward reasoned arguments against the signature of the pact. The document had probably been drafted by M. Konstantinovitch. But it was of interest that Mr Tsvetkovitch had signed this document at one period though at a later stage he had been weak enough to agree to signature of the pact. Dr Nintchitch expressed the view that Graf Toerring had won over the Prince Regent to signature or at least to a frame of mind which enabled the Prince to be persuaded by Hitler at the Berchtesgaden meeting. The coup d'état government had found nothing on record as to what passed there . . .[10]

Ninčić had spoken almost without a pause for an hour. Much of what he said was no more than malicious gossip but, fortunately for him, the Foreign Office were not disposed to see it as such. Back in March, judgement had been passed on Prince Paul and now the Foreign Office were not seeking the truth so much as evidence of his betrayal. The Cvetković-Konstantinović document served them well as, with Paul in Kenya and Cvetković under house arrest in Yugoslavia, there was nobody to explain that it was being taken out of context. In the case of Paul's meeting with Hitler on 4th March, the secrecy of the visit was, it seemed, proof enough that Paul had given way on every count. Whether or not Toerring* had been involved did not really matter, but it fitted well with the general picture. And so did the other points that Ninčić mentioned. Nobody chose to recall the fact that it had been the Turks not the Yugoslavs who had finally refused to co-operate over the Yugoslav-Turkish alliance. Likewise, nobody bothered to inquire why Mr Campbell thought that Hitler had let it be known that Russia was to be attacked by Germany towards the end of June. Had they done so, they would have found that the information reached Belgrade from Vauhnik, the military attaché who acted as the Yugoslav spy in Berlin. The Führer had not, after all, been whispering in the Prince Regent's ear.

The stimulus provided by the Yugoslav government caused a further burst of anti-Paul activity in the Foreign Office files. Rumours, supplied by the Yugoslavs, did the rounds of the civil servants and by sheer force of numbers became more credible at every turn. Paul had insisted on giving way to German demands against the will of Cvetković; Paul had ordered demobilization; Paul had coveted the crown of the Ukraine; Paul had been offered the kingship by Hitler; Paul had plotted to kill King Peter. . . . By the time the Duke of Kent delivered the other side of the story, the case against Paul was closed. The 'defence', such as it was, consisted of extracts of Paul's letter to the Duke of Kent of 18th August combined with his answer to some questions Marina had put to Olga:

> It's childish to talk of our 'flirting' with Germany and of my visit to Hitler as if it had been a 'partie de plaisir' and a meeting with a pretty woman! H. manifested for a long time

* According to German records and to Prince Paul's own account, Graf Toerring was not present at the meeting of 6th March, nor was he used by Hitler to influence Paul.

the wish to see me and I avoided doing so for ages. I sent my Min. of Foreign Affairs first; then the P.M. and the Min. of Foreign Affairs went together later. Hitler again insisted on seeing me and for a few weeks again I turned a deaf ear. At last I was asked by my Chief Mins. including Dr Maček to 'sacrifice myself' (that's the way they looked at it) and try and see if I could get round him. As to what concerns Anthony, it is again linked with our attitude and fright of Germany. We were surrounded by Germans, Italians and Hungarians; Bulgaria and Rumania already had German troops and it is nonsense to pretend we were not frightened— we were and I defy anyone not to be under the circumstances. We carried on negotiations with Germany and asked for terms which were very difficult for them to accept and which we were sure they couldn't accept but it gave us time to mobilize which we did, as when I left we had 750,000 men *mobilized* and *concentrated*. All the stories told since, that I gave orders to demobilize are pure fiction, probably to save the face of Gen. Simović and explain in some way (at my expense!) his failure . . .[11]

'Prince Paul pretends he acted on advice of his ministers but in fact his ministers were his lacqueys' wrote C. L. Rose of the Foreign Office. 'Unconvincing, especially claim that disastrous campaign proved that country did not want to fight; truth is that, owing to the partial demobilization secretly carried out by Prince Paul, Yugoslavs unable to put up proper resistance' added Pierson Dixon; 'unconvincing' commented Orme Sargent. The Foreign Office had distilled their own version of the truth.[12]

The Yugoslav government did not restrict their activities to the Foreign Office. Public opinion was important, and so, therefore, was the press. Within weeks of the government's arrival, the newspapers were carrying articles on the fall of Yugoslavia—the Yugoslav government's version. In a leader entitled 'How Yugoslavia Fell—The Prince Regent and his Prime Minister—Evidence of Betrayal from Above' *The Times* centred on the Cvetković-Konstantinović document:*

News from Yugoslav sources throws much light on the

* See above, pages 225 and 226.

causes of the rapid victory of the German armies in the Western Balkans, and some on the painful conditions now prevailing in the conquered territories. Croats, Serbs and Slovenes were betrayed from above. Mr Tsvetkovitch, the Prime Minister who signed the pact by which Yugoslavia joined the Axis, has been bitterly reproached for his action. But documentary evidence now available shows that he signed it against his own better judgement and will, because he had been overruled by the Prince Regent and dared not oppose him.

The evidence is a memorandum which he addressed to Prince Paul shortly before the Bulgarian government opened their frontiers to the Germans . . .

But Prince Paul would not listen. He disbelieved, he said, in the possibility of any alliance with Turkey although Mr Sarajoglu did not take that view in February. He seems to have seen Hitler on 6th March, and after the coup d'état he made, not for Greece, but for Brdo, on the exposed northern frontier. He was turned back and sent to Athens and is now in Kenya. Mr Tsvetkovitch who advised the better course and accepted the worst is believed to be in Belgrade . . .[13]

In another article, *The Times* reported General Simović's speech, of 4th July, to the Yugoslav people:

General Simovitch, the Prime Minister of Yugoslavia, and the man responsible, with King Peter, for the historic reversal of Yugoslav policy on 27th March, has broadcast to his people from London his own account of the brief Yugoslav campaign, and the effect which it had on the German plan of operations.

He seems to establish a good case for his claim that Yugoslavia contributed materially to upset Hitler's time-table and forced him to adopt a totally different plan in the Middle East and Russia from that which he had originally conceived . . .[14]

Broadcasting from the safety and comfort of London, General Simović had had to offer some kind of justification for the coup d'état and the devastation it had brought upon Yugoslavia. His claim that the events of 27th March had seriously delayed the opening of Hitler's campaign in Russia was a useful one for it sounded reasonable and it could not be tested. In all fairness, General Simović probably believed it. Churchill did, and so did the British public, for it was yet another touch of romance to the Yugoslav story. The story of the boy king who rebelled against his wicked uncle, the story of the small country who 'staked her very existence'.[15]

King Peter's firm support was essential for the Simović government. In Yugoslavia there had been no problems, for Peter had been alone and confused, but in England he was considerably more vulnerable. The campaign in the Foreign Office and the press was going well but Simović knew that Paul's circle of friends and family was wide and that his only hope was to keep Peter under constant supervision. This might have been difficult had it not been for the wholehearted co-operation of Queen Marie. 'I think the fat one* and Simović have talked a lot and told a lot of lies and suggested you wanted the throne etc, the Duke of Kent warned in a letter to Paul of 5th November 1941.[16]

With the exception of a few months in 1939, Queen Marie had been living in England since 1937, first in her own flat in London and then in the country with a female friend. During this time she had bombarded Paul with a series of rambling and intimate letters full of excuses for not coming home, requests for money, and details of illnesses. Paul had responded with regular sums of money (in addition to the £30,000 per annum that she received from the civil list) and had accepted the fact that she had virtually handed over the care of Peter to him: 'I have had such happy letters from Peter in which he tells me that you are like a father to him and the nicest man he knows— God bless you Paul for that. I can't tell you what a joy it was to me for Peter to say so, 'coz you know he is very undemonstrative and coming from him like that it means a good deal. I miss him quite dreadfully and long to be with him, but as I can't I must just stand it. What a handicap one's health can be—it never entered my head when I left last year that I would breakdown so completely.'[17]

* One of the names used by the Duke of Kent and Prince Paul for Queen Marie.

At the time of writing Queen Marie had seemed both affectionate and grateful, yet within nine months she was telling her friends, journalists, and any M.P.'s she could persuade to listen, that Paul had made her life a misery in Yugoslavia and that he had done his damnedest to steal the crown from Peter.

Strange as it may seem, Queen Marie probably bore no malice towards Paul. Her behaviour is much more readily explained by a desire to draw attention to herself. Almost from the outset in Yugoslavia she had had to live in Olga's shadow: Olga had been more beautiful; Olga had fascinated her husband; Olga's son had become her own husband's favourite; Olga's husband had become Prince Regent. With Olga out of the way she at last had the chance to be the queen she had never been, and for this she was quite prepared to concoct a few stories with General Simović, and tell a few lies.

Closeted with his scheming mother, or with ministers of the Yugoslav government, it is not altogether surprising that Peter was prepared to overlook certain inaccuracies in the stories that were being told about his uncle. If Paul had kept him better informed, he might have felt the need to speak out, but Paul had cushioned him from politics and affairs of state: indeed Paul had never really got through to him at all. Besides, Peter was enjoying his new rôle as king in exile. The British government were making every effort to keep him amused and the British public were only too willing to accept him as a hero. Young, interesting-looking and a great-great-grandson of Queen Victoria, he made perfect copy for the newspapers: 'King Peter visits Portsmouth', 'King Peter inspects London gun sites'; 'King Peter visits King George'; 'King Peter attends birthday service in Bayswater Greek Orthodox Cathedral'; his movements filled their pages.[18]

'Peter is eighteen today and officially of age, if only Pacey could have handed over to him in the way he hoped' Olga entered in her diary on 6th September 1941. Neither she nor Paul had had any word from Peter, but from Marina they had gathered that he was living in the country with his mother and that he was forbidden by his ministers to see the Kents or Chips or any other of Paul's close friends. 'Poor boy,' Olga continued later, 'his weakness of character is even more evident now, allowing himself to be so completely overruled by his ministers' opinions, as not to insist on being informed as to his uncle's whereabouts and means of living! . . . any affection or loyalty he may have had for P. seems to have faded away. And to think of all he owes him!'[19]

Harsh perhaps, but Olga had little cause to be charitable. She was beginning to wonder if Paul would ever recover his spirits. 'P in the depths of gloom—he usually stays in bed almost till lunch time, wish he would try to react.'[20]

Olga found it difficult to understand Paul's behaviour for she was much happier: in September they had at last moved out of dreadful Osserian. Their new home, Preston's house, was further around the lake and infinitely more pleasant. The lights worked, the water was fresh, the rooms were bright and the climate was less heavy and sticky than it had been at Osserian. Olga had looked upon the move as the end of an era, but Paul had hardly noticed. It was not the physical discomfort that he minded.

Paul had pinned a lot of hope on what the Duke of Kent had written in July: 'I know you were misjudged here at the time— but since then with the collapse of your country in three days— it was obvious that what you did was for the best—and to save the country for Peter'[21] but as the summer and autumn passed it became increasingly apparent that the Duke's statement had been more an attempt to raise Paul's spirits than an objective analysis. In fact, the press campaign against Paul was reaching its height and in Nairobi, as elsewhere, it had its champions. Extracts from the English newspapers appeared in the *Mombasa Times* and information from Kenya, in exaggerated form, was relayed back to London to furnish articles on 'How this quisling prince spends his time'.[22] Soon Paul could not go into the capital without encountering gossip and ill feeling. It hurt him terribly, and it hurt him even more when he found out that Alexander had been taunted and bullied at school on his account.

The publicity was not Paul's only preoccupation. He was desperately worried about money too. On the matter of expenses the Foreign Office had decided that Her Majesty's Government should pay for the rent of the house 'to mark the fact that it is, in a sense, prison'[23] but that Prince Paul should pay for its upkeep and for his own living expenses. The fact that the outgoings would be dictated by the size of the house and the distance from Nairobi did not enter their consideration. However, it tormented Paul. Simply keeping a house like Osserian or Prestons ticking over was costing him £200 per month and each trip to Nairobi was an extra £10 or £12. Then there were doctors, dentists and schools to pay and, on top of everything else, an income tax of £150 in every £1,000. For tax purposes, Paul was classed as a British resident; for every other purpose he was a prisoner.

In Yugoslavia Paul and Olga had lived on an allowance from the civil list, supplemented by income from money Paul had with Coutts & Co. in London. In cash terms they had never been fabulously rich, for Paul had spent any extra funds on pictures or furniture, or on one of the houses. Equally, they had never been short of money and Paul had always had the security that his art treasures were worth a fortune. About six months after leaving Yugoslavia, Paul had received word, via Sir Miles Lampson, that the occupation authorities had 'saved, inventoried and put in a safe place all his art collections and possessions of value'.[24] This, as Paul rightly assumed, meant that they had taken them to Germany and that he would never see them again. The only article that he had saved from Beli Dvor was a Gobelin tapestry, small enough to be rolled up and stuffed in a suitcase. Other than that, he owned about ten pictures which had been out of the country at the time of the coup d'état. Amongst these was his beloved Laocöon, which was on loan to the Mellon gallery in Washington.

Paul and Olga had, between them, brought only £200 out of Yugoslavia, and without any money from the Yugoslav government they were dependent entirely on Paul's London bank account. Far away from civilization and from the people that were controlling his life, Paul felt utterly vulnerable, and the idea of using up capital terrified him. He had no idea how long it was going to have to last and his greatest fear was that he would die leaving Olga and the children destitute. He toyed with the possibility of selling the Laocöon in America but decided against it because of the prohibitive duty on bringing the proceeds back to England.*

---

* Paul estimated its value at $200,000. He eventually sold it from South Africa in 1946.

As with his other problems, Paul turned to his brother-in-law:

My Dearest Georgie,

Here I am once more to bother you. Since I wrote, income tax has been raised so please send enclosed to Stephens.* Our position will become desperate. If only we could live in a small house or flat in a town but we are made to live in a large establishment miles away from everything. . . . Is Canada impossible or U.S.A. Could Roosevelt help us to get there? He was always so friendly to me in the past . . .[25]

By the time this letter was written, the Duke of Kent had already done his best to get Paul and Olga out of Kenya but he had met with little success: 'I had a long talk with Winston—and he said it would be much better if you stayed where you were. He wasn't very helpful—he is so busy with today and tomorrow that what happened yesterday or last week is of no interest. As to Anthony, he feels he was snubbed when you didn't see him and can't get over it—As he is entirely under W's spell, one can't get anything out of him.'[26]

However, over the money the Duke of Kent was able to be more constructive. After months of trying, he managed to get through to the Yugoslav government who agreed immediately to re-establish the allowance to which Paul was technically entitled. They had only stopped it, they explained, because they were not sure of Paul's address.†

No request, great or small, was too much trouble for Georgie. He settled the money question, he arranged for Alexander to join the R.A.F. and for Lilia‡ to travel from Egypt to Kenya and, besides all this, he wrote regular letters and even contrived to send Paul a present at Christmas:

On 20th February I got your letter of 29th December and

* Mr Stephens of Coutts bank.
† Despite the Duke of Kent's efforts the Yugoslav government did not keep up a regular payment of Paul's allowance, leaving him in an even more difficult position than before, as he never knew whether or not he could expect money.
‡ Mme Lilia Ralli.

also that lovely pen. How you knew that I ever wanted a pen beats me flat as O swears she never mentioned it to you. It is heavenly in colour and I simply love it. It was so unexpected and a great joy—thanks a million times. I wish I could express all we feel about your kindness to us and all the infinite trouble you are taking over us. If there is ever a change in our condition it will be entirely thanks to you. I hope that what they tell you about being so busy and having no time to bother about us is true and not an excuse. But then, in everything to do with us there are such contradictions and it is always the thing that harms and hurts us most that is chosen. For instance, we are prisoners but when it concerns money we are British residents and if we are intending to go to the seaside we immediately become enemy aliens who can't go to the coast—we might give signals to the Japs! ...[27]

It was largely the Duke of Kent's friendship that kept Paul going through the first year of his exile. Chips remained faithful and the King, whose hands were tied, sent affectionate messages. But nobody really battled for Paul like his brother-in-law and nobody understood so well the humiliation that Paul was going through. Nevertheless letters from other friends helped, specially when they were as sensitive and informative as the one Paul received from Kenneth Clark in November 1941.

We have thought of you very often in the past year, but didn't know how to get in touch with you. Now we hear from the Duchess of Kent that she will kindly forward you a letter, and I am very glad of the chance of writing. I know you won't want me to say anything about the state of the world in general, but you may be glad to know something about such fragments of our world as still exist.

First of all you will be glad to know that some time ago I got all the National Gallery pictures into a perfectly safe place—an old slate mine deep in the fastnesses of North Wales. There are a series of magnificent caves, about 1000 ft deep in the side of a mountain, and in these we have built galleries all air conditioned, so that all the pictures are hung up, and are actually in very much better condition than they have ever been in in their lives. It is a strange experience to [drive trucks] miles up into the mountains, then to enter a cave and go 400 yards down a passage, and finally to come on the whole National Gallery all hung and lit, in a lovely dry, temperate atmosphere, complete with restorers' rooms, etc. I have taken a film of the whole place which I shall hope to show you after the war. Did you know, by the way, that for a year or so I was in charge of our film propaganda? It was most interesting, and I was less bad at it than might be supposed. But for a variety of reasons I am now back at the National Gallery where there was a great deal to be done.

We have managed to persuade the government to spend a large sum of money on buying or commissioning modern painters—on the pretext that they are making a record of the war. This is really an experiment in state patronage, also in education, for the resulting pictures are not only shown at the National Gallery but are sent round the country. We have about a dozen shows travelling round and on the whole have managed to employ all the artists of talent, even saving some of them from the army. At least two of them, Henry Moore and Graham Sutherland, have real distinction, and I think are better than any painters of their generation in France.

The French artists, by the way, are still working. Bonnard is still alive and has just exchanged his model with Maillol—who is painting! Matisse is very prosperous, and is collaborating, as one would expect. (Valéry, on the other hand, has behaved with great courage and may, I fear, be in want. He has resigned from the Académie Française.) Rouault is unable to grasp what has happened and thinks it is all a posthumous trick by Vollard.

We have even managed to buy one or two pictures for the Gallery which I think you would like. The most important of these (which isn't quite bought yet) is David Crawford's Rembrandt portrait of Margaretha Trip which is even more subtle and beautiful than the one already in the Gallery. It is a miracle of painting. In a less serious vein we have bought a most ravishing mannerist landscape by Niccolo del'Abbate the friend of (Primaticcio) who went with him to Fontainebleau. It was painted about 1550 and almost like Tintoretto, with Fontainebleau figures—very large and cost £300 at a country sale. On the whole, however, there are very few pictures for sale and most dealers have gone to America. A good many lost their galleries in the bombing, including your friend Mr Sabin. All that corner of Bond Street looks like Ypres in the last war. Your other friend Mr Drey is still functioning and has some nice things, but on the whole there is very little to look at. The only public gallery still open is Hampton Court. I have taken away all the famous pictures—over 100—but have got some others out of the deposits which look very well and are really most beautiful in an unfashionable way.

I hope you will not think from all this that I am unaware of the dreadful state of the world or do not realize that our whole future still hangs in the balance. On the contrary, such considerations fill most of my working day; but I am sure you will wish to know about the small part of my life which is still spent in trying to keep alive the things we really believe in.

Jane joins me in sending our respects and warmest sympathy to Princess Olga.

. . . p.s. I hear BB* is still in Italy and so far unmolested, and leading the same life writing a great deal.[28]

Paul, though thrilled at all the news and especially at the news that Berenson was still alive, was too demoralized to answer this kind letter.† He was consumed with one idea and one idea only: to clear his name in Britain. And the key to this was the Duke of Kent.

It was thus with uncontrollable grief and misery that Paul heard, on 27th August 1942, that his beloved friend and brother-in-law had been killed. The flying boat, in which the Duke had been travelling to Iceland, had crashed near Dunrobin Castle in Scotland on the previous day. Everyone on board had been killed.

Marina was completely shattered. The King and Queen did their best to comfort her but it was obvious to them that she

* Since 1939, when he had first heard of the Fascist treatment of Jews, Paul had been worried for his friend's safety.

† Paul replied in October 1944.

needed someone from her own family. Yet who? Neither her mother, who was in Nazi-occupied Greece, nor her sister Elizabeth, who was in Germany, could come to England. The only possibility was Olga. King George acted swiftly. He obtained permission from the Prime Minister, dispatched a telegram to Kenya, and asked that priority transportation be made available to her.

Olga left Nairobi on 10th September with Lilia Ralli, expecting to be away no more than a month. But when she arrived in England she found Marina in such a pathetic state that she put off her departure first until November and then until December. Her presence in England did not, however, pass unnoticed. A certain Captain Cunningham-Reid was relentless with his questioning in Parliament. Protected by Parliamentary privilege, his slander was ruthless. It went unanswered and soon stirred the press into renewed anti-Paul activity. Once again articles on 'the quisling prince' appeared in the papers and the repercussions in Kenya were so bad that Paul had to cease going into Nairobi altogether.

Despite all this, Olga's visit did Paul's reputation more good than harm. Conscious that her first task was to comfort Marina, Olga took care not to crusade and thus embarrass her relations in any way. But quietly, at Coppins, she told Paul's story to those who came to hear it: Nancy Astor, Chips, Bobbety Cranborne, and the King. 'Bertie has been here twice—the day after I came and two days later for tea. Spoke so nicely of you, asked me about our life etc., all of which I told him stressing the isolation and patheticness of it all, Quissy's* treatment etc., all of which seemed to touch him. We spoke of the Mikros.† He said he is badly advised, the Gov. all hating each other and that he doesn't even know whom to trust among them. The second time he brought me a detailed list of the members of the Gov. (which I copied) and even asked me to mark those who were desirable and those not! To which I replied that I preferred not to mix up in that question.'[29]

By acting with discretion and dignity, Olga rose above the newspapers and the ever more hysterical attacks of Captain Cunningham-Reid. In the House, the Members tired of the

* Paul and Olga's son, Alexander.
† King Peter.

Captain's insatiable vindictiveness, and they let him know it. 'Has not this lady been allowed to be in a position whereby if she returns to Kenya she will be able to convey information to her quisling husband which might be invaluable to the Axis?' he asked heroically on 16th December. 'The circumstances are well known,' Mr Eden replied sharply. 'Princess Olga was the only sister of the Duchess of Kent who could come to this country at all, and it was with the government's full authority and with their approval and I have no apology to make for it.'[30] The House responded with loud cheers. Princess Marina had all their sympathy.

At about this time there was a gradual change in attitude at the Foreign Office, too. As Olga's description of their African existence got about, and Simović's government ministers continued to bicker amongst themselves, Paul's name began to feature once again, less one-sidedly, in Foreign Office files: 'Personally I have always felt that our treatment of Prince Paul has been "petty and unworthy of us". For years he was our loyal friend, giving us valuable information and helping our cause as far as he could, and if in the end he ratted on us, he did so, I am convinced, not through any malicious or treasonable motive, but merely through weakness of character and moral cowardice. It is scarcely for us to punish him for these defects, nor, as Lord Cranborne says, can we conceivably pretend that he is a dangerous enemy and a menace either to ourselves or our Allies.'[31] So wrote C. L. Rose. Dixon, Howard and Orme Sargent agreed. It was time to review the case of the Prince Regent. Surely they could remove the 'rather ineffective but humiliating restrictions' under which he was held and put him, as it were, on parole.[32] He would still be a political prisoner but he would be allowed to live where he chose, without surveillance, and with normal social relations with the Governor.

There was only one problem: they had just assured Captain Cunningham-Reid that Prince Paul was being treated in the same way as any other political prisoner, and as Howard pointed out 'it might prove embarrassing if it were discovered that very soon after that assurance was given we relaxed the restrictions'. But, as he went on to say 'need we take Capt. C-Reid seriously into account in this connection'?[33]

This question was still under consideration when a malicious article about Prince Paul appeared in the *Sunday Times*. The Foreign Office decided to put the matter aside until the publicity had died down. It remained aside until early in February 1943.

Without Olga's support and without Georgie's letters, Paul had given way completely to depression. Unable to show his face in Nairobi because of Captain Cunningham-Reid and his connections in Kenya, Paul had soon ceased bothering to get up at all. His days were spent in bed with a gun under the pillow, doing nothing, and consuming nothing besides the cup of hot chocolate that Elizabeth's nanny brought to him each morning. He even contemplated suicide, for he reasoned that by continuing to live he could only bring more harm to his innocent wife and children. The fact that he was now a prisoner at the behest of his 'beloved England' and that his children were, by association, outcasts was intolerable to him.

At the end of November 1942 Paul's doctor, Dr Bunny, was sufficiently disturbed to pay a personal visit to the Governor. As a result of this, Sir Henry Moore sent a telegram to England explaining Paul's condition and urging the immediate return of Princess Olga. But it was the middle of the war and what with difficulties over aeroplanes and bad winter weather, Olga did not leave England until 31st December. This delay still further aggravated Paul's condition for after the Duke of Kent's accident he had a morbid dread of flying. Olga's journey took twelve days and when she arrived at Prestons she received a shock: Paul met her at the door in his dressing-gown, wasted and thin, and leaning heavily on a stick. At forty-nine he had become an old man.

The Governor had hoped that with Princess Olga's return Paul would 'shake off his depression and rapidly recover his health'.[34] But Paul's condition continued to decline. Olga, who had come back full of hope after her warm reception in England, was at her wits' end. On 23rd January she wrote in her diary: 'Pulled through another day—the same eternal discussions on our future. Sh.* told P that the Gov. had a second wire from Oliver† instructing him to look for a house nearer Nairobi.

* Major Sharpe.
† Oliver Stanley S. of S. for the Colonies.

P can talk of nothing but the subject of his treatment—he doesn't care any more where he lives: only that he will die if he stays here. Eats less than ever and smokes all day—it wears one out and I can't keep Marina in the know each day: even when I do I know the wires are copied.'[35]

Towards the end of January, Dr Bunny informed the Governor that there had not been any improvement in Paul's health and that if no action were taken he would not be responsible for the consequences. On 6th February Dr Jex Blake visited Paul to give a second medical opinion and his diagnosis prompted the Governor to send a telegram marked 'Most secret and personal' to the Secretary of State for the Colonies on 9th February 1943:

Prince Paul.

Since person named, despite Princess Olga's return, has remained in bed in highly depressed condition, I arranged with the agreement of all concerned, for Dr Jex Blake to be called in. He reports that the general state of health of person named is now very low, that his mental state causes him grave anxiety, and that if his present state of acute depression is allowed to persist, the development of insanity in the form of melancholia is definitely to be feared.

I have received report in very similar terms from Dr Bunny, and full reports follow by first bag. I have discussed the situation with both independently, and their view is that if a clearer declaration by H.M. Government could be made for local publication here as to his status, including his recognition at Government House and more freedom to move about the Colony, this should do much to improve his mental condition. I undertook to convey to you this medical opinion, though I explained to them in confidence that I had hoped for a solution along these lines during my recent visit to London but without success. My personal view, in which Dr Jex Blake fully concurred, is that a complete change of scene and of environment is what is really required. Interests of person named are predominantly intellectual and aesthetic, and he is bored with country life. If, in view of his present grave condition, the earlier proposal that he should go to South Africa could be reconsidered, I believe that this would be best solution. Alternatively would America be now out of the question?[36]

The telegram, and the letter and doctor's reports which followed, were received with some alarm in London and it was generally agreed that Paul should be moved to South Africa. Only one person stood out against the proposal: the Prime Minister. In a personal minute to the Secretary of State for the Colonies, Winston Churchill expressed his view: 'I really do not see why we should worry about this man who did so much harm to his country, and deprived it of its chances of striking a united blow for its liberties. Considering the terrible things that are going on in Yugoslavia, I should think Prince Paul is very lucky to be confined under such easy conditions. If it is only a question of a few civilities from Government House, there is no need to worry about that.'[37] But, for once, Churchill was alone: even Eden thought it necessary to do something. With Oliver Stanley, the Secretary of State for the Colonies, Eden composed an eminently tactful reply: 'While we entirely agree with your minute of 12th February as to the part Prince Paul has played in the destruction of Yugoslavia and the absence therefore of any claims to special consideration, we both feel it would be extremely unfortunate if he became permanently insane while in our custody . . .'[38] Using, as an excuse, the unsuitable climate in Kenya, Eden and Stanley went on to advocate a move to South Africa. Reluctantly Churchill agreed, and in so doing probably spared Paul's life.

What was the nature of Churchill's profound antipathy towards Prince Paul and what were the reasons for his personal vindictiveness? If his minute of 12th February 1943 to the Foreign Secretary is any guide (and the Prime Minister knew that the likely consequence of his actions was the permanent loss of mind of a prisoner) his dislike of the ex-Prince Regent appears to have stemmed, in the main, from his belief that Paul had done 'so much harm to his country'. It is difficult to understand how Churchill could have meant to imply that the 'terrible things that are going on in Yugoslavia' could be laid at the feet of Paul simply because he had 'deprived [his country] of its chances of striking a united blow for its liberties'. It is difficult to believe that Churchill thought Paul had actually

288

harmed his country *because* he had prevented it from rising up against Hitler. For, thanks in large measure to the consistent disregard with which his repeated entreaties for military and economic assistance had been received in London during the late 1930s, Paul had lacked the means either of effective military attack or of national defence and had accordingly refused to push his government into a declaration of war against Germany.

It was precisely because Paul and his ministers had been unwilling to commit Yugoslavia to a path of national destruction, that they had refused to 'strike a united blow'. First, it would not have been united (for Maček and Kuloveć had said as much); and secondly, it would not have constituted much of a blow.

It is even more difficult to believe that Churchill thought Paul had done harm in Yugoslavia before 1941. The record of Paul's Regency years shows that his administration was benevolent and, as a unifying force, effective within Yugoslavia. In the conduct of foreign policy his own strongly pro-British sympathies had been consistently in evidence.

The inevitable conclusion is that Churchill somehow equated responsibility for Yugoslavia's not having risen against Nazi Germany, when first instructed to do so by London, with responsibility for its subsequent and terrible punishment.

Eden, and Stanley too, in their tactful reply took Churchill to mean that Paul had played the major part in the destruction of his country and they readily agreed with their leader's assessment. What they meant by this in 1943 remains unclear.

To be sure, Paul and his government had defied the British government. They had been instructed to declare war on Hitler and to fall upon the Italians in Albania. Without the means at their disposal and with no prospect of any Allied help, they had refused. They had played for time and, when at last their basic pre-conditions designed to render the Tripartite Pact ineffective had been agreed, they had been left with no alternative but to sign. They had thwarted the British plan and Churchill and Eden had had good reason to be vengeful. But Paul had played no part in the destruction of Yugoslavia.

Nor would Paul have behaved differently had he had (as he

K   289

was assumed in London to have had), or been prepared to exercise, dictatorial power. He thought in 1941, and continued to think for the rest of his life, that his government had acted in the best interests of its people.

And what of the 'liberties' of which the great British leader wrote and which had been trampled on by the Germans in the space of a few days after Paul had been bundled off into exile? They were never again, after the British had had their way, to be returned to his country except under the definition of a communist system of government.

There were, then, understandable reasons why the British Prime Minister should harbour a personal grudge against the Prince Regent. There were equally understandable reasons why the press, in the immediate wake of the coup, followed the official government line. It is possible, even, to explain the excesses in Parliament of Captain Cunningham-Reid whose own caddish marital behaviour had made the headlines for many weeks. (His speeches and questions in the House were essentially the result of ignorance and of a desire to bask, by association, in the glory of the 1941 conspirators.) In every case the judgement was identical: Prince Paul was a traitor, he had turned on his friends, he was pro-Nazi, a quisling and a coward. No one produced proof, for none appeared to be needed. Churchill had stated it to be so and, for most people, that was enough.

But in 1942 a book had been published, written by an acknowledged authority on Yugoslavia and one of Britain's greatest authors, which contained what appeared to be a serious and informative account of the facts. It was not a government publication. Nor was it a product of journalism. It was a massive and brilliant masterpiece of English Literature by Rebecca West,* and its epilogue was the *locus classicus* of the case against Paul.

When the book appeared, in two volumes, it was acclaimed by reviewers all over the world. 'One of the great books of this century', wrote Elizabeth Nicholas in the *Sunday Times*; the *Observer* hailed it as 'a major book in every sense . . . an

---

* *Black Lamb and Grey Falcon—A Journey through Yugoslavia*, by Rebecca West, was published by Macmillan in 1942, and re-issued in 1977.

artist's book; a philosopher's book; a book that holds a torch'.*
It was, to Paul and his family's unfathomable suffering and cost,
an instant best seller.

In Paul's own judgement, Rebecca West did more to blacken
and damage his name than anyone else. She described him as
having been 'pro-Axis',[39] of having had 'a genuine admiration
for Hitler's personality',[40] of having personally intervened to
withhold the Cvetković government 'permission to refuse
Germany's demands'[41] and of having 'persuaded Cvetković to
act against his judgement'.[42]

According to Rebecca West: 'There was also imposed on
Yugoslavia an ignominy peculiar to the moment. The Pact
bound it to permit the passage of German war-material on the
railways to Greece; and it was not to retain the right of
inspection of such traffic. This meant that troops also would
probably be carried. Thus Yugoslavia was forced to help
Germany to knife in the back a Balkan brother, her kin by
blood and tradition.'[43] In fact, in the agreement signed by
Cvetković and Cincar-Marković in Vienna there was no
reference to war-material or to a denial of the right of inspection,
and in the second of the appended notes from Ribbentrop it
was specifically stated that no demands were to be made on
Yugoslavia to permit the march or transportation of troops
through the Yugoslav state or territory†—to Greece or anywhere else.

A more vivid inaccuracy is to be found in the description of
the celebrations on the morning of the coup d'état: '. . . At
8.00 in the morning the exhilarated boy drove in radiant sunshine
through Belgrade, which rejoiced as if he were returning from
victory instead of being about to lead them to defeat. From
the city Palace he issued a Proclamation declaring that he was
about to assume royal power, that the Army and Navy had put
themselves at his disposal, and appealing to the Croats and
Slovenes and Serbs to stand firm round the throne. The crowd
that gathered in the street to see him show himself on the

* When this book was re-issued by Macmillan, the fly-leaf said:
'Its publication during one of the great climaxes in the story of
Western European culture was significant; the book was completed
while bombs fell on London and Yugoslavia fell.'
† See Appendix III, pages 313 to 315, below.

balcony, gave rapturous cheers . . .'[44] This passage about King Peter, who in reality spent most of the day waiting apprehensively with his aunt and cousins at Beli Dvor, belongs to a work of fiction.

But none of *Black Lamb and Grey Falcon* was sold as fiction, and it set the attitudes of a whole generation. Paul was powerless. 'What can you do against one of the best and most popular writers of English?' he asked. 'What can you do against a best-selling book?'

CHAPTER XIV

1943–1976

The Other Shore

In the late spring of 1943, Paul and Olga were informed that, thanks largely to General Smuts' intervention, they were to be allowed to travel south to the Cape. Immediately Paul's condition began to improve.

On 11th June 1943 Paul and Olga left Kenya for good. Seventeen days later they arrived in Johannesburg and took up residence in a dingy hotel and later in a small modern house that had been found for them in Young Street. Although Paul was not officially given his liberty until 1st June 1946, the worst part of his punishment was over. In South Africa, there was no Major Sharpe to check his mail and dog his every step, and there was no more isolation or bitterness. He and Olga were accepted as ordinary people and not as prisoners. General Smuts and his wife called on them on the day after their arrival.

Slowly Paul recovered his mental health. He began, in 1947, to correspond with Maček, who had fled to the United States, and later with Cvetković,* and he watched with interest and alarm the progression of events in Yugoslavia and the spread of communism in the world. But politics had only ever been his job. Art had been his passion and in Johannesburg Paul began to realize that at least in this one field his interest was

* After the German invasion of Yugoslavia, Cvetković had been placed under house arrest. In May 1942 he was sent to a prison camp outside Belgrade. He was released after three months and lived quietly until September 1944 when two of Mihailović's men suggested that he should join in the anti-German movement in Bulgaria. Cvetković accepted but when he reached Bulgaria the Russians had already declared war. Cvetković fled to Turkey on a Bulgarian passport. He stayed in Ankara until 1946 trying to drum up support against the Communists. After the war he moved with his wife, Mara, to Paris, where they saw a lot of Prince Paul and Princess Olga.

undiminished, his friendships intact and his reputation unaffected. He met a talented local artist and commissioned a portrait of Olga; he presented a picture by Neville Lewis to the Johannesburg Art Gallery, and he finally replied to the long and informative letter that Kenneth Clark had written to him in November 1941. But more important than all this, he reestablished contact with Bernard Berenson. In the autumn of 1945 he received a letter from his old friend, and he answered immediately on 14th October:

Oh the joy of hearing from you altho' your letter was several months old. . . . To know that you are alive and well in your beautiful home and looked after by a beloved friend was one of the rare things I heard for years which cheered me up. The death of your poor Mary was less of a surprise after knowing of her ill health for so many years and I often wondered if she would survive these ordeals. And yet with her a whole epoch has departed and I can never forget her great and charming personality and her immeasurable kindness to me thro' so many years.

I shuddered when I read a description of all your troubles and am trying not to dwell on them so as to give myself up entirely to the happiness of knowing that you are at I Tatti again. If only I could spend the rest of my days near you! Will that be possible I wonder? The future of my own land looks dim but the shock that came was expected by me altho' it didn't make it less of a shock when it came. For the rest of the world I have never been less able to visualize the future I must admit. . . . We live in a suburb of J. and have a small garden. We lead a quiet life seeing only a few people and reading a lot. I think that without my passion for art and books I would have gone mad, especially in Kenya where we spent more than two, very hard, years. Here, it is a great improvement and this country has many good points. I appreciate the Union (at least what I know of it) for not being exotic, a thing I dislike intensely, but all the same I can never become a good African at my age and only realize now how European I am . . .[1]

'If only I could spend the rest of my days near you'. It was

Paul's ultimate wish, and it was one that kept him going. But before he could return to live in Europe, he needed not only to be free, but also to feel that, at least in the opinion of his friends, he had not behaved with dishonour. He had been treated, for reasons of state, as an enemy of Britain. For reasons of state, too, slander had been allowed to pass unanswered in the Commons, in the press and on the radio. If anything, it had been encouraged by a British government anxious to show that the 1941 coup in Belgrade had been worthwhile.

In 1946, the press, which had without exception accepted the 'treacherous quisling' line about Paul, seemed again to be out for his blood. On 3rd March the *Sunday Times* published an article describing Paul as a war criminal. On 21st April, Olga noted in her diary 'a fourth article about Paul being a quisling and will be tried at Nurnberg in two months'. By the end of August, the press campaign had reached a crescendo and Elizabeth, aged ten, was beginning to face bullying at school. On 23rd August she struck a girl for suggesting that 'her father had been friends with Hitler'.

It was, of course, time for the winners to start rounding up and closing in on the losers. It was the start of the Nurnberg trials. By 16th September, Goering had taken his own life and ten of his colleagues had been hanged.

Yet not all the victors were blameless; not all the vanquished delinquent. Back in March, Paul had heard of the capture of Mihailović by Tito. By 17th July Mihailović had been shot alongside eight of his Chetniks. 'He was once such a hero' noted Olga with bitterness. For reasons which were none too clear at the time, the interests of King Peter had been effectively dumped by the British in favour of a communist partisan.

How was it possible that the British, who by any definition of national morality had had an obligation to hand back to King Peter the remnants of his war ravaged nation, were now so readily prepared to support a communist in Yugoslavia? The answer, quite simply, was that for the British, the absolute test of 'loyalty' in Nazi-occupied Yugoslavia during the 1941–5 period had been immediate and visible military action against the German armed forces (exactly, as under different circumstances, it had been in March 1941). Against this paramount consideration, Tito's activities had certainly seemed more convincing than those of Mihailović. The radio messages and 'field reports' from the headquarters of the two rival guerilla leaders, as transmitted to London, had showed that the communist had been considerably more effective in his anti-Nazi activities than the monarchist.

But the fact that all such communications had had to pass through British Intelligence in Cairo and that the Cairo desk had all along been staffed by a committed and well known communist, James Klugman,[2] had been totally disregarded in London. This was hardly surprising, for the British were waging a military war against Germany and not an ideological war against communism. Besides, the British Secret Service had for some time been recruiting not only communists and anti-royalists, but fully fledged comintern agents as well.*

To Paul, the death of Mihailović, in July 1946, was a tragedy. It marked ultimate victory for communism in Yugoslavia. Yet this, which he now accepted as inevitable, was his own ultimate vindication. The single-minded pursuit by the Allies, and by the British in particular, of immediate military advantage over Germany had dictated policies which had led in 1941 to the military annihilation of his country and now to its abandonment to an alien and abhorrent ideology and system of government.

Was it conceivable that now, at last, his own position might be better understood? Even if his actions, and those of his government, had run counter to the specific instructions emanating from London in 1941, had he not nevertheless behaved with honour and in the immediate interests of his country as Prince Regent? Could it not also now be said that, in the long run, his policies might have yielded better results not only for Yugoslavia but even for Western Europe as well?

But in 1946 nobody was inclined to re-evaluate Paul's position. His guilt was already established and it looked, as the year progressed, as if he might be called upon to defend not only his honour but his life as well. The Nurnberg trials were in full swing and Olga's prayer 'Pitus† will protect us!' was entered in her diary on 21st April 1946, in a moment of utter desperation.

* Guy Burgess joined S.I.S. in 1939, Kim Philby in 1940.
† General Jan Smuts.

General Smuts, who certainly believed that his distinguished guest had been judged unfairly and treated shabbily by Britain, was at a loss to understand how the truth, as Paul described it and as he believed it, could have been so distorted. The early reaction of the British government, Cunningham-Reid's parliamentary vindictiveness, newspaper articles and Rebecca West were all, in different measure, to blame.

Not surprisingly, it was inconceivable to Paul in 1946 that he, or anyone else for that matter, would ever be able to set the record straight. He realized that the 'popular view' would prevail. All the more, then, he cared that at least his close friends should be aware of the truth. Their sympathy he knew he could count on. But the thought that those whose views and judgement mattered to him might one day objectively understand the truth and help him to hold his head up in London seemed far fetched. People were not prepared to believe that he had acted in good faith and in Yugoslavia's interests.

Yet the moment when symbolically and emotionally Britain's hand of friendship was once more held out to Paul was not far off. Early in 1947, King George VI and Queen Elizabeth arrived on a State visit to South Africa. It was, in terms of strict protocol and Foreign Office agenda, almost impossible for them to receive their Yugoslav friends. Yet, true to their basic instincts and to their old friendship, King George and Queen Elizabeth insisted on it. In many ways this display of faith and loyalty changed Paul's life. It marked the beginning of a process of reinstatement that was to continue and gain ground throughout the remaining thirty years of his life. For the rest of his days Paul was to be welcomed and treated by the King and Queen, and later by Queen Elizabeth II, as a friend, a royal prince, and a Garter Knight.

Yet his own deep wounds took years to heal, as did his self-respect and confidence. Even with dear friends like Archie Balfour his first attempts at correspondence were diffident and faltering and full of fears of rejection. 'You must realize that I have been through such awful times these last years and, though I have survived it, I am no longer what I was and have reached the other shore a very changed man with innumerable complexes, one of them being a complete inability to write.

K*   297

I know that it's idiotic and difficult to understand, but there it is. In your case, I felt, besides, that in writing to you, I might do harm to Jock. So you must forgive a crazy old man whose feelings to you and your beloved family have never altered.'[3]*

By February 1948 Paul had begun to set his sights on a return to Europe, and by October of that year the plans were made. Paul and Olga had been issued with South African passports and visas to enter Switzerland. Towards the end of the month Paul, Olga, Elizabeth, Nursie and Lilia arrived in Geneva at the Hotel des Bergues. A huge bunch of orchids awaited them there, a present from Bernard Berenson. Paul immediately and excitedly made plans to receive his ageing friend. 'It was wonderful seeing you again after all these years and I can't tell you how touched I was by your arrival here in this cold weather,' wrote Paul on 2nd November 1948. 'How I enjoyed seeing you both and how I miss you. Bless you a thousand times for being such a wonderful friend and especially keep well and look after yourself.'[4]

Paul began at once to show his face in galleries and showrooms, and within a week of his arrival he had written to Berenson: 'I discovered a remarkable antiquarian in Lausanne called Valloton (nephew of the painter) who showed me some lovely things including an Ingres drawing, Cézannes, Renoirs and Veuillards. So unexpected and prices quite reasonable.'[5] His interest in art was not without humour and before very long he had unearthed an intriguing piece of information about his old friend, Sir Joseph Duveen: 'Now something which will amuse you. In 1935 I asked Duveen to bid for me at an auction for a Sèvres service and he sent me the bill for £2,500. Now, I have just discovered the proof that at the sale the service fetched less than £1,000!!'[6]

But Paul was no longer in a position to invest in pictures. Even after only four weeks at the Hotel des Bergues he had begun to realize that the expense would be too great. He was undergoing a cure, which was in itself expensive, for his liver and blood had been badly poisoned by malaria during his seven years in Africa. Apart from his few pictures scattered about

* This letter was one of condolence. Paul had just learned of Archie's mother's death.

Europe and the U.S.A., he had some capital investments which were held in London and which yielded him some sterling income. This was enough to live on but it was both difficult and expensive to transfer into Swiss francs. He therefore turned to his friends in the world of art for guidance, no longer as a buyer but as a potential seller. 'As my cure is going to be a lengthy one and as my Swiss francs are dwindling I very much fear that I'll have to part with one of my pictures. What do you advise me to do and could you help me in U.S.A.?'[7] He had already received back his Mantegna as well as one or two other pictures which had been with friends or professional cleaners or on exhibit outside Yugoslavia at the time of the 1941 coup.* He kept these in a cupboard, unframed and wrapped up in some old silk shirts. By May 1949 with Elizabeth at school at Clarens near Montreux and Nicky, who had in January that year obtained a first-class degree in economics in South Africa, due to go up to Christ Church, Oxford in the autumn, Paul began seriously to think of settling down.

Paul had heard through government channels that his presence in France would be welcome so in the spring of 1949, after Olga had left to spend some time with her mother in Athens, he made a number of trips to Paris. Any initial apprehension that he might not 're-succumb to its charms'[8] was dispelled on his first visit: 'Paris was absolute Heaven: the chestnut trees in full bloom and the long avenues filtering the light through the tender green of the leaves had an aquatic look'[9] Paul had made up his mind where they should live.

While Paul was house-hunting in Paris in May he saw a lot of King Peter ('so that is patched up again')[10] and on 17th Nicky arrived back from Cape Town. Nicky was artistic, intellectual and his father's favourite. He mixed in well with Paul's aesthetic world—Berenson had taken a particular liking to him—and he understood his father's tastes and values. In contrast, Alexander was tall, strong and more obviously an extrovert. He was also less intellectual and, in his efforts to

* The little *Head of St Jerome* by Mantegna, as well as his P. Breughel the Elder had been sent by Paul to Newton Don in March 1939 for safekeeping. The two pictures were returned to Paul by Archie at the beginning of 1949.

strike out for independence, frequently fell foul of his father's critical eye. Alexander was kept on a small allowance and, as a consequence of his previous seven years' existence, lacked qualifications. Not surprisingly, he had difficulty finding a job.

Paul planned the summer of 1949 with care. Elizabeth was sent to England to be with her Aunt Marina and cousin Alexandra, who was exactly the same age. Nicky was sent to Athens to see his mother for a few weeks prior to joining friends in the South of France. Paul, meanwhile, revelled in the glories of Paris. On 16th July he wrote to Berenson: 'I am still here and can't tear myself away from this heavenly town . . . it was difficult to resist all the mondanities as people are so kind and hospitable and besides the local society, masses of English friends have been pouring in all summer. The galleries are wonderful and there is always something on.'[11] Marina came to Paris on an official visit in early July and she saw a lot of her brother-in-law. Paul was received with great affection and warmth by the British Ambassador, Duff Cooper, and his beautiful wife Diana, and it was at their home in Chantilly that he met Berenson's friend, Johnny Walker,* for the first time. Kenneth Clark, too, came out to Paris and he arranged with Paul to return in October when Berenson was expected to be in town. Paul spent part of August with Marie Bonaparte in St Tropez and in September went, accompanied by Nicky, to stay with the Comte de Paris in Portugal. Here a huge cross-section of Spanish, Italian, Balkan and other royal families had begun to foregather and it was an excellent opportunity for Paul, and especially for Nicky, to make up for the seven years of isolation. To Paul's delight, Nicky was an immediate success with everyone. For Paul the relief was immeasurable: he at last had proof that the African experience had inflicted no permanent damage on his favourite son.

In October 1949 Olga returned from Greece rested, and happy to have seen her mother again. The formidable and remarkable Princess Nicholas had spent the war under Italian and German occupation in Athens and had suffered terrible privations. She had seen neither of her two youngest daughters for eight years and she had only seen Olga once, in 1947, when

* Curator of the National Gallery, Washington D.C.

through the intervention of General Smuts, Olga had managed to get away to Athens for four months.*

Princess Nicholas had always wanted the best for her beautiful eldest daughter and, though she was proud of the way Olga had coped as wife and mother since 1941, she resented the lot that had befallen her. In her heart she felt that Paul had behaved dishonourably in Yugoslavia, and before Olga left she reminded her once again of her duty to herself as well as to her husband. She made it clear that she considered Olga's duty as a wife to have been fully discharged already. But Olga's loyalty to Paul was not motivated by duty alone. Back in Paris she immediately fell in with his plans to rent a corner house near the Trocadero.

As if determined to make up for lost time, Paul took his entire family skiing that winter to Gstaad ('I personally hate the snow, but my children love it').[12] It was not until the following November, two years since their return from Africa, that Paul saw his other sister-in-law, Elizabeth. Ten years, the war, and family anxiety had played havoc with Woolly. 'I found [her] looking old and haggard. It is so depressing to see a lovely creature grow old prematurely.'[13] Not only Paul, it seemed, had been through hard times. By the end of 1950, Paul had managed, through Wildenstein, to sell his 'Cupid', for 90,000 Swiss francs. Wildenstein, Paul was convinced, would never have looked at it had not both Berenson and Clark shown interest in it. But though Berenson ascribed it to Bellini, Clark had thought it was a copy by Palma of the 'missing' Cupid in the Dresden Venus revealed by X-rays. Whoever was right, the price was good and Paul's immediate future became suddenly less precarious.

Elizabeth was at boarding school in England, and Nicky well ensconced at Oxford and a member of all his favourite clubs. By the end of 1950, too, Alexander was involved 'in a romance with the eldest Luxembourg girl . . . they met par hasard and no one ever thought of arranging it.'[14] He had shown that he was capable not only of deciding his own fate but also, to the surprise of his father, of selecting for himself a perfectly

* General Smuts, captivated by the young and vivacious Queen Frederika who had spent several years in exile in his capital, became a friend and protector to several members of the Greek royal family.

suitable girl-friend. Nevertheless, his ambition, after leaving the R.A.F., seemed to be to become an airline pilot and Paul found this unpalatable. Through contacts and friends, positions were to be found for him in the years ahead in less demeaning and more appropriate occupations, yet Alexander was repeatedly to disappoint his father, whose tastes he was neither suited nor inclined to follow. Not for nothing had he been the apple of King Alexander's eye.

Paul was happy enough. True, his doctors had already diagnosed the start of a blood and liver deterioration which caused Paul considerable pain and insomnia and which would, in 1976, eventually bring about his death. But at that time the nature of the disease was still unknown. Paul would certainly have been happier in England, but this was quite obviously out of the question. He had 'reached the other shore', though probably not the shore he would have hoped to reach, and he had begun at last to shed the pall of sorrow under which he had had to live for so many lonely wretched years. He was restored in the affections and regard of all his friends and this was certainly the first and, from his point of view, the most important hurdle. He had still to visit England and it was obviously only a matter of time before he would.

The pretext was provided by the death on 6th February 1952, of King George VI, his loyal and trusting friend. The funeral took place at Windsor and Paul was invited to attend both by Queen Elizabeth (by now the Queen Mother) and by the young Queen. He stayed a fortnight and, upon his return to Paris, wrote to Berenson: 'I felt like a ghost returning after so many years and so many events. I got a wonderful reception and everyone was unbelievably kind to me.'[15] He had seen most of his friends and had come to realize that at least among those who knew him personally he was remembered with affection. Both his sons were living in England—'the eldest still a pilot in B.E.A. and seems to enjoy that sort of life and to be a success . . . the younger is working with a man called Niarchos who appears to be a rising star on the financial horizon and owns a fleet of tankers.'[16]

He returned to London the following year for the coronation of the Queen in June and, with all his family, to spend Christmas at Coppins with Marina. Early in the New Year of 1954 he decided to visit friends in Scotland and on 6th January he wrote to Archie: 'I am off to Bowhill and Drumlanrig on Friday night and have asked them to take me to Newton Don one day. I am looking forward to it and dreading it at the same time . . .'[17]

Yet though at Windsor and Buckingham Palace Paul was received with genuine warmth, and though everywhere his friends were keen to show him that he was as welcome as ever before, there was a strong cross-section of British opinion which remained openly hostile. Thus, on 17th January 1954, John Gordon of the *Sunday Express* complained that Paul was in Britain staying with the Duchess of Kent and weekending with the Queen at Sandringham: 'I am with those who take a sour view of this princeling as a visitor. He is an ex-enemy with . . . some rather murky stains on his record'. The column went on to advise that the Duchess of Kent 'would be wise to persuade Prince Paul to work out his penance elsewhere than in Britain'.[18]

It was the prevalence of this kind of attitude in Britain, the result of so many years of unthinking and unanswered censure, that prevented Paul from establishing his permanent home in London. It was painful enough when the attacks were directed merely against himself but it was unbearable when they were directed against members of the royal family and those who welcomed him into their homes. Yet though he was always careful (to the point of secrecy) about his visits to London, he continued to make them, and for the rest of his life he was an especially welcome visitor at the private and official homes of his friends.

With a home in Paris, his children in England and proof that his most important friendships were intact, his spirits and self-confidence were restored.

But fate had one last cruel blow in store for Paul and Olga. On 12th April 1954, Nicky was driving back to London from a dinner party near Datchet. His car skidded round a bend, left the road and overturned into a watery ditch. Nicky, trapped inside and knocked unconscious, was drowned. The family, utterly grief-stricken, gathered at Coppins for the funeral. Paul and Olga, who had lost an adored and favourite son, were disconsolate; Alexander began to feel that it might have been better if he had been killed instead; and Elizabeth took years to get over the death of a brother who had consistently championed her cause. In a sense, the family never recovered. Without Nicky, who had understood his father so well, the bonds between parents and children were never the same again. Nicky had been the go-between and he was missed by his brother and sister as desperately as he was by his parents. Months after the funeral, Paul wrote to Berenson: 'The season *bat son plein*, I'm told, but we never see anybody as we don't feel like it any longer. There are things from which one can never recover and one goes on living mechanically because one has to but without any purpose or any desire.'[19]

At the time of Nicky's death, Paul was sixty-one and was to live for another twenty-two years. The pattern of his life was not to change much. It consisted of a prodigious amount of reading, regular correspondence with his friends, and a certain amount of travel between Florence, Paris, Geneva and London. He maintained, to the end, a keen interest in the latest developments in the world of art, whilst in the political field his dread of communism, became, if anything, more acute. For fourteen happy years after the death of his Aunt Moïna in 1955 he was to spend his summers at Pratolino.* Here at last he became a neighbour of Berenson's and during the last seven years of his friend's existence Paul marvelled at the old man's astonishing capacity for work.

He himself consistently refused to write about his life and he repeatedly discouraged others from trying to do so directly.†
He realized he could not engage in such a work without reopening old wounds and giving new life to a controversy from which he felt he could not derive any benefit.

Apart from the unavoidable sadness during these last remaining years of outliving his dearest friends and contemporaries, which he gradually learned to accept without

* Pratolino and most of its contents were sold in 1969 through Sotheby's.

† Paul refused numerous offers such as that from Sir Cecil Parrott to help him with his memoirs and that from Virginia Cowles to write his biography. He did, however, give J. B. Hoptner valuable assistance in the editing of his private papers at Columbia University and willingly underwent cross-questioning 'on the record' from Phyllis Auty.

bitterness, he came by stages to take a keen interest in the life of his grandchildren, of which at his death he had seven.

As he felt his life drawing gradually to a close (though with his faculties remarkably undiminished) he began to make some important donations to his favourite galleries and museums. To the Ashmolean at Oxford he gave an extremely rare Japanese painting, of the Muromachi period classical school ('our only example of . . . a type that is extremely difficult to obtain now', wrote the Assistant Keeper in 1970);[20] to the Musée National de la Légion d'Honneur he gave a collection of pendants, miniatures and catalogues which had once been the personal property of Napoleon Bonaparte ('un enrichissement aussi prestigieux qu' émouvant', acknowledged the Curator);[21] to the new owners of Pratolino, the Società Generale Immobiliare, he gave two paintings representing *A masked ball in Paris* which the Director General undertook to display there in memory of the Demidoff family; and to Christ Church, his old Oxford college, he made an important contribution to the 'Blue Boar Appeal' in memory of his son Nicky, whose name is now inscribed above room 11 of staircase 2. And he bequeathed his proudest possession, his Garter medallion (which he had had set into a silver cigarette box)* to Queen Elizabeth II.

Paul was admitted to the American Hospital in Neuilly on the evening of 11th September 1976. As his life began to ebb, on the morning of the 14th, his semi-conscious mind began to wander. Olga, who never left his side, heard him repeatedly cry out with horror at the memory of the 1903 Obrenović murders in Belgrade and for the last time in her life, and as the terrified ten-year-old must have longed for seventy-three years before, she held his hand in comfort and support.

---

* After Paul's death, his Garter Banner was returned, as is the custom, to Princess Olga, who gave it to Christ Church Chapel at Oxford, where it hangs today.

APPENDIX I

Genealogical Tables

A. KARAGEORGEVIC FAMILY TREE (SERBIA/YUGOSLAVIA).

B. KING GEORGE I OF GREECE AND ISSUE.

C. KING FERDINAND OF RUMANIA AND ISSUE.

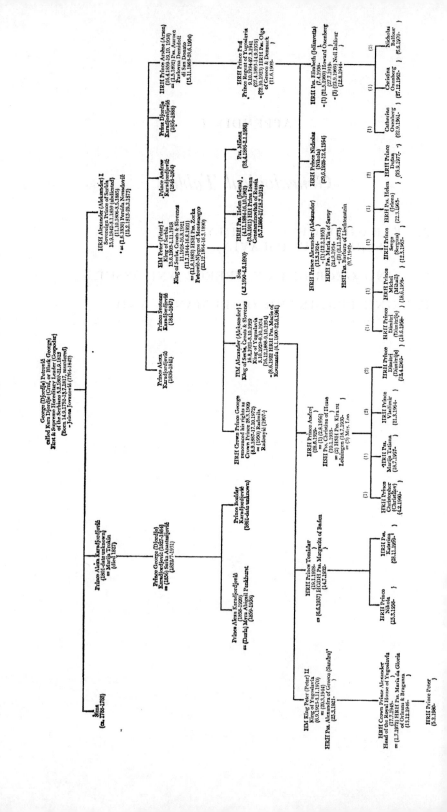

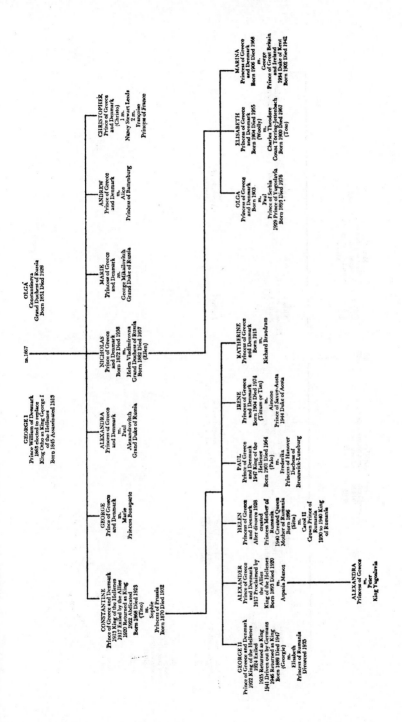

GEORGE I
Prince William of Denmark
1863 elected to replace
King Otho as King George I
of the Hellenes
Born 1845 Assassinated 1913

m.1867

OLGA
Constantinova
Grand Duchess of Russia
Born 1851 Died 1926

CONSTANTINE
Prince of Greece and Denmark
1913 King of the Hellenes
1917 Exiled by the Allies
1920 Returned as King
1922 Abdicated
Born 1868 Died 1923
(Tino)
m.
Sophie
Princess of Prussia
Born 1870 Died 1932

GEORGE
Prince of Greece
and Denmark
m.
Marie
Princess Bonaparte

ALEXANDRA
Princess of Greece
and Denmark
m.
Paul
Alexandrovitch
Grand Duke of Russia

NICHOLAS
Prince of Greece
and Denmark
Born 1872 Died 1938
m.
Helen Vladimirovna
Grand Duchess of Russia
Born 1882 Died 1957
(Ellen)

MARIE
Princess of Greece
and Denmark
m.
George Mikailovitch
Grand Duke of Russia

ANDREW
Prince of Greece
and Denmark
m.
Alice
Princess of Battenburg

CHRISTOPHER
Prince of Greece
and Denmark
(Christo)
1 m.
Nancy Stewart Leeds
2 m.
Françoise
Princess of France

GEORGE II
Prince of Greece and Denmark
1922 King of the Hellenes
1924 Exiled
1935 Returned as King
1941 Driven out by Germans
1946 Returned as King
Born 1890 Died 1947
(George)
m.
Elisabeth
Princess of Rumania
Divorced 1935

ALEXANDER
Prince of Greece
and Denmark
1917 Proclaimed by
the Allies
King of the Hellenes
Born 1893 Died 1920
m.
Aspasia Manos

HELEN
Princess of Greece
and Denmark
After divorce 1928
created
Princess Mother of
Rumania
1940 Created Queen
Mother of Rumania
Born 1896
m.
Carol II
Crown Prince of
Rumania
1930 to 1940 King
of Rumania

PAUL
Prince of Greece
and Denmark
1947 King of the
Hellenes
Born 1901 Died 1964
(Palo)
m.
Frederika
Princess of Hanover
Duchess of
Brunswick-Luneburg

IRENE
Princess of Greece
and Denmark
Born 1904 Died 1974
(Titina or Tim)
m.
Aimone
Prince of Savoy-Aosta
1944 Duke of Aosta

KATHERINE
Princess of Greece
and Denmark
Born 1913
m.
Richard Brandram

OLGA
Princess of Greece
and Denmark
Born 1903
m.
Paul
Prince of Serbia
1929 Prince of Yugoslavia
Born 1893 Died 1976

ELISABETH
Princess of Greece
and Denmark
Born 1904 Died 1955
(Woolly)
m.
Charles Theodore
Count Törring-Jettenbach
Born 1900 Died 1967
(Toto)

MARINA
Princess of Greece
and Denmark
Born 1906 Died 1968
m.
George
Prince of Great Britain
and Ireland
1934 Duke of Kent
Born 1902 Died 1942

ALEXANDRA
Princess of Greece
m.
Peter
King Yugoslavia

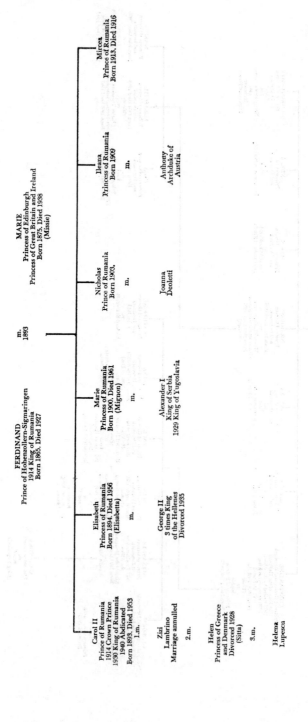

FERDINAND
Prince of Hohenzollern-Sigmaringen
1914 King of Rumania
Born 1865. Died 1927

m.
1893

MARIE
Princess of Edinburgh
Princess of Great Britain and Ireland
Born 1875. Died 1938
(Missie)

Carol II
Prince of Rumania
1914 Crown Prince
1930 King of Rumania
1940 Abdicated
Born 1893. Died 1953
1.m.

Zizi
Lambrino
Marriage annulled
2.m.

Helen
Princess of Greece
and Denmark
Divorced 1928
(Sitta)
3.m.

Helena
Lupescu

Elisabeth
Princess of Rumania
Born 1894. Died 1956
(Elisabetta)
m.

George II
3 times King
of the Hellenes
Divorced 1935

Marie
Princess of Rumania
Born 1900. Died 1961
(Mignon)
m.

Alexander I
King of Serbia
1929 King of Yugoslavia

Nicholas
Prince of Rumania
Born 1903,
m.

Joanna
Deoletti

Ileana
Princess of Rumania
Born 1909
m.

Anthony
Archduke of
Austria

Mircea
Prince of Rumania
Born 1913. Died 1916

APPENDIX II

[The following is an incomplete list, prepared by Prince Paul in 1926, of the donations to the Prince Paul Museum in Belgrade. (Columbia, Box 109).]

Donor	Artist	Subject
H.M. the King	Paul Jouvé	Tigre
H.M. the King	Georges Scott	Amandiers en fleurs
H.M. the Queen	Beatrice Bland	Flowers
Prince Paul	Jacques Blanche	Princess Olga
Prince Paul	G. Buscaglione	Countryside
Pss. Daria Karageorgević	Marie Bashkirtzeff	Prince Bozidar
Pss. Daria Karageorgević	Corcos	Prince Alexis
Lady Cunard	Augustus John	Children's drawing
Lady Cunard	Sir J. Lavery	Interior
Lady Cunard	Duncan Grant	Country Scene
Lady Cunard	Hammond	Trafalgar Square
Lady Cunard	Hammond	Flowers
Lady Cunard	Miss John	—
H.M. the King	Paul Jovanovich	The Vendetta
Arthur Acton	Arthur Acton	'Nature Morte'
Arthur Acton	Alfred Muller	Fiesole
Arthur Acton	Rolshoven	Naked Woman
Lord Ivor Churchill	W. Steer	Country Scene
J. Manson	J. Manson	Flowers
L. Pissarro	L. Pissarro	—
Tonks	Tonks	Rustic Scene
Pearson	Neville Lewis	Kaffir Woman
Sir Michael Sadler	Roger Fry	—
Sir Joseph Duveen	Mrs Stewart Walker	—
Sir Joseph Duveen	Mrs Stewart Walker	—
Sir Joseph Duveen	Mrs Stewart Walker	—
Sir Joseph Duveen	Miss Vicaji	—
Sir Joseph Duveen	Miss Vicaji	—
Sir Joseph Duveen	E. B. Lintot	—
Sir Joseph Duveen	Ch. Sims	—

Donor	Artist	Subject
Sir Joseph Duveen	Ch. Sims	—
Sir Joseph Duveen	Cautairs	Chinese Subject
Sir Joseph Duveen	R. d'Erlanger	Country Scene
Serte	Serte	Decoration
Muirhead Bone	Muirhead Bone	—
Paul Jovanovich	Paul Jovanovich	The wife of the artist
F. Hindley Smith	G. F. Watts	Lady Garvagh
H. Vellen	Holloway	Seaside
Samuel Courtauld	—	—
Holliday	Burne Jones	—
Holliday	Cox	—
Mrs. Fisher	Maria Fisher	Bathing Boy
H.M. the Queen	Popesco	Country Scene
H.M. the Queen	Popesco	Country Scene
H.M. the Queen	Popesco	'Carriere'
H.M. the Queen	—	Roman Countryside
H.M. the Queen of Italy	—	Villa Borghese
H.M. Queen of Italy	—	Alpine Countryside
Mariani	Mariani	Seaside View
H.M. the Queen	Kousnetsoff	Portrait of a Man
H.M. the Queen	Kousnetsoff	Portrait of a Woman
B. Berenson	Conder	—
Pss. Abamaleck	Harlamoff	Portrait of a Woman
B. Berenson	Camille Pissarro	Country Scene

APPENDIX III

PROTOCOL OF ADHESION OF YUGOSLAVIA TO THE TRIPARTITE PACT, VIENNA, MARCH 25, 1941*

The Governments of Germany, Italy, and Japan on the one hand and the Government of Yugoslavia on the other hand, through their plenipotentiaries, acknowledge the following:

Article 1. Yugoslavia adheres to the Tripartite Pact, which was signed September 27, 1940, at Berlin, between Germany, Italy, and Japan.

Article 2. Representatives of Yugoslavia will be present at conferences of commissions for common technical questions created under Article 4 of the Tripartite Pact so far as the commission deals with matters touching Yugoslavia's interests.

Article 3. The text of the Tripartite Pact is added as an annex to this protocol. This protocol is drawn up in the German, Italian, Japanese and Yugoslav languages, each of which is authentic. The present protocol comes into effect on the day of signing.

THREE NOTES FROM GERMAN FOREIGN MINISTER RIBBENTROP TO YUGOSLAV PRIME MINISTER CVETKOVIĆ, VIENNA, MARCH 25, 1941*

Mr Prime Minister:

In the name of the German Government and at its behest I have the honour to inform Your Excellency of the following:

On the occasion of the Yugoslav adherence today to the Tripartite Pact the German Government confirms its decision to respect the sovereignty and territorial integrity of Yugoslavia at all times.

Mr Prime Minister:

With reference to the conversations that occurred in connection with Yugoslav adherence to the Tripartite Pact I have the honour to confirm to Your Excellency herewith in the name of the Reich Government that in the agreement between the Governments of the Axis powers and the Royal Yugoslav Government the Axis power governments during this war will not demand of Yugoslavia to

313

permit the march or transportation of troops through the Yugoslav State or territory.

Mr Prime Minister:

With reference to the conversations that occurred in connection with Yugoslav adherence to the Tripartite Pact, I have the honour to confirm to Your Excellency herewith in the name of the Reich Government that in the agreement between the Governments of the Axis powers and the Royal Yugoslav Government:

Italy and Germany assure the Government of Yugoslavia that out of consideration of the military situation, they do not wish to advance, on their part, any request whatsoever regarding military assistance.

If, however, the Government of Yugoslavia, would consider, at any moment, that it is in its own interest to take part in the military operations of the powers of the Tripartite Pact, the Yugoslav Government will be free to conclude such military agreements as necessary, and with these powers themselves.

Meanwhile, I beg you to keep the preceding communication strictly secret, and to make it public only with agreement of the Governments of the Axis powers.

THE TRIPARTITE PACT BETWEEN GERMANY, ITALY, AND JAPAN, SIGNED AT BERLIN, SEPTEMBER 27, 1940*

The Governments of Germany, Italy, and Japan consider it the pre-requisite of a lasting peace that every nation in the world shall receive the space to which it is entitled. They have, therefore, decided to stand by and cooperate with one another in their efforts in Greater East Asia and the regions of Europe respectively. In doing this it is their prime purpose to establish and maintain a new order of things, calculated to promote the mutual prosperity and welfare of the people concerned.

It is, furthermore, the desire of the three Governments to extend cooperation to nations in other spheres of the world who are inclined to direct their efforts along lines similar to their own for the purpose of realising their ultimate object, world peace.

Accordingly, the Governments of Germany, Italy, and Japan have agreed as follows:

Article 1. Japan recognises and respects the leadership of Germany and Italy in the establishment of a new order in Europe.

Article 2. Germany and Italy recognise and respect the leadership of Japan in the establishment of a new order in Greater East Asia.

Article 3. Germany, Italy, and Japan agree to cooperate in their efforts on aforesaid lines. They further undertake to assist one another with all political, economic, and military means if one of the three Contracting Powers is attacked by a Power at present not involved in the European War or in the Chinese–Japanese conflict.

Article 4. With the view to implementing the present pact, joint technical commissions, to be appointed by the respective Governments of Germany, Italy, and Japan, will meet without delay.

Article 5. Germany, Italy, and Japan affirm that the above agreement affects in no way the political status existing at present between each of the three Contracting Parties and Soviet Russia.

Article 6. The present pact shall become valid immediately upon signature and shall remain in force ten years from the date on which it becomes effective.

In due time, before the expiration of said term, the High Contracting Parties shall, at the request of any one of them, enter into negotiations for its renewal.

* Auswärtiges Amt, Docs. 68–71.

REFERENCES

Chapter I

Reference has been made to a number of unpublished family papers (biographical essays, genealogical tables and notes) in the possession of Princess Olga and amongst Prince Paul's papers at Columbia University, Boxes 109 and 111 and the usual Dictionaries of National Biography.

Chapter II

1. Bakhmeteff Archive, Rare Book and Manuscript Library, Columbia University, New York. Collection of H.R.H. Prince Paul of Yugoslavia, Box 111. Margot Asquith to Prince Paul, 6th November 1914.
2. Sir Nevile Henderson, *Water Under the Bridges*, Hodder and Stoughton, 1945, p. 74.
3. Balfour family papers, Newton Don, Kelso. A. Balfour to Lady Nina Balfour, 12th May 1915.
4. I Tatti Institute, Florence. Prince Paul to Mrs Berenson, 18th January 1917.
5. Balfour papers. C. B. Balfour to J. Balfour, 6th May 1917.
6. Balfour papers. C. B. Balfour to J. Balfour, 26th August 1917.
7. I Tatti, Prince Paul to Mrs Berenson, 28th December 1918.
8. *Chips, The Diaries of Sir Henry Channon.* Ed. R. Rhodes James, Weidenfeld and Nicolson, 1967.
9. Ibid.
10. Ibid.

Chapter III

1. Princess Olga's private diaries 1922 and 1923.

Chapter IV

1. Princess Olga's diaries, 1924.
2. I Tatti, Prince Paul to B. Berenson, 4th September 1924.

3. Princess Olga's diaries, 1925.
4. Ibid.
5. Ibid.
6. Ibid.
7. Ibid.
8. Ibid.
9. Ibid.
10. Ibid.
11. Princess Olga's diaries, 1926.
12. Princess Olga's diaries, 1928.
13. I Tatti, Prince Paul to Mrs Berenson, 4th May 1928.
14. I Tatti, Prince Paul to B. Berenson, August 1928.
15. Princess Olga's diaries, 1928.
16. Princess Olga's private papers, Prince Nicholas to Princess Nicholas, June 1929.
17. I Tatti, Prince Paul to B. Berenson, January 1926.
18. Columbia, Box 109, Emerald Cunard to Prince Paul, 1st September 1925.
19. Columbia, Box 109, Emerald Cunard to Prince Paul, 9th September 1925.
20. Columbia, Box 109, Sir Joseph Duveen to Prince Paul, 1st October 1925.
21. Columbia, Box 109.
22. Columbia, Box 109, C. Aitken to A. Balfour, 18th November 1925.
23. I Tatti, Prince Paul to Mrs Berenson, 22nd April 1929.
24. I Tatti, Prince Paul to B. Berenson, September 1929.
25. I Tatti, Prince Paul to B. Berenson, 1929.
26. I Tatti, Prince Paul to B. Berenson, 1930.

CHAPTER V

1. Princess Olga's diaries, 1933.
2. I Tatti, Prince Paul to B. Berenson, 30th July 1932.
3. I Tatti, Prince Paul to Mrs Berenson, 1st August 1933.
4. Princess Olga's diaries, 1933.
5. Ibid.
6. Ibid.
7. Ibid.
8. Ibid.
9. Ibid.
10. Princess Olga's private papers, Prince Paul to Princess Olga, July 1933.

11. Chips' diaries, 8th May 1934 (part unpublished).
12. Columbia, Box 112, Duke of Kent to Prince Paul, 26th September 1934.

CHAPTER VI

1. Columbia, Box 108, King Alexander to Prince Paul, 23rd December 1933.
2. Princess Olga to authors.
3. Public Record Office (P.R.O.) FO 371/18452 Sir N. Henderson to Foreign Secretary, October 1934.
4. Columbia, Box 112.
5. Columbia, Box 109, Prince Paul to Chips Channon, 25th June 1945.
6. Balfour papers, Prince Paul to A. Balfour, 3rd November 1934.
7. P.R.O. FO 371/18456, Sir J. Simon to Mr Cowan (Belgrade), 26th November 1934.
8. Ibid.
9. Columbia, Box 108, Prince Paul's diaries, December 1934.
10. Columbia, Box 108, Prince Paul's diaries, 12th December 1934.
11. Columbia, Box 108, Prince Paul's diaries, 17th May 1935.
12. P.R.O. FO 371/18456, Sir J. Simon to Mr Cowan (Belgrade) 26th November 1934.

CHAPTER VII

1. Columbia, Box 108, Prince Paul's diaries, 15th January, 1935.
2. Columbia, Box 113, Stojadinović to Prince Paul, 22nd May 1935.
3. Columbia, Box 108, Prince Paul's diaries, 21st June 1935.
4. I Tatti, Prince Paul to B. Berenson, 26th June 1935.
5. Henderson, Sir Nevile, *Water Under the Bridges*, Hodder and Stoughton, 1945.
6. P.R.O. FO 371/20436 Eden to Sir R. H. Campbell, 17th November 1936.
7. Columbia, Box 112, Philip of Hesse to Prince Paul, 1st January 1935.
8. Columbia, Box 108, Prince Paul's diaries, June 1935.
9. Columbia, Box 113, Stojadinović to Prince Paul, 20th September 1935.
10. Columbia, Box 108, Prince Paul's diaries, 18th October 1935.
11. I Tatti, Prince Paul to Mrs Berenson, February 1935.
12. I Tatti, Prince Paul to B. Berenson, 17th March 1935.

13. I Tatti, Prince Paul to B. Berenson, 10th September 1935.
14. Princess Olga's diaries, 27th October 1935.
15. Chips' diaries, 5th April 1935.
16. P.R.O. FO 371/19580, Sir R. Vansittart, 5th November 1935.
17. I Tatti, Prince Paul to B. Berenson, 15th November 1935.
18. Columbia, Box 111, Kenneth Clark to Prince Paul, 15th December 1935.
19. Chips' diaries, 28th January 1936.
20. I Tatti, Prince Paul to B. Berenson.
21. Sir John Balfour's unpublished papers, 'Encounters with the Duke and Duchess of Windsor'.
22. Ibid.
23. P.R.O. FO 371/20436, Sir R. H. Campbell to Eden, 20th November 1936.
24. Columbia, Box 113, Purić to Stojadinović, 15th May 1936.
25. Columbia, Box 113, Stojadinović to Prince Paul.
26. P.R.O. FO 371/20436, Sir R. H. Campbell to Eden, 20th November 1936.
27. P.R.O. FO 371/20436, Eden to Sir R. H. Campbell, 17th November 1936.
28. Columbia, Box 108, Prince Paul's diaries, 17th November 1936.
29. Chips' diaries, 13th November 1936.
30. Princess Olga's diaries, 13th November 1936.
31. Columbia, Box 108, Prince Paul's diaries, 17th November 1936.
32. Princess Olga's private papers, Duke of Kent to Prince Paul, 16th December 1936.
33. Nicolson, H., *Diaries and Letters 1930–1939*, ed. N. Nicolson (Collins, 1966), H. Nicolson to V. Sackville-West, 9th December 1936.
34. Columbia, Box 112, Duke of Windsor to Prince Paul, 18th March 1937.
35. Columbia, Box 111, Godfrey Thomas to Prince Paul, 21st April 1937.

CHAPTER VIII

1. Columbia, Box 113, Stojadinović to Prince Paul, 24th December 1936.
2. Columbia, Box 113, Stojadinović to Subbotić, February 1937.
3. Ciano, Galeazzo. L'Europa Verza la Catastrofe. Verona: Mondadori (1948), pp. 151–162.
4. Columbia, Box 111, Sir N. Henderson to Prince Paul, 6th February 1935.

5. Columbia, Box 111, Sir N. Henderson to Prince Paul, 13th April 1937

6. Columbia, Box 108, Prince Paul's diaries, May 1937.

7. P.R.O. FO 371/21196, Sir E. Phipps to Foreign Office, 15th May 1937.

8. Columbia, Box 108, Prince Paul's diaries, 26th May 1937.

9. Chips' diaries, 28th August 1937 (unpublished).

10. Chips' diaries, 27th August 1937.

11. P.R.O. FO 371/21197, Conversation between Prince Paul and Mr Shone, 1st September 1937.

12. Columbia, Box 108, Prince Paul's diaries, conversation with Dr Šubašić, 29th August 1937.

13. Columbia, Box 113, Cvetković to Prince Paul, 7th August 1937 and 16th November 1937.

14. Documents on German Foreign Policy (D.G.F.P.), D, V, Doc 153 Government Printing Office, Washington D.C.

15. D.G.F.P. D,V, Doc 163.

16. Columbia, Box 112, Infante Alfonso to Prince Paul, 5th March 1937.

17. Columbia, Box 111, Sir N. Henderson to Prince Paul, 3rd June 1937.

18. Henderson, Sir Nevile, *Failure of a Mission*, Hodder & Stoughton, 1940, pp. 124–125.

19. Columbia, Box 111, Sir N. Henderson to Prince Paul, 8th March 1938.

20. Memoirs of Dr Eduard Beneš, G. Allen and Unwin Ltd (1954), pp. 31–33.

21. Columbia, Box 108, Prince Paul's diaries, 6th April 1938.

22. Columbia, Box 112, King Carol of Rumania to Prince Paul, 24th August 1938.

23. Columbia, Box 109, Cecil Parrott to Prince Paul, 10th March 1938.

24. I Tatti, Prince Paul to B. Berenson, 21st April 1938.

25. Columbia, Box 108, Prince Paul's note on a conversation with Chamberlain at Buckingham Palace, 1938.

26. P.R.O. FO 371/22476, Sir R. H. Campbell to Foreign Office, 5th November 1938.

27. Hansard CCCXL, 1st November 1938. Col. 80, H.M.S.O.

28. Columbia, Box 108, Prince Paul to J. B. Hoptner, 14th October 1960.

29. Columbia, Box 113, Acimović to Prince Paul, 24th November 1938.

30. Columbia, Box 113, Stojadinović to Prince Paul, 16th December 1938.

Chapter IX

1. Columbia, Box 113, Cvetković to Prince Paul, 2nd February 1939.
2. Columbia, Box 109, Cecil Parrott to Prince Paul, 18th February 1939.
3. Columbia, Box 109, Cecil Parrott to Prince Paul, February/ March 1939.
4. P.R.O. FO 371/23888, Sir R. H. Campbell, Personality Report 1939.
5. P.R.O. FO 371/21197, T. Shone to S of S, September 1937.
6. P.R.O. FO 371/22965, Sir R. H. Campbell to Halifax, 16th February 1939.
7. Columbia, Box 113, Subbotić's Report, 5th May 1939.
8. P.R.O. FO 371/23884, Sir R. H. Campbell to Foreign Office, 5th June 1939.
9. Documents on British Foreign Policy (D.B.F.P.), III, 4, Docs 426, 511 and 542, H.M.S.O.
10. P.R.O. FO 371/23884, Sir P. Loraine to Foreign Office, 18th May 1939.
11. P.R.O. FO 371/23884, Sir R. H. Campbell to Foreign Office, 6th June 1939.
12. Princess Olga's diaries, 1st–8th June 1939.
13. Princess Olga to authors 1978.
14. Irving, David, *The War Path*, Michael Joseph, 1978, p. 209.
15. Columbia, Box 112, Infante Alfonso to Prince Paul, 29th December 1954.
16. Columbia, Box 112, Prime Minister's secretary to Prince Paul, 19th July 1939.
17. Foreign Relations of the United States (F.R.U.S.), pp. 287–288, Kennedy to S of S, 20th July 1939, Government Printing Office, Washington D.C.
18. F.R.U.S., pp. 199–200, Kennedy to S of S, 21st July 1939.
19. F.R.U.S., pp. 198–199, Lane to S of S, 16th July 1939.
20. I Tatti, Prince Paul to B. Berenson, 31st August 1939.
21. Columbia, Box 111, Sir R. H. Campbell to Prince Paul, 26th January 1940.
22. Columbia, Box 111, Sir N. Henderson to Prince Paul, 23rd September 1939.

Chapter X

1. P.R.O. FO 371/25029, R. I. Campbell to Halifax, 25th January 1940.

2. P.R.O. FO 371/25029, Sir P. Loraine to Foreign Office, 23rd January 1940.
3. P.R.O. FO 371/25029, R. I. Campbell to Halifax, 25th January 1940.
4. Princess Olga's diaries, 15th January 1940.
5. P.R.O. FO 371/25029, R. I. Campbell to Halifax, 25th January 1940.
6. P.R.O. FO 371/25030, R. I. Campbell to Halifax, 4th April 1940.
7. Columbia, Box 113, Brugère to Paris, 3rd September 1939.
8. Ibid.
9. P.R.O. FO 371/23884, T. Shone to Halifax, 20th May 1939.
10. P.R.O. FO 371/29750, Rendel to Eden, 27th March 1941.
11. P.R.O. FO 371/24884, R. I. Campbell to Foreign Office, 3rd January 1940.
12. German White Book, 7, Doc 58 from 16th April 1940 and Doc 60 from 19th April 1940.
13. Columbia, Box 112, Duke of Kent to Prince Paul, 5th December 1939, 10th March 1939, 2nd April 1940.
14. Princess Olga's private papers, Prince Paul to Princess Olga, 15th April 1940.
15. Princess Olga's private papers, Prince Paul to Princess Olga, 21st April 1940.
16. Princess Olga's diaries, 10th May 1940.
17. P.R.O. FO 371/25031, Halifax minute, 17th May 1940.
18. Columbia, Box 111, Sir R. H. Campbell to Prince Paul, 8th April 1940.
19. Princess Olga's diaries, 4th October 1940.
20. Columbia, Box 112, King George VI to Prince Paul, 3rd July 1940.
21. Columbia, Box 111, Sir R. H. Campbell to Prince Paul, 8th April 1940.
22. Columbia, Box 112, Duke of Kent to Prince Paul, 17th July 1940.
23. Princess Olga's diaries, 4th September 1940.
24. Columbia, Box 112, King George VI to Prince Paul, 14 Nov. 1940.
25. P.R.O. FO 371/25034, Nichols' minute 8th November 1940, Dixon minute 19th November 1940.
26. P.R.O. FO 371/25031, R. I. Campbell to Foreign Office, 23rd November 1940.
27. P.R.O. FO 371/25031, Foreign Office to Belgrade, 24th November 1940.
28. *Hitler e Mussolini Lettere e Documenti, Milan*: Rizzola 1946, Hitler to Mussolini, 5th December 1940.

29. D.G.F.P., D, XII, No. 467, Von Heeren to Foreign Ministry, 7th December 1940.

30. D.G.F.P., D, XII, No. 467, Ribbentrop to Heeren, 21st December 1940.

CHAPTER XI

1. Columbia, Box 117.
2. Chips' diaries, 12th January 1941.
3. P.R.O. FO 371/30089, P.M. Personal Minute Serial No. M55/1, 14th January 1941.
4. Churchill, W. S. *The Second World War I. The Gathering Storm*, p. 213, Cassell & Co. Ltd, 1948.
5. Churchill, W. S. *The Second World War I. The Gathering Storm*, p. 274, Cassell & Co. Ltd, 1948.
6. Eden, Anthony (Earl of Avon), *Memoirs: The Reckoning*. Cassell & Co. Ltd, 1965.
7. P.R.O. FO 371/33145, Memo by Field-Marshal Sir John Dill, 21st April 1941.
8. P.R.O. FO 371/25034, Dixon minute, 30th November 1940.
9. D.G.F.P., D, XII, No. 47, 14th February 1941.
10. Columbia, Box 111, R. I. Campbell to Prince Paul, 27th February 1941.
11. Columbia, Box 111, R. I. Campbell to Prince Paul, 2nd March 1941.
12. P.R.O. FO 371/30231, Sir H. Knatchbull-Hugessen to Foreign Office, 22nd January 1941.
13. P.R.O. FO 371/30231, Sir H. Knatchbull-Hugessen to Foreign Office, 24th January 1941.
14. P.R.O. FO 371/30231, R. I. Campbell to Foreign Office, 12th February 1941.
15. P.R.O. FO 371/30231, Sir H. Knatchbull-Hugessen to Foreign Office, 15th February 1941.
16. P.R.O. FO 371/30231, R. I. Campbell to Foreign Office, 17th February 1941.
17. D.G.F.P., D, XII, No. 119, 2nd March 1941.
18. Hoptner, J. B., *Yugoslavia in Crisis 1934–1941*, Columbia University Press , 1962, p. 216, Cvetković to Hoptner.
19. Columbia, Box 108, Prince Paul to J. B. Hoptner, 21st October 1971.
20. Professor Phyllis Auty's conversations with Prince Paul, 1975. Professor Auty to authors.

21. Van Creveld, Martin, *Hitler's Strategy 1940–1941—The Balkan Clue*, p. 128, Cambridge University Press, 1973.
22. Hoptner, J. B. *Yugoslavia in Crisis 1934–1941*, Columbia University Press, 1962, p. 221, Maček to J. B. Hoptner.
23. Princess Olga's diaries, 9th March 1941.
24. P.R.O. FO 371/30255, 13th March 1941.
25. P.R.O. FO 371/29780, R. I. Campbell to S of S, 15th March 1941.
26. P.R.O. FO 371/30231, Foreign Office minute, 24th March 1941.
27. Princess Olga's diaries, 18th March 1941.
28. Columbia, Box 111, Eden to Prince Paul, 17th March 1941.
29. P.R.O. FO 371/30231, Sir H. Knatchbull-Hugessen to Cairo, 23rd March 1941.
30. P.R.O. FO 371/30206, R. I. Campbell to Eden, 23rd March 1941, from T. Shone.
31. Hoptner, J. B., *Yugoslavia in Crisis 1934–1941*, Columbia University Press, 1962, p. 236.
32. Columbia, Box 112, King George VI to Prince Paul, 23rd March 1941.
33. P.R.O. FO 371/30253, Eden to R. I. Campbell, 24th March 1941.
34. P.R.O., P.R.E.M. 3/510/511, Nos. 428–30.

Chapter XII

1. Hoptner, J. B., *Yugoslavia in Crisis 1934–1941*, Columbia University Press, 1962, p. 260, Maček to J. B. Hoptner.
2. P.R.O. FO 371/30255, H.M. Consul, Zagreb, H.M. Minister, Belgrade, 27th March 1941.
3. Mirković Papers, Colonel Dragutin P. Savić to Captain Miodrag. C. Urosević, 10th September 1960.
4. Mirković Papers, Captain Bozidar Delibasić to Captain Miodrag. C. Urosević, 1961
5. Princess Olga's diaries, 1941.
6. *New York Times*, 28th March 1941.
7. *Slavic Review*, No. 3, September 1977. D. Stafford, S.O.E. and British involvement in the Belgrade Coup d'Etat of March 1941. G. Taylor to D. Stafford.
8. P.R.O. FO 371/30206, R. I. Campbell to Foreign Office, 15th March 1941.
9. P.R.O. FO 371/30253, Air Attaché to Foreign Office, 26th March 1941.
10. P.R.O. FO 371/33490, R. I. Campbell to O. Sargent, 1st July 1942.

11. P.R.O. FO 371/30253, Air Attaché to Foreign Office, 26th March 1941.
12. P.R.O. DO (41) 10th March 27th 1941, in CAB 69/2.
13. London School of Economics and Political Science. Dalton Diary, 27th March 1941.
14. Professor Phyllis Auty's conversations with Prince Paul, 1975, Professor Auty to authors.
15. Churchill, W. S. *The Second World War III, The Grand Alliance*, p. 142, Cassell & Co. Ltd, 1950.
16. P.R.O. CAB 65(18) 32(41), 27th March 1941.
17. P.R.O. FO 371/30255, Eden to R. I. Campbell, 27th March 1941.
18. P.R.O. FO 371/30255, Foreign Office minute, 28th March 1941.
19. P.R.O. FO 371/30255, Sir M. Palairet to Foreign Office, 9th April 1941.
20. P.R.O. FO 371/30255, Sir M. Palairet to Sir M. Lampson, 10th April 1941.
21. P.R.O. FO 371/30255, Sir M. Lampson to Foreign Office, personal for S of S, 16th April 1941.
22. P.R.O. FO 371/30255, Foreign Office to Sir M. Lampson, 17th April 1941.
23. D.G.F.P., D, XII, No. 211, Von Heeren to Foreign Ministry, 30th March 1941.
24. Von Heeren to Berlin, 26th March 1941, quoted in German White Paper, P.R.O. FO 371/29803.
25. ed. Trevor-Roper, H. R., *Hitler's War Directives 1939–1945*, Sidgwick & Jackson Ltd, 1964.
26. Columbia, Box 113, Minutes of Meetings of Council of Ministers, 6th–11th April 1941.
27. Miss Ede to authors, 1977.
28. Princess Olga's diaries, 28th April 1941.

Chapter XIII

1. P.R.O. FO 371/30255, P. Dixon minute, 19th April 1941.
2. Princess Olga's diaries, 28th April 1941.
3. Princess Olga's diaries, 25th May 1941.
4. Princess Olga's diaries, end of May 1941.
5. Columbia, Box 108, Prince Paul to Duke of Kent, 18th August 1941.
6. P.R.O. FO 371/30255, P. Dixon minute, 19th April 1941.
7. P.R.O. FO 371/30255, Eden comment, 2nd May 1941.
8. P.R.O. FO 371/30255, S of S Colonies to Sir H. Moore, 5th May 1941.

9. P.R.O. FO 371/30255, H.M. Consul Zagreb to Foreign Office, 27th March 1941.
10. P.R.O. FO 371/30265, 27th June 1941.
11. Columbia, Box 108, Prince Paul to Duke of Kent, 21st September 1941.
12. P.R.O. FO 371/30265, 27th June 1941.
13. *The Times*, 15th July 1941.
14. *The Times*, 11th August 1941.
15. Simović broadcast, 4th July 1941.
16. Columbia, Box 112, Duke of Kent to Prince Paul, 5th November 1941.
17. Columbia, Box 112, Queen Marie to Prince Paul, 17th October 1941.
18. *The Times*, 23rd July 1941, 27th August 1941, 16th September 1941, 7th September 1941.
19. Princess Olga's diaries. Review of the past year, 1st January 1942.
20. Princess Olga's diaries, 28th October 1941.
21. Columbia, Box 112, Duke of Kent to Prince Paul, 1st July 1941.
22. *Evening Standard*, 26th September 1941.
23. P.R.O. FO 371/30255.
24. P.R.O. FO 371/30255.
25. Columbia, Box 108, Prince Paul to Duke of Kent, 21st November 1941.
26. Columbia, Box 112, Duke of Kent to Prince Paul, 5th November 1941.
27. Columbia, Box 108, Prince Paul to Duke of Kent, 2nd March 1942.
28. Columbia, Box 109, K. Clark to Prince Paul, 30th November 1941.
29. Princess Olga private papers, Princess Olga to Prince Paul, 25th September 1942.
30. *The Times*, 7th December 1942.
31. P.R.O. FO 371/33448, 16th October 1942.
32. Ibid.
33. P.R.O. FO 371/33448, 17th October 1942.
34. P.R.O. FO 371/37627, Governor of Kenya to S of S Colonies, 10th February 1943.
35. Princess Olga's diaries, 23rd January 1943.
36. P.R.O. FO 371/37627, Governor of Kenya to S of S Colonies, 9th February 1943.
37. P.R.O. FO 371/37627, Prime Minister's personal minute, 12th February 1943.
38. P.R.O. FO 371/37627, Eden to Churchill, 17th February 1943.

39. West, R. *Black Lamb and Grey Falcon*, Macmillan, 1943, p. 1141.
40. Ibid.
41. West, R. *Black Lamb and Grey Falcon*, Macmillan, 1943, p. 1142.
42. Ibid.
43. West, R. *Black Lamb and Grey Falcon*, Macmillan, 1943, p. 1135.
44. West, R. *Black Lamb and Grey Falcon*, Macmillan, 1943, p. 1140.
45. Prince Paul to N. R. Balfour, 15th April 1973.

CHAPTER XIV

1. I Tatti, Prince Paul to B. Berenson, 14th October 1945.
2. Martin, D. *Patriot or Traitor—The Case of General Mihailović*, Hoover Archival Documentaries, Publication 191 (1979).
3. Balfour family papers, Prince Paul to A. Balfour, 1948.
4. I Tatti, Prince Paul to B. Berenson, 2nd November 1948.
5. Ibid.
6. I Tatti, Prince Paul to B. Berenson, 27th November 1951.
7. I Tatti, Prince Paul to B. Berenson, 9th April 1949.
8. I Tatti, Prince Paul to B. Berenson, 26th March 1949.
9. I Tatti, Prince Paul to B. Berenson, 18th May 1949.
10. Ibid.
11. I Tatti, Prince Paul to B. Berenson, 16th July 1949.
12. I Tatti, Prince Paul to B. Berenson, 29th November 1949.
13. I Tatti, Prince Paul to B. Berenson, 12th November 1950.
14. Ibid.
15. I Tatti, Prince Paul to B. Berenson, 24th March 1952.
16. I Tatti, Prince Paul to B. Berenson, 16th November 1953.
17. Balfour family papers, Prince Paul to A. Balfour, 6th January 1954.
18. *Sunday Express*, 17th January 1954.
19. I Tatti, Prince Paul to B. Berenson.
20. Columbia, Box 109, Assistant Keeper of Ashmolean Museum, Department of Eastern Art, to Prince Paul, 23rd January 1970.
21. Columbia, Box 109, Le Conservateur, Musée National de la Légion D'Honneur to Prince Paul, 10th July 1974.

BIBLIOGRAPHY

Amery, H. J., *Sons of the Eagle*, Macmillan, 1948.

Barker, E., *British Policy in South-East Europe in the Second World War*, Macmillan, 1976.

Breccia, Alfredo, *Yugoslavia 1939-1941—Diplomazia della Neutralità*, Giuffre.

Brugère, Raymond, *Veni, Vidi, Vichy*, Vanves: Calmann-Levy, 1944.

Beneš, Eduard, *Memoirs of Dr Eduard Beneš*, Allen & Unwin, 1954.

Churchill, W. S., *Second World War*, Vol. I, Cassell, 1948.

Churchill, W. S., *Second World War* Vol. III, Cassell, 1950.

Ciano, Galeazzo, *Ciano's Diary 1937-38*, Methuen, 1952.

Ciano, Galeazzo, *Ciano's Diary 1939-43*, Heinemann, 1947.

Dalton, Hugh, *The Fateful Years*, Frederick Muller, 1957.

Darby, H. C., ed., Seton-Watson, R. W., et al, *A Short History of Yugoslavia*, Cambridge University Press, 1966.

Dilks, David, ed., *The Diaries of Sir Alexander Cadogan 1938-1945*, Cassell, 1971.

Eden, Anthony (Earl of Avon), *Memoirs: The Reckoning*, Cassell, 1965.

Henderson, Sir N., *Water Under the Bridges*, Hodder and Stoughton, 1945.

Henderson, Sir N., *Failure of a Mission*, Hodder and Stoughton, 1940.

Hoptner, J. B., *Yugoslavia in Crisis 1934-1941*, Columbia University Press, 1962.

Irving, David, *The War Path*, Michael Joseph, 1978.

Maček, V., *In the Struggle for Freedom*, Speller and Sons, N.Y., 1957.

Mariano, Nicky, *Forty Years with Berenson*, H. Hamilton, 1966.

Nicolson, Nigel., ed., *Harold Nicolson Diaries and Letters 1930-1939*, Collins, 1966.

Parrott, Cecil, *The Tightrope*, Faber and Faber, 1975.

Pavlowitch, Stefan K., *Yugoslavia*, Ernest Benn, 1971.

Peter II, *King of Yugoslavia, A King's Heritage*, Cassell, 1955.

Rhodes, James Robert, ed., *Chips, The Diaries of Sir Henry Channon*, Weidenfeld & Nicolson, 1967.

Seton-Watson, Hugh, *Eastern Europe Between the Wars, 1918-41*, Cambridge University Press, 1945.

Sweet-Escott, Bickham, *Baker Street Irregular*, Methuen, 1965.

Templewood, Viscount, *Nine Troubled Years*, Collins, 1954.

Trevor-Roper, H. R., ed., *Hitler's War Directives 1939–45*, Sidgwick and Jackson, 1964.

Van Creveld, Martin L., *Hitler's Strategy 1940–1941, The Balkan Clue*, Cambridge University Press, 1973.

Barker, E., *British Wartime Policy towards Yugoslavia* (Paper delivered to the School of Slavonic and East European Studies, February 1979).

Barker, E., *The Belgrade Coup and The British: The Military Coup d'Etat of 27th March 1941* (unpublished) 1979.

Martin, D., *Patriot or Traitor—The Case of General Mihailović.* (Hoover Archival Documentaries, Publication 191), 1979.

Prince Paul of Yugoslavia (Paper printed in London for private circulation), 1942.

Slavic Review No. 3. September 1977.

INDEX

Margherita, Queen of Italy, 57, 65, 70
Marie, Queen of Rumania, 55, 56, 103, 152, 153
Marie, Queen of Yugoslavia, 54–56, 58, 59, 61, 65, 66, 69, 71, 72, 74, 86, 87, 91, 98, 100, 102, 103, 106, 119, 124, 154, 166, 204, 276, 277
Marina, Princess, Duchess of Kent, as Princess of Greece, 43–45, 47, 48, 50, 54, 55, 62, 66, 71, 72, 86, 87, 89, 90, 92–94; as Duchess of Kent, 117, 119–121, 123, 125, 133, 153, 157, 181, 195, 204, 270, 273, 277, 283–285, 287, 300, 302, 303
Mary, Queen of Great Britain, 51, 61, 93, 120, 123, 134, 136, 137
Masterson, Thomas, 253, 254, 256
Maud, Queen of Norway, 123
Mellon Gallery, Washington DC, 279
Mestrović, Ivan, 32
Metaxas, Jean, 207
Michael, Crown Prince of Rumania, 70; as King of Rumania, 72, 206
Middle East, the, 202, 233, 275
Mihailović, Dragoljub, 295, 296
Milena, Queen of Montenegro, 50
Millington Drake, Eugen, 27
Mirković, Bora, 244–248, 254, 255
Monastir, 264; Gap 36
Moore, Sir Henry, 267, 272, 286, 287
Mountbatten, Earl and Countess, 195
Munich Conference, 152, 167, 173
Murray, John, 28, 34, 39
Musée National de la Légion d'Honneur, 305
Mussolini, Benito, 68, 97, 98, 105, 106, 114–116, 129, 130, 132, 133, 147–149, 167, 168, 173, 177, 178, 190, 191, 196–199, 205, 206, 211–213

Narodna Odbrana, 253
National Gallery (London), 78, 157, 281, 282
Nedić, Milan, 193, 208–210, 215, 245
Neuilly, Treaty of, 113
Neurath, Baron von, 147, 148, 151
Nicholas, Prince of Greece, 43, 46, 48–50, 53, 55, 56, 64–66, 70, 73, 80, 87, 90–92, 119, 125, 152, 153
Nicholas, Princess of Greece, 43–56, 64–66, 70, 72, 73, 87, 90–92, 119–121, 125, 152–154, 181, 195, 204, 207, 260, 284, 299, 301
Nicholas, Prince of Yugoslavia, 72, 90, 91, 154, 156, 157, 181, 195, 203, 251, 268, 271, 299–301, 303–305
Ninčić, Momćilo, 259, 261, 272, 273
North Africa, 17, 115, 199, 218–219
Norway, 194–196, 198

Obolensky, Prince Serge, 28, 41, 61
Obrenović, Alexander, King of Serbia, 21
Obrenović, Miloš, reigning Prince of Serbia, 17, 18
Old Palace, Belgrade, 55, 64, 73, 85, 102, 124
Olga, Princess of Yugoslavia, as Princess of Greece, 43–55; as Princess of Serbia (1929 Yugoslavia), 56–62, 64–73, 81, 85–8, 90–93, 99, 100; during regency, 102–4, 117–21, 123–6, 128, 133–7, 152–8, 160, 165, 166, 169, 173, 175–9, 181, 184–8, 195–8, 200, 203–7, 229, 231, 234, 240, 247; in exile, 251, 252, 260–2, 267–71, 273, 277–81, 283–6, 293–6; leaves South Africa, 298, 299, 301, 303, 305
Olga, Queen of Greece (exiled), 71
Operation Marita, 214, 220, 239
Order of the White Eagle with Swords, 253
Orthodox Church, 145, 199
Oxford, 24–28, 33–35, 39–41, 61, 74, 117, 135, 143, 156, 299, 301, 305

Pact of Steel, 167
Polairet, Sir Michael, 260
Paris, 17–20, 25, 32, 40, 44, 47, 48, 54, 56, 58, 61, 64–66, 69, 70, 73, 75, 81, 87–89, 91, 92, 94, 100, 105, 116, 117, 121, 122, 126, 136, 143–145, 147, 153, 154, 181, 183, 184, 188, 190, 196–198, 203, 299, 300–304
Paris, Comte de, 300
Parrott, Cecil, 103, 124, 154, 155, 165, 166
Parrott, Ellen, 124
Pašić, Nikola, 38, 81–83
Paul, Prince of Greece, 152
Paul, Prince of Yugoslavia, as Prince Paul Karageorgević, 17, 19, 20; to Belgrade as Prince Paul of Serbia (1929 Yugoslavia), 21; to Oxford, 27; flat in London, 41; marriage, 54–57; organizes Museum of Modern Art, 74–9; appointed Prince Regent, 101; negotiates with Croats, 107–11, 146, 147, 164, 174, 182, 183; signs Sporazum, 182; instructs Stojadinović to form government, 111, 112; at George V's funeral, 123, 124; receives Edward VIII in Yugoslavia, 126–8; in London during abdication crisis, 134–9; asks British for arms, 133, 171, 172; and Italo-Yugoslav Pact, 140, 142; at coronation of George VI, 143; and King Peter's education, 154–6, 165, 166; contrives